SCRIPT GIRLS

script girls

WOMEN SCREENWRITERS IN HOLLYWOOD

LIZZIE FRANCKE

BRITISH FILM INSTITUTE

bfi

BFI PUBLISHING

First published in 1994 by the
British Film Institute
21 Stephen Street
London W1P 1PL

The British Film Institute exists to encourage the development of film,
television and video in the United Kingdom, and to promote knowledge,
understanding and enjoyment of the culture of the moving image. Its
activities include the National Film and Television Archive; the National
Film Theatre; the Museum of the Moving Image; the London Film Festival;
the production and distribution of film and video; funding and support for
regional activities; Library and Information Services; Stills, Posters and
Designs; Research; Publishing and Education; and the monthly *Sight and
Sound* magazine.

British Library Cataloguing-in-Publication Data.
A catalogue record for this book is available from the British Library.

ISBN 0-85170-477-8
    0-85170-478-6 pbk

Cover design by Sophie Herxheimer
Typeset in 10/11.5 pt Zapf Book by Goodfellow & Egan, Cambridge
Printed in Great Britain by The Trinity Press, Worcester

Contents

Acknowledgments

This book found its origin in the 'Give a Girl Her Credit' season programmed by myself and Kate Ogborn at the National Film Theatre in 1990. I would like to give Kate her credit for helping me get *Script Girls* off the ground, and for her advice in the early stages of its conception.

I would like to thank the following archives and libraries: in the US: Janet Lorenz and staff and Center for Motion Picture Study, Margaret Herrick Library, Academy of Motion Picture Arts and Sciences; Madeline F. Matz, Motion Picture Division, Library of Congress, Washington D.C.; Alice Lotvin Birney, Manuscript Division, Library of Congress; Sara S. Hodson, The Huntington Library, San Marino, California (Zoë Akins, Sonya Levien collections); staff at Billy Rose Theatre Collection of the Performing Arts Research Center, The New York Public Library at Lincoln Center (with special thanks to Angelita Sierra in the Reprographic Services); staff at the Research and Study Center, Powell Library, UCLA Film and Television Archive; Bridgette Kueppers, Theater Arts Library, UCLA; Anne Schlosser, Ned Comstock at Cinema and TV Library, Doheny Library, University of Southern California; Mary J. Walker, Special Collections Librarian, Williamson Science Fiction Library, Eastern New Mexico University (Leigh Brackett collection); Ben Brewster, Wisconsin Center for Film and Theatre Research (Vera Caspary, Ruth Goetz, Frances Goodrich collections); staff at Film Studies Center, Museum of Modern Art, NYC; George M. Barringer, Special Collection, Lauinger Library, Georgetown University Library. The photographs on pages 15, 21, 23, 31, 43, 48, 58, 62 are courtesy of Quigley Photographic Archive, Special Collections Division, Georgetown University Library, Washington D.C., and on pages 19, 20, 39, 57, 68 and 71, courtesy of The Museum of Modern Art, New York. In the UK: Gillian Hartnoll and her staff at the British Film Institute Library.

I would also like to thank the staff at the Writers Guild of America (West) and Mona Mangan, Executive Director of the Writers Guild of America (East).

For pointing me in the right direction and for advice and addresses offered on the way I would like to thank the following: Ally Acker, Kevin

Brownlow, Virginia Clark, Tina Daniell, Graham Fuller, Paul Jarrico, Pat McGilligan, Paul Taylor, Mae Woods. Special thanks to Pat McGilligan for all his suggestions and to him and Tina Daniell for allowing me access to their unpublished interviews with Marguerite Roberts and Vera Caspary; also to Bob Thomas for allowing access to his interview notes with Virginia Van Upp.

Many thanks to the following who were interviewed for the book: Jay Presson Allen, Alice Arlen, Leora Barish, Sheila Benson, Hindy Brooke, Jean Rouverol Butler, Helen Deutsch, Leslie Dixon, Philip Dunne, Carole Eastman, Nora Ephron, Maggie Greenwald, Hilary Henkin, Georgia Jeffries, Callie Khouri, Mary Loos, William Ludwig, Ida Lupino, Clair Noto, Arthur Orloff, Stephanie Rothman, John Sanford, Joan Scott, Mary David Sheiner, Amanda Silver, Edith Somer, Caroline Thompson, Catherine Turney.

Special thanks to Barbara Baruch, Alysse Bezahler, Lori Bezahler, Debbie and Harvey Bezahler for making my US stay so easy, happy and possible, also to my dear parents for putting up with me back in London! Finally a very special thanks to the following for giving me support and confidence in my writing over the last three years: Pam Cook, my exceptionally patient editor Roma Gibson, Mary Beth Hamilton, Ruth Picardie, Andrea Stuart, and Julie Wheelwright.

Script Girls is dedicated to Cora Ogborn James and her generation, with hope and love.

Introduction

Think of the Hollywood screenwriter and invariably the image is of some dashing fellow in rolled white shirt sleeves, green eye shield perched on his forehead, cigarette hanging louchely out of his mouth and whisky at the elbow. He's brother to the newsroom hacks and pulp fiction writers, only he bashes away at his typewriter in some shady corner of the lime grove that is forever Hollywood. Or perhaps, if one veers towards *Sunset Boulevard*, one finds the desperate guy who sold his soul for a share in Babylon, soaking it up face downward in a topaz-blue pool. In this movie mythology, the screenwriter finds his hero in Billy Wilder's Joe G. Gillis, or lately in the Coen Brothers' Barton Fink. Men who lose it to the system, who end up dumbfounded or dead.

But rewind the film for a moment, and look at the figures in the background. In *Sunset Boulevard*, the linen-fresh, apple-eating Betty Schaefer always interested me; neatly stowed away in the script department on the Paramount lot where she files away others' stories. She's the girl who tells Joe, 'I don't want to be a reader all my life, I want to write.' Smart and ambitious, she burns the midnight oil and brews the coffee as she and Joe resuscitate some plot about teachers. Whether Betty made it to the studio writers' block we'll never know. But chances are she did.

For those determined young women who wanted to play a role behind the camera, screenwriting has been one profession open to them throughout the history of Hollywood. (They've been allowed to be editors too, but sewing up films in a dark room under the judicious eyes of the director obviously limited their participation in the story-telling process.) Survey the screenwriting credits of a random selection of classics and the script girls will be there: *Gilda* (Virginia Van Upp), *The Big Sleep*, *Rio Bravo* (Leigh Brackett), *Mildred Pierce* (Catherine Turney), *Singin' in the Rain* (Betty Comden), *Bringing Up Baby* (Hagar Wilde). Then there are the countless women whose novels and short stories have been adapted for the screen – from Margaret Mitchell's *Gone with the Wind* to Dorothy B. Hughes's *In a Lonely Place*.[1] While this latter category is not the focus here, it is worth remembering how Hollywood has ravenously consumed women's ideas.

The fact that women have had such a crucial involvement in the history of Hollywood always seems to surprise people. 'It must be a short book' was a comment I heard rather too often when explaining my project to friends. It certainly wasn't just the audiences who thought the actors made up the words as they went along. For the writer Mary McCall Jnr, it was all too sadly par for the course when during the 1940s a New York reviewer commented of one of her *Maisie* films, which starred Anne Southern as the eponymous heroine: 'Miss Southern's unceasing flow of bright sayings redeems a dull script.'

It was only with the publication of the American critic Richard Corliss's *Talking Pictures* in 1974 that screenwriters began to attract substantial critical attention, but even so, they continue to get short shrift: 'Somewhere just below the publicists but above the hairdresser,' as writer Jay Presson Allen quipped. Or, as the writer Eleanor Perry once overheard in a Beverly Hills hotel lobby: 'Writers are the women of the film industry.' To be a screenwriter *and* a woman, then, doesn't bode too well. One's status is low and one's contributions are shrouded.

Of course, there have been women writers who have received some notoriety: Anita Loos, Dorothy Parker and Lillian Hellman's experiences in Hollywood are well documented.[2] These women were exceptions, however, phenomena unto themselves, with their own particular mythologies. With her fiction, and especially her novel *Gentlemen Prefer Blondes*, Loos found a reputation for herself beyond the movie industry, while Parker and Hellman were already established literary doyennes of New York before making the sortie out west.

The roll-call of women who worked in writing partnerships is also lengthy: Frances Goodrich and Albert Hackett, Sarah Y. Mason and Victor Heerman, Ruth Gordon and Garson Kanin, Edna and Edward Anhalt, Harriet Frank Jnr and Irving Ravetch, Nancy Myers and Charles Shyer – to a name a few.[3] Mostly in married teams, the musical specialists Betty Comden and Adolph Green being an exception, these women's contributions are no less important, but their careers are protected by the partnership. Frances Goodrich, who wrote from the 30s through to the 50s, once commented that as a woman she was never discriminated against, though adding that the presence of Hackett might have made a difference.[4] A few of the women did write solo, but only after making a name for themselves with their husbands or, in the case of the actress Ruth Gordon, establishing their Hollywood credentials in other ways as well. (The only two women who merit attention in Corliss's book were in writing teams – Betty Comden and Ruth Gordon, though Gordon's name only appears in brackets alongside Kanin's.)

The case for examining the careers of women screenwriters is clear. This book isn't, however, devoted to cataloguing the incidences of discrimination. It was conceived in a celebratory mode, to put women writers back into the Hollywood picture, and to give the debates about women working in the film industry some sort of socio-historical perspective.

Starting in the 1900s with Gene Gauntier, whose version of *Ben Hur* precipitated the copyrighting of scripts, *Script Girls* focuses on a range of writers whose careers highlight some of the salient issues for women as the Hollywood film industry developed and changed. Here that history is traced from the silent era, which was a boom time for women who worked in a variety of roles behind the camera, through to what is considered to be the golden age of the studios in the 30s and 40s and its aftermath with the arrival of television.[5] The book looks at the impact of feminism on writers in the 60s and 70s and concludes with an examination of the current situation, constructed out of interviews with Callie Khouri, Leslie Dixon, Nora Ephron and Caroline Thompson amongst others. The fact that Ephron and Thompson are now directing as well indicates a certain amount of optimism for women working in Hollywood in the 90s as cinema approaches its 100th birthday.

Constructing the history of a neglected subject has had its difficulties. It would have been easier to write this book ten years ago when many of the women who worked in Hollywood's heyday were still alive or young enough to recall their thoughts. Primary sources proved to be pretty scarce in 1990 when I first started my research. I tracked down one writer who had worked during the 30s and 40s, and our discussion seemed to be going well despite her obvious frailty. She recalled how she had suggested the idea for *Cat People* to Val Lewton at a dinner party, which roused my curiosity, but then she also informed me that she had come up with several of the endings to Hitchcock's films, while professing to know nothing about one screenplay that she is credited with. One can double-check with material on Hitchcock and Val Lewton to contest such assertions, but her claims still intrigue me. What other truth existed there?

If this is an attempt to put a record straight, it is also an attempt to examine some truisms. 'Women screenwriters only wrote women's stories' is one familiar remark. *Script Girls* tests the thesis about such typecasting. And if they were just writing 'women's stories', how many were interested – or able – within the studio system to challenge the conventional approach to 'women's' material? Unfortunately it has not been possible within the scope of this book to rifle through all the film production files to ascertain whether women writers who wanted to twist convention were finally forced to stick to the director/producer's line. Nor has it been possible to check all the films written by women for hidden subtexts. But does it make a difference to one's perception of a film to know that it has been written by a woman? Does one's reading of *Play Misty for Me*, directed by Clint Eastwood, suddenly become revised on discovering that it was written by Jo (and not Joe, as some books have it) Heims? There's the twist. *Play Misty for Me* is a fascinating study of jealousy and demented desire, as much as a gripping thriller, in which Eastwood is finally allowed to reveal the vunerable cracks in his steely screen persona. In this instance I believe that Heims's contribution is an important factor to consider, adding to an understanding of the film as a critique of masculinity. The woman screenwriter can be allowed to make her mark by the right director. Her presence in the credits allows for a few nuances in the film's interpretation. But by no means all women writers had feminist agendas; many were just trying to make their mark and a better living – script girls like Betty Schaefer, who dreamed of getting out of the reading and typing pools and splashing out on their own.

3

Notes

1. See Jill Robinson Fenton's *Women Writers: From Page to Screen* (New York: Garland Publishing, 1990) for a comprehensive reference list of women writers' works that have been adapted for screen.
2. For the writers in their own words see the following memoirs: Lillian Hellman, *Three* ('An Unfinished Woman', 'Pentimento', and 'Scoundrel Time'; Boston and Toronto: Little Brown, 1979); Anita Loos: *A Girl Like I* (New York: Viking, 1966), *Kiss Hollywood Goodbye* (New York: Viking, 1974), *Cast of Thousands* (New York: Grosset and Dunlap, 1977). For Dorothy Parker's experiences in Hollywood see Marion Mead, *Dorothy Parker: What Fresh Hell Is This?* (London: Heinemann, 1988).
3. These partnerships' credits are included in the filmographies at the end of the book.
4. Melissa Sue Kort, '"Shadows of the Substance": Women Screenwriters in the 1930s', in Janet Todd (ed.), *Women and Film* (New York; London: Holmes and Meier, 1988).
5. Television provided enormous opportunities for women screenwriters and deserves a separate study. For women who might have considered feature-writing careers, the small screen became an easier and therefore more attractive option. It was a burgeoning industry with a high turnover and needed writers. The principal area in which women could first find work was – and still is – in daytime soaps, a genre derided as much as its cinematic foremother, the 'woman's movie' (and consequently not lucrative despite the fact that the income generated from daytime advertising supports the evening's programming). During the 50s and 60s screenwriters such as Edith Sommer, Jean Rouverol Butler and Fay Kanin made the transition to television as movie work became scarce. But for a writer such as Kanin who had a manifest interest in 'social issues', the medium proved more accommodating to her ideas. Indeed, in the 70s the growing influence of feminism was more marked on the small screen than the large.

    It is important to note that the ground-breaking series *Cagney and Lacey* (1981–88), which took the cop-show format and turned the genre, as the *Village Voice* critic noted, 'not upside down so much as inside out', started as a film script. The show's originators, Barbara Evedon and Barbara Corday, came up with the premise after reading Molly Haskell's *From Reverence to Rape: The Treatment of Women in the Movies* (New York: Holt, Rinehart and Winston, 1974) and discovering that there had never been a women's 'buddy' movie. But they and their producer, Barney Rosenzweig, couldn't find finance for what they believed could be the first 'real hit feminist film'. Hence the idea eventually evolved into a TV series; see Julie D'Acci's 'The Case of Cagney and Lacey' in Helen Baehr and Gillian Dyer (eds.), *Boxed In* (London: Pandora, 1987).

1

'No finer calling for a woman'

The Silent Era

In the early days of film many of the scenarists were women.
Frances Marion wrote most of Mary Pickford's films. June
Mathis wrote Valentino's stories and Anita Loos wrote for
Douglas Fairbanks. Nowadays the pictures are run by men and
they are made for men and they seem to defile human relationships. But it was not always so. D. W. Griffith felt that if women
didn't like a movie it would be a failure; if they liked it, it would
become a success. Have the women in the audience been forgotten? If this is so, I think that is more a struggle between business and art in movies than between masculine and feminine.

Lillian Gish.[1]

1912 was an auspicious year for the scenario writer, as the screenwriter of
the silent era was called. It was the year in which the American Copyright
Law was officially amended to recognise motion pictures so that features
and shorts were at last perceived to be the products of authors, rather
than stories that just happened to be made up by the actors on the screen.
This historical achievement followed a test case in which a suit was filed
against the Kalem film company, which had produced the gladiatorial epic
Ben Hur (1907). The film's scenario had been adapted from a Lew Wallace
novel by Kalem's writer Gene Gauntier. No permission had been sought,
so the Wallace estate contested that this had been a breach of its author's
copyright. The Wallace estate won the case and Kalem paid $25,000 for its
oversight. From then on all films produced in the United States had to be
registered for copyright. Producers were legally bound to lodge materials
related to their films at the Copyright Office at the Library of Congress in
Washington, DC. This, in the silent era, included synopses and scenarios –
precursors to the film script.[2] Between 1911 and 1929, when the silent
period drew to a close, more than 25,000 films were registered.

The Copyright Office conserves stacks of these films' scenarios in its
vaults. But the pages are beginning to fade now, the mimeographed words
becoming less distinct. As with the films shot on nitrate stock that have
vaporised with age, other relics of the early days of cinema are becoming

more elusive. How easy it is, then, for a history to become hazy. That half of those 25,000 scripts stored away in the Library of Congress Copyright Office were written by women can be too soon forgotten.[3]

When analysing prospects for women behind the camera in the US film industry in the 1990s, it is all too easy to overlook the integral role that women played in the industry's embryonic years; indeed, women were the making of cinema. As an essential element in the audience they ensured that the novelty of cinema caught on,[4] while they were also often the creative forces in front of and behind the camera – directors, producers, editors, publicists and location managers. Women were even being hired as camera operators. 'Women's chances of making a living have been increased by the rise of the cinematograph machines,'[5] commented one of the earliest directors, Alice Guy Blaché, in 1908. It was the time of the 'New Woman' – the independent, career-minded and mostly middle-class females who were striding into the twentieth century. For these women the arts-oriented professions were the most accessible, and cinema, the newest art form, seemed to provide them with a multitude of opportunities.

But women were also helped by the fact that this youthful industry was regarded as a rather unsophisticated pastime, and therefore deemed perfect for them, as the experiences of Alice Guy Blaché illustrate. In 1895 Blaché was working as a secretary for the Gaumont organisation in Paris. There she had access to a prototype of the movie camera and sought her boss Gaumont's permission to film a couple of plays. He consented with the revealing comment, 'It's a child's toy anyhow.'[6] Blaché later recalled: 'If the developments which evolved from this proposal could have been foreseen, then I would probably never have obtained his agreement. My youth, my lack of experience, my sex all conspired against me.'[7]

Little conspired against women in the early days of the medium and work was easy to find, even if at first they were mainly employed as performers. Cinema's instant popularity saw the formation of many film production companies in the United States, first in major cities such as New York and Chicago, then in 1906 spreading out west to the sunnier climes of California and that new town, Hollywood. These enterprises were relatively small-scale, 'family' affairs in which, very much like the travelling stock theatre groups that were popular at the time, members chipped in with a variety of tasks. Thus women who joined the film companies as actors soon found that they were often doing more work behind the camera than in front of it. New skills could be swiftly obtained; as the scenarist Beulah Marie Dix described her days at Famous Players-Lasky to Kevin Brownlow: 'It was all very informal, in those early days. There were no unions. Anybody on the set did anything he or she was called upon to do. I've walked on as an extra, I've tended lights (I've never shifted scenery) and anybody not doing anything else wrote down the director's notes on the script. Script girls were then only slowly coming into being. I also spent a good deal of time in the cutting room.'[8] In such a relatively egalitarian atmosphere women seemed destined to become equal partners with men in this new industry.

Gene Gauntier, one of the earliest scenarists, who had been responsible for the cribbed *Ben Hur*, started her career in the movies around 1905. She worked briefly for the future film writer/director Lois Weber in her repertory theatre company, performing in the cautionary melodrama *Why Girls Leave Home or a Danger Signal on the Path of Folly*, and was still a teenager when she joined the New York-based Kalem Film Company as an actress.

Gauntier had left her home to pursue a theatrical career after graduating from the Kansas City School of Oratory. Her parents, though not actors themselves, did not harbour the then still prevalent middle-class anxieties about the impropriety of a stage life for their daughter, and Gene and her sister Marguerite (who was an opera singer) were both encouraged in their artistic ambitions. Gauntier, however, later commented to the press that while she was training to be an actress she often fantasised about the kind of success that 'would have the whole world at her feet and the people of her home town humbled (those who were scandalised because she avowed that she was going on the stage)'.[9]

Gene Gauntier, scenarist of Ben Hur *(1907).*

Gauntier responded by enjoying a highly successful career. Her life took a new direction in 1907 when she was persuaded into scenario writing by one of the bosses at Kalem, Frank Marion. He was having some trouble satisfying the movie theatres' demand for Kalem films. '[So I] turned in a crude script from the plot of a melodrama I had once appeared in – *Why Girls Leave Home*.'[10] Her first attempt at scenario writing proved to be unacceptable, but the head of the company and lead director, Sidney Olcott, gave her a second shot and asked her to adapt *Tom Sawyer*, the ever popular novel by Mark Twain.

'[The result] might have been called "simple bits from *Tom Sawyer*".' She notes in her aptly titled unpublished memoirs, *Blazing the Trail*, that in translating the Twain novel into a movie she was keen to keep out the sections that would be difficult or, mindful of the budget, too expensive to shoot. 'It was pretty dreadful but it was what Marion and Olcott wanted. And I had caught the knack. From henceforth I was the mainstay of the Kalem scenario department. *Tom Sawyer* was the first of three hundred that I wrote and produced or sold to other companies.'[11] Gauntier was prolific, often writing three scenarios for the short one-reeler films in a day to ensure that the Kalem company and the theatres that it supplied were kept busy. When her own imagination faltered, she turned for ideas to whatever happened to be at hand. 'A poem, a picture, a short story, a scene from a current play, a headline in a newspaper. There was no copyright law to protect authors and I could, and I did, infringe on everything.' *Ben Hur* being a case in point.

The Kalem company relied extensively on Gauntier, and were none too happy when she was wined and lunched and wooed away to the larger Biograph Company, which by then had its own studios in New York. She was hired as scenario editor, studio manager and supervising director. 'But no acting, we can get plenty good for that,' quipped Henry Marvin, the general manager at Biograph.[12] There, she not only wrote scenarios but also acted as a talent scout and apparently recommended that one actor in the company, a certain D. W. Griffith, should be allowed to direct. But her career in this bigger organisation was not entirely fulfilling. Gauntier didn't like the routine nature of the work, and felt more like a factory hand punching the clock at the beginning and end of the day. At Biograph she had lost the autonomy that she had enjoyed at Kalem. She also missed the acting.

After her short stint at Biograph, Gauntier was back at Kalem as their leading lady and scenarist on a weekly wage of $70 ($50 for acting, $20 for writing). Almost immediately after her return in 1908, she was sent down to Jacksonville, Florida with some of the 'Kalem gang' to film a series of location stories. It was there that she came up with the idea of writing and performing *The Adventures of a Girl Spy*. The tale, according to Gauntier, was based on the life of Belle Boyd, a young Southern woman who disguised herself as a boy in order to work as a spy for the Confederate army during the American Civil War. Such incidents had occurred quite frequently during the war and both 'highbrow' and 'lowbrow' novels inspired by these women's stories had already proved popular.[13] Indeed

Boyd may well have been a fictional creation herself. Gauntier took a well-worn literary genre and successfully cashed in on the public's fascination with the phenomenon.

> It made a tremendous hit and the exhibitors wrote in for more. Thus began the first 'series' made in films and I kept them up for two years, until, tired of the sprains and bruises and with the brains sucked dry of any more adventures for the intrepid young woman, I married her off and ended the war. And I thought that this would finish. Not so! The demand for them still came in and I was compelled to come back with one called *A Hitherto Unrelated Incident of the Girl Spy*. There's always a way, in pictures.[14]

Nan, the girl spy, was indeed an intrepid soul and Gauntier was as intrepid as her creation. The audience wanted excitement so Gauntier gave them scenes that 'embodied all of the difficult and dangerous stunts that I could conjure up. ... Every moment not spent in active service I was pounding away on my little "Blick", evolving stories I hated to write, hair-breath escapes that I feared to do, cudgelling brains for fresh situations and new characterisation.'[15] For the sake of her art and her public, Gauntier, who did all her own stunts, was quite adept at jumping into the shark-infested Florida waters. But it wasn't just the stunts that kept the punters happy. Her story-telling skills frequently received critical praise. The influential journal *The Moving Picture World* commented of one of the later films in the series, *A Daughter of the Confederacy* (1913):

> There is a great deal of suspense and it keeps the spectator on the knife edge. This is wholly due to the sharp, unexpected turns of the narrative. After the first jolt that we get, we are made to sit up, expecting every moment that another surprise will be sprung upon us. The scenario writer has seen to it that the next does come at the right, psychological instant and just before we realize that this is the method being fol-lowed. We are never permitted to feel anything but concern for the characters and are made to forget that it is a story.[16]

Gauntier had established that a woman writer was as adept with the thrills and spills of the action-adventure genre as her male colleagues. Nan was a robust heroine and the series ran on and off for over four years. But although Gauntier professed to hate writing the girl spy stories towards the end, the alternative proved to be less attractive to her. In her memoirs she mentions that in 1909 there were 'censorship worries' which led to constraints on the kind of material that Kalem wanted her to write while she was still based at Jacksonville. Indeed the issue of censorship had become a pertinent one at that time.

In 1907 three films were released that caused great consternation to America's moral guardians, made up of church and women's groups. *The Unwritten Law*, *The Thaw-White Tragedy* and *The Great Thaw Trail* were all based on the previous year's infamous Stanford White murder case, in which the celebrated architect had been shot by the debonair Manhattan socialite, Harry K. Thaw. The story contained all the magic ingredients of a nefarious scandal, with the glittering names of the case tarnished by the grubby facts. It was revealed that the middle-aged White had raped Thaw's young wife, the actress Evelyn Nesbitt, prior to their marriage. As Kevin Brownlow explains in *Behind the Mask of Innocence*:

> The Thaw films obliged the establishment to take a new interest in the moving picture; they realised it was capable of untold damage. Most obviously it was eroding the lower classes' faith in authority. A survey of working-class amusements in New York, conducted by the People's Institute, an adult education centre at Cooper Union, warned that the moving picture was 'potentially too great an influence of popular attitudes to be left unsupervised'.[17]

The uproar over the films prompted the Mayor of New York, George Brinton McClellan, to close all cinemas in 1908. The city's cinema owners swiftly responded to McClellan's decree by setting up in the following year their own monitoring organisation – the New York Board of Censorship of Programs of Motion Picture Shows – later the National Board of Censorship. Representatives on the board were drawn from such philanthropic and predominantly liberal organisations as the Children's Aid Society, the City Vigilance League, the League for Political Education, the Neighbourhood Workers' Association, the Public Education Association, the Society for Prevention of Crime, the Women's Municipal League and the People's Institute.

The National Board of Censorship was the first attempt by the movie industry to put its own house in order with a system of voluntary trade regulation. The producers and exhibitors paid the costs; they wanted their business to be publicly accountable. For them it was important to uphold the reputation of the industry and be seen to monitor those members of their profession who might have occasion to sully it. As Daniel J. Czitrom has commented in *Media and the American Mind*, the creation of the board was part of the industry's bid to court the upper and middle classes 'to improve the average quality of the films in order that a larger and larger number of the total population [would] patronise motion pictures.'[18]

The board's central concern was with the depiction of sex, drugs, violence and crime, regardless of the treatment of the subject. Production companies were therefore encouraged to avoid themes that were likely to provoke censorship. That was the message Kalem passed on to their writer down in Florida. Gauntier describes how she laboured to play down the 'thrills' in her scenarios and was obliged to stretch her adventurous imagination to genteel and uncontroversial stories:

> It daily grows difficult to write exterior stuff with no thrills and yet make it interesting. My mind has got to the point where it can only think of situations calling for 'beautiful Southern women' (and we have used them down here again and again), breakfast and tea scenes and

walks and proposals. I don't know which way to turn. And no matter how much I plead they never send down a scenario.[19]

Gauntier found the task unappealing. While the hardy heroine Nan was to resurface later, stories about 'beautiful Southern women' were for the moment perceived to have the requisite refinement to attract the new kind of audiences. But soon Frank Marion was offering Gauntier a new challenge: 'Mr Marion thought it would be a good idea for me to produce a picture entirely alone, writing the scenario, planning the sets, directing, cutting, getting up the advertising, etc. He said that it would be the first time any woman had ever done it and it could be advertised as a novelty.' (Though Mr Marion's promotional tactics were founded on an error – Alice Guy Blaché had been directing films since 1896.) But Gauntier did not enjoy the experience that had been afforded her. 'I wrote *The Grandmother* (1909), a rather prettily sentimental story with a strong heart interest. The picture was successful but I did not care for directing, and refused Mr Marion's offer for a unit of my own.'[20]

Gauntier, however, recognised how important Frank Marion's supporting role was in the progress of her career, even though his enlightened attitude may have been prompted more by commercial than ideological concerns. Marion believed that a film by a woman could be successfully promoted and win favour with the female film fans, so – with good business in mind – he proved to be a useful benefactor to women who wanted to work in film. 'Mr Marion had a great deal of faith in the ability of women and had, while we were away, taken on another girl as a scenario writer, a Miss Ponthier who had lived long in South America. She supplied the northern company.'[21]

But while Marion wanted to promote women, when Gauntier turned down her patron's offer of her own unit in 1910, she commented that producing and directing was 'not work for women'. Yet later, after venturing abroad to film various location-based stories for Kalem, including the first biblical epic to be shot in Egypt, *From the Manger to the Cross* (1912), she and Sidney Olcott broke away from Kalem and founded the Gene Gauntier Features Players Company, building themselves a studio in an old church on West 54th Street in Manhattan. The change of heart came about after the release of *From the Manger to the Cross*, which had proved to be a great money spinner for Kalem. But Gauntier comments that, for reasons she was never able to understand, Kalem sent the film out without credits and thus 'no publicity [was] given to those that deserve it'. For the new organisation Gauntier used her name to capitalise on her tremendous popularity, but it was the actress/writer's company in more than just title. 'Since I've had my own company, the work has been even more fascinating than ever, though also much harder because of the tremendous responsibility it has entailed.'[22]

Gauntier took her duties very seriously, often going to extraordinary lengths to do research for her scenarios. Her endeavours made the headlines:

11

In order to fully understand the life and the habits of New York's poor, Miss Gene Gauntier, author, playwright and actress, abandoned her home on Fifth Avenue two weeks ago and disguised in rags and a shawl, invaded lower Hester Street, where she secured lodgings in a garret at a rental figure of one dollar a month.[23]

Gauntier may have had an eye to the publicity that such a stunt would generate for her 1914 film *The Fight for a Birthright* (her sojourn received extensive coverage in both the trade and New York press), but she also proved to be quite scrupulous in her research to illuminate the appalling conditions of a life lived between the flop-house and the sweat-shop.

In one place on Madison street they offered me 50 cents a day to work from 7 a.m. to 9 p.m., providing I could sew 700 buttons on 140 waist-coats during that time. They explained their girls had to average ten vests an hour with five buttons to a vest. I took the job and worked one day fourteen hours, but only managed to sew on 280 buttons. That night they paid me 20 cents for my labour.[24]

Given her flair for reportage, it is not surprising that when Gauntier decided in 1918 to retire from the movies, she turned to journalism, including a brief stint as a war correspondent.

Gauntier capitalised on her screen power to secure a position for herself as a scenarist, which in turn meant that she had a degree of control over the material she acted in. During the silent period it became common for actresses to wield such power. As the owner of her own corporation Gauntier was to set a trend that was followed by stars such as Clara Kimball Young and, most famously, 'America's sweetheart' Mary Pickford, who eventually became one of the cornerstones of the Big Four Organization, later called United Artists (along with Charles Chaplin, Douglas Fairbanks and D. W. Griffith). Many actresses also turned to directing – including Mabel Normand, who directed comedies for Mack Sennett, Lillian Gish and Dorothy Davenport (also known as Mrs Wallace Reid) – while some just scripted their own material, such as Dorothy Gish and Ruth Roland.

For some actresses the move to scenario writing also ensured that they could have a life in the industry long after their screen allure had faded. Exchanging the set for the writer's office was considered a good career move. Cecil B. DeMille's chief scenarist, Jeanie Macpherson, was to take such a path from '"wop" parts to bossing the job' – as the tag-line of a *Photoplay* magazine profile put it. Her career with DeMille saw her retreat from the screen and flourish as a scenarist. She wrote for DeMille until her death in 1946.

Macpherson had an archetypal upper middle-class childhood, raised in the comfortable and cosmopolitan world of Boston high society. According to the few press profiles of Macpherson, her father was Scottish and claimed to be a descendant of Bonnie Prince Charlie, while her mother, of French and Spanish descent, was the daughter of the publishing magnate Samuel J. Tomlinson. The Macphersons planned to groom Jeanie for a sophisticated Boston life and sent her off to complete her education at Mlle De Jacques' school in Paris, an academic institution with an esteemed reputation (Mark Twain had sent his daughter there). But before the young Macpherson could contemplate university, a financial misadventure left her family bankrupt and she had to return to America and find some form of employment. For a bright young woman with considerable ambition but no formal training, the allure of the stage seemed preferable to the dull routine of a stenographer.

After spending some time in the chorus of the Chicago Opera House, Macpherson ventured to New York. There she found small parts in various Broadway plays and musicals. But like Gauntier, Macpherson discovered that more challenging employment could be found at the city's many film companies.

> All I knew was that I wanted to act. Then someone told me about motion pictures, how drama was filmed. I was fascinated. I liked mechanics anyway. I hunted all over New York for a studio – but could not find one. At last a super told me a man named Griffith was doing pictures for the Biograph company. I promptly went there. Mr Griffith wasn't in. His assistant was. I told him my stage experience. He ignored it, scorned it. 'We want to know what you can do in front of a camera,' he said. I said: 'If you get me on my Scotch day, I can't do anything, but if you get me on my French day, I can do "wop" parts.' He told me he would see what could be done.[25]

According to Carolyn Lowrey in her *The First One Hundred Noted Men and Women of the Screen* (1920), the determined Macpherson sat on the studio manager's doorstep until finally Griffith granted her an interview. Such a tale may be apocryphal, but Macpherson was eventually hired to work for Biograph where she stayed for two years, mostly playing what she described as 'emotional roles'. After a brief stint at another New York-based studio, the Edison Company, Macpherson decided to make the move west and found herself a contract with the recently established Universal Studios. It was there that she started writing her own scenarios, partly because, once again, the demand was exceeding the supply and partly because 'she wanted to do good sea and mountain stories and these were particularly hard to find.'[26] Like Gauntier, Macpherson, who was a skilled aviatrix in her spare time and had ambitions to fly the Atlantic, favoured adventure over sentiment.

It was while at Universal that Macpherson was presented with the opportunity to direct, albeit in somewhat bizarre circumstances. She had written and starred in *The Tarantula* (some newspaper cuttings of the time record this as the tale of a creature that is half spider, half woman, others suggest that the film is a Western), directed by Edwin August. Before the film was released, however, the negative was accidentally destroyed in a fire. Meanwhile August had left Universal to work for a rival company. The studio turned to Macpherson and asked her to direct a remake, bidding her to reconstruct the film from memory. Unlike

Gauntier, Macpherson did not shy away from the task. With the remake of *The Tarantula* completed, she was subsequently given her own unit at Universal and wrote, directed and produced films there for two years.

Ill health finally forced her to quit directing. Suffering from nervous and physical exhaustion, Macpherson had to take a break from Universal. On recovery she sought work at various other establishments, including the Lasky Features Company, then home to the blustery and bright show-man Cecil B. DeMille. The interview with DeMille proved to be a tellingly brusque affair:

> I sat and began to tell him what a great director and actress I was. He listened patiently, then said, 'Maybe you can act and direct, but I'll bet you can't write.' 'What! Didn't you see my last picture?' He had. 'What did you think of the writing in that?' 'Judging by the picture,' he answered, 'I think that you write like a plumber. But you've got a great imagination, and that may be an asset. A good writer is one of the rarest things in the world, and it's what the movies need right now. I don't need another director or actress, I need a writer. Want to go to school and learn to be one?'[27]

Despite his contemptuous manner, Macpherson leapt at the invitation. Thus began a long and sometimes difficult creative partnership between Macpherson and the maestro of the overblown epic film. Their collabor-ation was so close that it has been suggested their relationship was more than professional. In his biography of DeMille, the writer Charles Higham describes Macpherson as being a woman of 'extremely limited talent' as a writer. Her skills, Higham would like us to believe, lay elsewhere:

> An emancipate, she took on men as her equals in the life struggle. Though not quite beautiful, and somewhat frumpish and mannish in her dress, she still had considerable allure: her flashing blue eyes, elec-tric personality, and air of being totally available worked effectively on the men with whom she dealt. The suggestion she gave of a school marm who underneath pulsed with the vitality of a real woman, of a perennial virgin asking to be relieved of her virginity, earned her imme-diate professional success.[28]

Such a portrait reveals more about the way that some critics have obscured the contributions to film history of women like Macpherson. DeMille liked to have bright, industrious people around him (he employed women in other key, if somewhat female-oriented, roles – notably Claire West as costume designer and Anne Bauchens as film editor). No doubt he found Macpherson's spirited and ambitious character appealing. They may indeed even have had an affair; certainly Macpherson was obviously more to DeMille than just an employee. Theirs was an enduring, if trou-bled, friendship until the end; indeed, with no family of her own it was DeMille who visited Macpherson on her deathbed (she was only 59 when she died of cancer). But to suggest that Macpherson's sexual allure was all that she had to offer and that she set out to 'seduce her celebrated employer' is a travesty.

It is telling that in his assessment of Macpherson's career, Higham omits to mention that she had two years' experience as a director with her own production unit before she went to work for DeMille. Macpherson was 32 when she joined DeMille's company and hardly the ingénue desperate to get into movies. DeMille, who had also been making films for only two years, had already established a certain reputation for himself. For Macpherson, the idea of working for him presented a challenge she could not resist even if she did find herself demoted from the position of director/producer to writer. She found that her new boss was a tireless, even sadistic perfectionist – she had to rewrite her first script for him six times before it met with approval. But after such an inauspicious start, DeMille came to rely almost exclusively on his new recruit. If she had one fault, a colleague observed, it was that she couldn't punctuate. 'After the titles for a picture had been worked out, Jeanie stood across the room and threw periods and commas at them as if at dart boards.'[29]

While Macpherson wrote and appeared in a few DeMille productions – *Rose of the Rancho* (1914), *The Girl of the Golden West* (1914), *The Captive* (1915) and *Carmen* (1915) – she soon gave up performing to devote herself entirely to scenario writing. She told one reporter: 'I write out every piece of business and almost every gesture and then Mr DeMille and I will go carefully over it and discuss it from every angle. In addition, a detailed synopsis of

Jeanie Macpherson followed C.B. DeMille's taste for breeches and knee-high leather boots.

the whole thing is prepared, hitting the high spots, for a bird's-eye view of the scenario.[30] Her involvement in each film, however, would extend beyond the typewriter and the story conference room. As the scenario supervisor she was always on set to ensure that her script was shot as written, as well as taking on other tasks such as checking the authenticity of the costumes in the elaborate historical films. While she had a reputation for attending premieres wearing ornate picture hats that were more suitable apparel for a day at the races, publicity photographs show her dressed for the set in breeches and knee-high leather boots, thus imitating her boss' celebrated fashion taste.

Macpherson's scenarios also had to follow the DeMille trend. While DeMille productions are popularly remembered for their extravagant style, such as that displayed in the biblical epics *The Ten Commandments* (1923) and *The King of Kings* (1926), the output over the many years Macpherson worked for the director was far more varied. Admittedly the collaborators favoured the costume picture genre. Macpherson enjoyed the historical research and, more importantly, the fans hankered to see their idols dressed in the lavish finery of a 'bygone' age. Even contemporary stories would include flashbacks to the past. *Male and Female* (1919), Macpherson's adaptation of J. M. Barrie's *The Admirable Crichton*, is most remembered for its Babylonian sequences complete with live lions.

Jeanie Macpherson and C.B. DeMille, whose collaboration lasted nearly forty years.

But Macpherson and DeMille also enjoyed the modern mode. They tapped into the frivolous mood of the period and introduced the 'sex comedy' to an accommodating public. Faddish films with what were then considered racy titles, such as *Old Wives for New* (1918) and *Don't Change Your Husband* (1918), paraded the 'new woman' – the flapper girl with bobbed hair and skirt who enjoyed the new freedoms of the changing social and economic climate of the postwar period – who finally got the vote in 1920. The thoroughly modern Macpherson created the roles on paper but Gloria Swanson embodied the type on screen, most memorably in scenes in which she luxuriated in bathrooms so ornate that they were appositely described by Cecil's brother William as 'shrines'. The stories dealt brazenly with marital relations and illicit love, but always saw the estranged spouses happily reconciled in the end. These films were designed to tantalise, not shock, audiences who were acquiring, as the National Board of Censorship had hoped, an increasingly middle-class and therefore 'respectable' profile.

Unfortunately, as with many of the other early writers, there is little evidence in the available documents on Macpherson to suggest what she felt about the subject-matter of the scenarios she wrote. She contributed ideas but was ultimately beholden to DeMille for approval. But for a project like *Joan, the Woman* (1916), in which the opera singer turned film star Geraldine Farrar played the young French martyr, it is apparent that Macpherson exercised a strong influence on the material. With a great flourish she told the press: '*Joan, the Woman* is not a production – it's an inspiration.'[31] She wanted to make Joan less a plaster saint than a vulnerable mortal with her own desires and fears. The film was also a rallying call for the British troops who were at the time out in the French trenches. In the first scene, set during the First World War, a young soldier has a vision of Joan in which she tells him that he must die for France to atone for England's sins against her. The story then follows the events leading up to Joan's betrayal by her English lover and her eventual execution. But despite, or perhaps even because of, the film's war cry, *Joan, the Woman* struck a chord particularly among women in the audience who could find inspiration in this valiant heroine. Indeed it was one of Macpherson's most successful films and a personal favourite of its star, Geraldine Farrar. Sophie Irene Loeb, critic of the *New York World*, commented: 'To me it represented the last word in the picture field and I was glad when I saw that it was the work of a woman.'[32] She suggested that Macpherson brought to the scenario a particularly female perception that enhanced the story.

Macpherson's own comments on her craft, however, extended mainly to the development of the scenario-writing technique as silent film became more sophisticated. She explained to one paper in 1917:

I have watched the scenario work from the beginning, from the days when the main purpose of the script was to keep some prominent object moving before the eyes of the delighted audience. Naturally at that time any subtlety of motion would be wasted on a plot whose main situation took the form of a ball rolling down the hill with a frenzied mob chasing it. I now feel that scenario work is coming into its own.[33]

In the same year she contributed a column to the *Moving Picture World* in which she described how the scenario was evolving.

Illustrating sub-titles by means of moving pictures is also passed. No longer do we have to describe a scene of a sub-title and then act out the scene. Now a sub-title is being dropped wherever possible and everything told in terms of action. If a woman is going down town to buy a new hat because her old one is worn out, we no longer have to have our actors make a lot of gestures and use two or three spoken titles. It is simply necessary for them to show the worn, torn ribbon of the hat, with, of course, the necessary expression to show what is to be conveyed.[34]

Macpherson may have had problems with punctuation, but like the other early film-makers she was laying down the grammatical rules for the new language of cinema. As scenarios and the films made from them became more complex, Macpherson concluded that the scenarist's job would be considered more prestigious:

Within the next two years I expect to see a school of photo-dramatists as well known and as distinguished as the dramatists of the speaking stage. Already this school is being developed and established, and within that time it will be set on a firm foundation and photodramatic writers will be given their proper place and will be remembered for their contributions toward this new art.[35]

Macpherson prophesied correctly. By the early 1920s, scenario writing was regarded as a more specialised and 'professional' craft as Hollywood became a more organised industry. The film magazines devoted pages of advice to the would-be writer, while the publication of books by big names advising on how to craft scenarios became an industry in itself. Anita Loos and John Emerson's *Breaking in the Movies*, Catherine Carr's *The Art of Photoplay Writing*, Clara Beranger's *Writing for the Screen*, Frances Marion's *How to Write and Sell Film Scripts*, among others, plied advice to the hopeful writer, while competitions were run in the magazines which enticingly promised the production of the prize-winning script.[36]

Meanwhile, the heads of the larger studios were courting 'classy' names in a bid to give their nickelodeon organisations the respectability of the literary salon. Samuel Goldwyn was first with his Eminent Authors, who included detective story writer Mary Roberts Rhinehart, novelist Gertrude Atherton and playwright Elmer Rice. Goldwyn's rival, Adolph Zukor at Famous Players-Lasky, tried to trump him, bringing Elinor Glyn, then reigning queen of romance, over from Britain in 1920 to write original stories for films.

'Elinor Glyn's name is synonymous with the discovery of sex appeal for the cinema,'[37] wrote a piqued Goldwyn. Glyn, however, thought 'sex

Anita Loos, one of the most prominent screenwriters of her generation.

appeal' a rather cheap notion – and a more appropriate description for the DeMille creations which she considered were 'raw and crude'.[38] She preferred to refer to the 'It' factor and conjured up the concept of the 'It' girl which was to be personified on screen by the actress Clara Bow.

> To have 'It' the fortunate possessor must have that strange magnetism which attracts both sexes; he or she must be entirely unselfconscious and full of self-confidence, indifferent to the effect he or she is producing, and uninfluenced by others. There must be physical attraction, but beauty is unnecessary. Conceit or self-consciousness destroys 'It' immediately. In the animal world 'It' demonstrates tigers and cats – both animals being fascinating and mysterious, and quite unbiddable.

Glyn's stories reflected her very particular view of romance, in which only those with 'It' joined together in rapturous reverie. A typical Glyn scenario – such as *The Romance of the Queen*, adapted from her most celebrated novel *Three Weeks* and described by some at the time as 'sheer pornography' – featured heroines languishing on tiger skins, 'quivering with emotion and passion' and ready to succumb to the amorous advances of some courtly lovers.[39] Really there was only a fine line between the extravagance of Glyn's tiger skins and DeMille's bathrooms. Either way, sex was certainly in. Producers worried about losing their male audiences relied upon writers such as Glyn to create romances that were 'good and sexy'.[40] But not all found Glyn's stories so steamy. 'How would you like to sin on a tiger skin? Or would you prefer to err on some other fur?' quipped one Hollywood wit.

June Mathis rose to prominence as both a screenwriter and producer. She is also credited with 'discovering' Rudolph Valentino.

When not peddling her ideas through her fictions, Glyn was writing advice books for her American public. She even had her own *Elinor Glyn System of Writing*. In the section dealing with scenarios, she outlines nineteen plots that the novice writer should avoid. In this she proved to be a tireless campaigner against mawkishness. Scenarios about long-lost siblings and good children who reform their elders were off limits, while her strongest command was: 'Do not under any circumstances build a story around a pair of baby shoes.' But there was also *The Wrinkle Book*, in which Glyn entreated those who wanted to maintain a youthful complexion to scrub their faces hard with a dry nailbrush until the skin glowed crimson, and *The Philosophy of Love*, in which she declared that women could be divided into three groups: 'lover-women, mother-women and neuter-women'.[41] Certainly, Glyn hardly radicalised the depiction of women.

Glyn herself was represented as an independent woman with a glamorous and highly desirable life-style. Indeed, scenario writers were beginning to be portrayed in a very glamorous fashion in the cinema magazines. In 1923 *Photoplay* published a four-page spread – 'How Twelve Famous Women Scenario Writers Succeeded In This Profession of Unlimited Opportunity and Reward', asking the question, 'Where do successful screenwriters come from?' It concluded, 'every-place', and gave brief career sketches of such eminent names as Anita Loos, Frances Marion, Ouida Bergère, June Mathis, Olga Printzlau, Margaret Turnbull,

Clara Beranger, Jane Murfin, Beulah Marie Dix, Marion Fairfax, Eve Unsell and Sada Cowan. 'All of them normal, regular women. Not temperamental "artistes", not short-haired advanced feminists, not faddists. Just regular women of good education and adaptability who have caught the trick of writing and understand the picture mind. These twelve women are essentially the feminine brains of the motion picture, making good equally with men.'[42]

The *Photoplay* article indeed emphasised how 'regular' these writers were. The new generation of writers were mostly college-educated women and were more likely to have backgrounds in journalism, short story or theatrical writing than performing (of the above, only June Mathis and Ouida Bergère were actors before turning to scenario writing). They were bright but certainly, as we are assured, not recruits from the monstrous regiment of feminists – though the piece doesn't care to ask the women themselves about the subject.

Other press features took pains to stress just how feminine and charming women scenarists could be. 'You Are So Pretty – You Should Go in Pictures', blazed one piece that looked at career prospects for women behind the camera:

> Her profile is like Norma Talmadge's. Daintily patrician, with the faint touch of arrogance that distinguishes beauties of that type. Ruby, the

Elinor Glyn brought the 'It' factor to Hollywood. One of the few to pen books on both writing and beauty tips.

cigarette girl at the Montmartre, confided to me that when the Norma-like girl dances … gracefully beneath the festooned canopy … she is showered with questions as to her identity. No, she is not an actress, nor does she aspire to be a great film mummer. She writes for her daily bread!

So glows the prose heaped on one Dorothy Manners, a 'beauty-sacrificing scribe'. While an interview with Eve Unsell describes her as

> so *womanly* – without the slightest trace of 'pose' or 'literariness', and gives one a 'homey' feeling at once. And I like her pretty frock, with its bunch of flowers stuck in the belt, and her dainty shoes. … And how we talked! – of babies and kittens (both of which she adores); of roses; of English women's complexions … and a hundred and one delightfully feminine topics.[43]

The press or, more pertinently, the studios' publicity hand-outs were constructing film star-like personas for their women writers. With the enfranchisement of American women in 1920, there were fears about exactly what all these career girls were up to. Glamorising the women writers in such a way and turning them into star personalities drew attention to their enormous contribution to the picture business, but at the same time made them safe and acceptable to the public and their colleagues. An interview with Frances Marion, who was one of the highest paid and most powerful writers in Hollywood in the 20s (and later in the 30s, after she made the successful transition from silent scenarist to talkie screenwriter), typically begins: 'She looks like the kind of woman who has nothing more important to think of than an appointment at the couturier's.' Marion was particularly singled out for the glittering treatment, the many cuttings on her describing her bright blue eyes as much as her writing. 'Women who can earn a quarter of a million a year and have brains enough to make most men look like second-raters are not supposed to be beautiful,' said one typical profile.

In Marion's case, it wasn't just the press who harped on her looks. In her memoirs, *Off With Their Heads!*, Marion recalls her interview with William Fox of the Fox Corporation. His opening gambit understandably vexed the young literary woman.

> 'Why does a pretty girl like you want to be a writer?' 'Because I like to write.'
>
> He shook his head with mock pity. 'Now answer me this. Why ain't you in a dress from a stylish store? Why don't I see no jewelry?'
>
> 'That's because I haven't any.'
>
> 'Tsk, tsk, tsk,' he clicked, 'a girl like you should have rings on her fingers –'
>
> 'Bells on her toes?'
>
> 'Ha, sassy! From a homely face I wouldn't take it. From prettiness it's cute. Do you know how you should look? In the most expensive outfits

they got at Saks Fifth Avenue, earrings, bracelets – no phonies, all real stuff.' The look in his eyes said more than his words. 'Well what do you think?'

'I'm paid to think, Mr Fox. Two hundred dollars a week? Are you willing to sign me for that figure – as a scenario writer?'

He smiled indulgently. 'Listen, cuteness, don't try to be a foolish somebody. Nobody cares nothing about female writers. Actresses – yes, they got glamour – but writers, the poor schlemiels!'[44]

Marion recalls that luckily she had another interview that day which proved to be more successful.

But not all the women succumbed to the charm school treatment. Beulah Marie Dix was a self-confessed blue stocking. As a young girl she was 'bored to the teeth by what was then thought properly female – primping, nattering, and petticoats.' Instead she created for herself a boy hero, and wrote about the adventures she wished she could have. A prodigious child, at the age of sixteen she was packed off to Radcliffe (which at the time, the 1890s, was still the Harvard annexe for women) by a forward-thinking father. Henry Dix, a

Beulah Marie Dix was concerned not to present an over-feminine image of herself in order to be taken seriously.

factory foreman, could barely afford the fees but he believed his exceptionally bright daughter deserved such an education. She repaid him by graduating *summa cum laude*, Phi Beta Kappa, as well as being the first woman to
win Harvard's Sohier literary prize. She sold her first short story while she
was still a student, so a writing career was planned.

Dix, who had been involved in student theatre at Radcliffe, was soon to
make a name for herself as a dramatist, first as a collaborator with the
contemporary popular playwright Evelyn Greenleaf Sutherland, then on
her own. Her play *Across the Border*, written in 1914, dealt with the atroci-
ties of war. A devoted pacifist, Dix did not expect to see the play performed
and was surprised when it was immediately accepted by a theatre producer in Boston. When it opened, it was greeted with a good deal of critical attention, though much of it scornfully commented on Dix's politics.
One reviewer said of her anti-war stance: 'She preaches a good deal of
pernicious nonsense.'

Dix had meanwhile established herself as one of the few women playwrights with a thorough knowledge of military policies; *Across the Border*
was followed by *Moloch*, which dealt with the same themes. Her daughter,
Evelyn F. Scott, comments in her memoirs on her mother's beliefs: 'In her
mind, thanks to her research, were all those sordid facts it was not going
to be patriotic to speak about for years (though she did) – namely, that
looting, sadism, rape, massacre, and systematic starvation were not
weapons merely of a depraved enemy; and that all of it was futile.'[45]

Given that she was now married to a German, Herr Flebbe, Dix was
treading a dangerous line with her plays. Her pacifism could all too easily
have been construed as treachery, and in a patriotic climate the plays
were destined not to be financial successes. Dix, however, was to put aside
idealism and East Coast intellectuality and to embrace commercialism. In
1916, on the invitation of her agent and friend Bibi DeMille (mother of
Cecil and William), Dix took her daughter on the train heading out west
and joined Famous Players–Lasky as a writer. Her husband joined her
later.

William DeMille was in charge of the scenario department at Lasky's. A
playwright himself, he wanted writers with similar backgrounds working
for him. Dix found herself in the company of Margaret Turnbull, Gladys
Unger and Marion Fairfax, among others, while elsewhere at the studio
Jeanie Macpherson was working for William's brother Cecil B. Even with
so much female company, Dix felt the need to be seen as one of the boys.
She smoked, 'in order to look as busy and wise during silences at story
conferences as men lighting up their cigarettes or knocking out their
pipes'.[46] She liked to hang out with the crew, 'a craftsman (*sic*) among
mutually respecting craftsmen'.[47] While worried about the kind of clothes
she should wear to work, she finally chose a uniform of 'corduroy skirt, a
blouse with an orange tie, a leather jacket and boots.'[48]

Dix was obviously concerned about what was appropriate to men and
women writers in terms both of their behaviour and the subjects about
which they wrote. As a playwright she had occasionally written under a
male pseudonym; according to Evelyn Scott, she did so for one play popu-

lar on the repertory circuits of the time – *Breed of Treshams* – since it was 'better suited to so much steel and leather'. Dix preferred writing for actors – her assignments included those for the famous stars of the day, Wallace Reid and Sessue Hayakawa – but found that she was more likely to be asked to write for women. Scott recalls her mother's delight after one actress made a dramatic exit from the set. 'Mother wasn't really sorry. That was one less female for whom, being female herself, she might be called upon to write. The "money men" kept seeing her gift for violence, as in *The Cost of Hatred*, and tried not to believe it. Surely a woman named Beulah Marie Dix would *want* to write for a star named Mary Miles Minter?'[49]

It was not always presumed that women should want to write mainly for their own sex, though Dix's experience was becoming more the rule. Certain writers developed unique relationships with stars or directors that transcended such assumptions. June Mathis wrote for and, according to Hollywood fable, discovered Rudolph Valentino; Anita Loos worked with D. W. Griffith, providing her famously witty intertitles for a range of projects, both male and female led. The Western – the most masculine of genres – attracted many women writers from the silent period onwards. One of the first was Adele Buffington, who began in the film business at the age of nineteen, first as a cashier at a movie house, then as a full-time scenarist after selling her first script for $300 in 1919. Working mainly for Thomas Ince and Fox, she wrote a 'darn lot of horse operas', as she described them, for such early stars in the saddle as Tom Mix and Buck Jones.[50] Unfortunately, there is little material on her and questions about her interest in the genre remain unanswered. What is known is that later in her career she became infamous in the industry for her right-wing opinions.

Dix's main reason for resisting female lead stories was that they tended to deal with lighter subject matter. But this was not always the case for other women writers. As Kevin Brownlow writes in *Behind the Mask of Innocence*, during the silent era there were hard-hitting films that dealt with a range of contentious social issues. Women were writing stories dealing with such concerns as drug abuse (Dorothy Davenport Reid's *Human Wreckage*, 1923) or juvenile delinquency (Jeanie Macpherson's *The Godless Girl*, 1928). But they were also contributing to projects concerning issues more obviously relevant to their gender, such as birth control and female emancipation, and the films played an important role in the various campaigns for reform.

Indeed the women leading these campaigns turned to film to promote their causes, believing that the medium could help take their message far further than their pamphlets and lectures. The suffragette picture *Votes for Women* (1912) was written by Mary Ware Dennett, Secretary of the New York State League, and involved many key suffrage leaders on the East Coast, both on and behind the screen. The woman behind *Birth Control* (1916) was Margaret Sanger, the champion of contraception, who wrote, produced and starred in the film that dramatised aspects of her tireless involvement in her crusade – including a spell in prison. The British campaigner Marie Stopes wrote *Maisie's Marriage* (1923), a melodrama with a hidden birth control message about a young woman who aspires to escape from her life in 'slumland'.

But it was the theatre actress turned film-maker Lois Weber who was most prominent in the area of social conscience films. Indeed Brownlow comments of her: 'Only one film-maker in America devoted an entire career to making what were known as "thought films".'[51] As the title of a lecture that Weber delivered in 1913 to the Women's City Club of Los Angeles indicates, she believed in 'The Making of Picture Plays that will have an influence for good on the public mind'. Weber had experienced the ignominies of poverty first-hand. In her early life, her own impecunious circumstances had once forced her to beg on the street, while later she worked as a social worker in slum areas of New York and Pittsburgh. Her films – which she wrote, directed, produced and often appeared in – were testimony to her conviction that social change was both necessary and possible. She found and tackled inequality in all areas of life. She advocated birth control (though opposed abortion in *Where are My Children?*, 1916) and presented a fictionalised account of the life of Margaret Sanger, whom she also played, in *The Hand that Rocks the Cradle* (1917).[52] *The Jew's Christmas* (1913) was a protest against racial prejudice for which Weber and her husband and occasional collaborator, Phillip Smalley, called in a group of rabbis for advice, while in *The People vs. John Doe* (1916) she made a forceful case against capital punishment.

With these and other titles, Weber is seen as one of the most important early film-makers, though the pattern of her career is a sad reflection on the changes that were to affect women as the cinema industry grew up. When Weber started out in the early 1910s, the prospects for women writer/directors were promising. By 1920, the director Ida May Park could state in Catherine Filene's *Careers for Women* that directing could present 'no finer calling' for women, and she encouraged her readers in that particular vocation. But during the 1920s there was little else to inspire these young hopefuls, as the names that had emerged in the previous decade – including Weber and Park – faded away. When Filene updated her guide in 1934, now entitled *Careers for Women – New Ideas, New Methods, New Opportunities to Fit a New World*, the situation for women in the film industry in the new era of the 'talkie' seemed to have regressed. The entry on directing was no longer included. It was replaced with a piece on screenwriting, as the craft was now called. A pattern was thus established in which screenwriting became the predominant outlet for women wanting to shape the substance of the images on the screen. It was a pattern that wasn't to be properly disrupted for another forty years.

Notes

1. *Man's World, Woman's Place, Film Library Quarterly*, Winter 1971–2, p. 27.
2. The film historian Kevin Brownlow defines the term scenario more specifically:

'The word scenario – replaced today by the term screenplay – did not mean shooting script. It was the sequence of scenes, the story told in visual terms, originally devised to explain as clearly as possible what its author had in mind.' *The Parade's Gone By* (London: Secker and Warburg, 1968), pp. 270–1.

3.   While no data have been compiled to support this assumption, it is a rough estimate that is commonly agreed upon. See Ann Martin and Virginia Clark, *What Women Wrote: Scenarios, 1912–1929* (University Publications of America, Cinema History Microfilm series, 1987), p. v. of Introduction.

4.   See Kathy Peiss's excellent study *Cheap Amusements* (Temple University Press, 1986), p. 148. 'When pictures moved from the arcade's kinescopes to nickelodeon screens, women's attendance soared; women comprised 40 per cent of the working-class movie audience in 1910.'

5.   *Views and Film Index*, 3 October 1908.

6.   Sharon Smith, *Women Who Make Movies* (New York: Hopkinson and Blake, 1975), p. 2.

7.   Alice Guy Blaché, 'Alice Guy: La naissance du cinéma', *Image et Son* 283, April 1974, p. 42.

8.   Brownlow, *The Parade's Gone By*, pp. 275–6.

9.   *Photoplay*, January 1915, p. 72

10.   Gene Gauntier, *Blazing the Trail* (unpublished memoirs at MOMA, New York).

11.   Ibid.

12.   Ibid.

13.   See Julie Wheelwright's *Amazons and Military Maids* for more information about this.

14.   From Gene Gauntier's unpublished memoirs.

15.   Ibid.

16.   *Moving Picture World*, March 1913.

17.   Kevin Brownlow, *Behind the Mask of Innocence* (London: Jonathan Cape, 1990), p. 4.

18.   Daniel J. Czitrom, *Media and the American Mind* (Chapel Hill: University of North Carolina Press, 1982), p. 53.

19.   From Gene Gauntier's unpublished memoirs.

20.   Ibid.

21.   Ibid.

22.   *Photoplay*, January 1915, p. 72.

23.   *Moving Picture World*, 2 May 1914.

24.   *New York Telegraph*, 19 April 1914.

25.   Alice Martin, 'From "Wop" Parts to Bossing the Job', *Photoplay*, October 1916.

26.   Unidentified clipping, Billy Rose Theatre collection, New York.

27.   Jeanie Macpherson, 'Back Stage Glimpse of My Boss', *Hollywood Reporter*, 8 October 1940.

28.   Charles Higham, *Cecil B. DeMille* (London: W. H. Allen, 1974), p. 38.

29.   Evelyn F. Scott, *Hollywood: When the Silents Were Golden* (New York: McGraw-Hill, 1972), p. 70.

30.   *Herald Tribune*, 30 November 1919.

31.   Untitled and undated clipping in the Jeanie Macpherson file from the Billy Rose Theatre Collection, New York.

32.   *New York World*, 20 October 1917.

33.   *New York Telegraph*, 21 October 1917.

34.   *Moving Picture World*, 21 July 1917.

35.   Ibid.

36.   John Emerson and Anita Loos, *Breaking into Movies* (New York: James A. McCann Co., 1921); Catherine Carr, *The Art of Photoplay Writing* (New York: Hannis Jordan Co., 1914); Clara Beranger *Writing for the Screen* (Dubuque, IA: William C. Brown, 1950); Frances Marion, *How to Write and Sell Film Scripts* (New York: Garland, 1978, reprint).

37.   Antony Glyn, *Elinor Glyn* (London: Hutchinson, 1955), p. 279.

38.   Ivan St Johns, 'It Isn't Sex – It's Good Pictures', *Photoplay*, March 1926.

39. Ibid. p. 287
40. Frances Marion, *Off With Their Heads! A Serio-Comic Tale of Hollywood* (New York: Macmillan, 1972), p. 75.
41. Ibid., p. 292.
42. *Photoplay*, August 1923.
43. 'Introducing Eve Unsell', *Picture Show*, 18 October 1919.
44. Marion, *Off With Their Heads!*, pp. 28–9.
45. Scott, *Hollywood: When the Silents Were Golden*, p. 40.
46. Ibid., p. 34.
47. Ibid., p. 73.
48. Ibid., p. 58.
49. Ibid., p. 73.
50. Los Angeles *Herald Examiner*, 23 November 1972.
51. Brownlow, *Behind the Mask of Innocence*, p. xxi.
52. No relation to the 1992 film of the same title.

2

The Golden Ghetto

Working for the Studios in the 1930s and 1940s

> When we carried the scripts on which we were doing rewrites, we made sure that they were in unmarked, plain covers. But we knew male writers were complaining about the 'tyranny of the woman writer' supposedly prevalent at all studios then, and particularly at MGM.
>
> Frances Marion

In 1927 a new dimension was brought to Hollywood cinema with the release of the first sound film, *The Jazz Singer*. The success of the 'talkies' brought such increased wealth to the already prosperous industry that it was almost immune to the chaotic aftermath of the Wall Street crash of 1929. Riding high on record box-office figures and huge profits, the industry was believed to be 'Depression-proof' as the new decade began. The dampened economic climate, however, was to affect the overall structure of the industry by the early 1930s. As the smaller companies folded, the studio system came into being with Fox, Warners, MGM, Paramount and RKO emerging as the biggest names. Streamlined for maximum efficiency, each studio was beginning to develop its own discernible house style, often reflecting the preoccupations and tastes of the studio head. At the outset of the 30s MGM, under the guidance of Irving Thalberg, favoured the lavish melodrama typified by such films as *Grand Hotel* (1932). Meanwhile the most powerful man at Warners, Darryl F. Zanuck, fostered the gritty and hard-edged realism found in such movies as *The Public Enemy* (1931).

Within these larger and more formally organised concerns there was no longer the flexibility of roles that had been enjoyed in the previous decades, and the division of labour became more marked. With the growing sophistication of film-making techniques, each of the creative departments became more specialised. None more so than screenwriting, which was radicalised with the advent of the 'talkie'. But, to begin with, the transition from silents to talkies had put the screenwriting departments into hiatus. 'Everyone was floundering, there was no theory about anything,' recalled the screenwriter Marguerite Roberts, who had joined the Fox

29

Film Corporation in 1927, first as a secretary to the studio head Winfield Sheehan, then as a reader in the script department where she worked alongside chief script editor Al Lewis.

The advent of talkies meant that Lewis needed writers with a talent for crisp and persuasive dialogue. His roster of silent scenarists had yet to prove that they could spin lines. So, like the department heads at the other studios, he sent out scouts to New York, which was famed for its witty and erudite wordsmiths. There they swept Broadway for playwrights and dialogue directors (who were employed specifically to coach actors on their diction – but were soon abandoned as they disrupted the work of the overall directors), while also combing the magazines and newspapers for the wisest of wise-cracking journalists. Anyone who could string an elegant sentence together had a chance. But arriving in Hollywood, this new wave of writers was to find a doubtful place reserved for them. There was some inverted snobbery in the industry stalwarts' attitudes to the influx of graduate types. Roberts recalled that inscribed over the doorway of the then newly constructed writers' building at Fox was the line: 'One picture is worth a thousand words.' The Depression, however, had so badly affected the literary and publishing world on the East Coast that this word-rush seemed like manna to the voracious scribes who made their way west.

Women featured in this new migration, having already established themselves in the relevant literary fields. The playwrights Zoë Akins, Frances Goodrich (who collaborated throughout her career with her husband Albert Hackett), the short story writers Tess Slesinger, Mary McCall Jnr, Hagar Wilde (without whom there would have been no *Bringing Up Baby*), Viña Delmar (who wrote *The Awful Truth*), Vera Caspary (whose novel *Laura* would be turned into one of the film noir classics of the 40s) and the infamous wit Dorothy Parker were among the many who received the call to go to Hollywood. Meanwhile, various women scenarists from the silent era successfully shifted to sound. They included Frances Marion, Sonya Levien, Lenore Coffee, Bess Meredyth and Anita Loos, who were talented but, more importantly, good business-women who could sell themselves as indispensable assets during this period of industrial evolution.

Sonya Levien, for instance, was undaunted by the new preoccupation with dialogue. It was her theory that one couldn't depend solely on it since she believed that the image was still essential to the telling of the story: dialogue only enhanced the images. For her, therefore, the silent scenarist's training was the best. Indeed she came to be relied upon by producers for her skilful construction of scripts. But she still faced stiff competition in the new climate. A letter written by Levien in 1928 to Chandler Sprague, a Fox production executive, reveals more than just a grim determination to secure a post at the studio after a less than happy interview.

I am sorry that I was such a dumb dora when I saw you yesterday afternoon. It isn't that I am over-modest, but I have such a horror of the female scenarist who pierces you with a fanatical eye and tells you, foaming at the mouth, what a brilliant 100 per center she is, that I usu-

Sonya Levien gave up a career as a lawyer to pursue screenwriting which she found to be a more acceptable profession for a woman.

ally act perversely when it comes to selling myself. And since I was the fifth female in the line within a period of half an hour, I was conscious that you had your fill of the poisonous species.[1]

The letter has a sharply competitive edge to it as Levien puts down the other women in classically misogynist fashion, presumably to court favour with Sprague and distinguish herself from the rest of the rabid brood even if she demeans herself in the process. But despite what she describes as a deluge of female applicants, when in the following year Fox unveiled the new studio at Culver City and its line-up of talent, only five of thirty-three writers featured in the publicity were women. Levien was hired, along with fellow veteran of the silents, Elinor Glyn, and the playwrights Akins, Marion Orth and Clare Kummer. Levien's letter might belie the fact that she was once a suffragette who left the legal profession to become a writer because she couldn't stand the constant jibbing and teasing from her male peers. She found journalism and screenwriting far more tolerant professions. Indeed, writing was accepted as a far more 'feminine' activity than battling it out in the courtroom. But even so, in her reflections on the changing prospects for career women in the industry in the late 20s she comments: 'The novelty of their being in business is over. They must compete with men on equal terms. It's a struggle between men and women in every profession.'[2] It seems from Levien's letter to Sprague, however, that women were more likely to have to compete with women, not men, for a prized place. As was the case with other professions, the film industry just couldn't be seen to be employing too many of them in prominent positions. 'When I first started, men didn't fear us because we were a novelty and they treated us with amusement and courtesy, but now we are a thorn in the field of competition, another factor to fight.'[3] This observation could be related to all other spheres that professional women had encroached upon as the Depression took its hold.

In this new competitive studio atmosphere, it seemed that women writers were less likely to encourage each other. During the 1910s and 20s, there had been more opportunities for women to advance other women's careers. Anita Loos commented that through the silent era 'the two most important executives I knew in the movies were Mary Pickford and Lillian Gish'. Frances Marion was also indebted to Pickford, though it was to Lois Weber that she owed her vocational calling in the first place. Starting out as a commercial artist, Marion was taken on by Weber, who trained her in the craft of movie-making. Later, Marion honoured her mentor by paying for Weber's funeral expenses when the veteran director died a destitute in 1939. In the 60s, Marion was moved to observe:

> While it's perfectly true that many important men like Oliver Morosco, William A. Brady, William Randolph Hearst, Samuel Goldwyn and Irving Thalberg helped and encouraged me, it's consoling to know how many women gave me real aid when I stood at the crossroads. Too many women go around saying that women in important positions don't help their own sex, but that was never my experience. In my case they were Marie Dressler, Lois Weber, Mary Pickford, Elsie Janis, Mary Roberts Rinehart, Adela Rogers St John, Hedda Hopper, Bess Meredyth, Anita Loos … the list is endless, believe me![4]

During the 20s Marion was a well-known hostess of 'hen parties', to which the cream of female talent, both on and off camera, were invited. Indeed, because women were involved in various aspects of production during that period there was a far greater sense of professional and social networking. From the 30s on, the more common alliance would be between the writers and the actresses at the studio, as will be discussed later.

Meanwhile women were more likely to be taking their place as the secretarial and administrative minions at the studios (as they were in other industries), unsung but essential to the smooth running of the departments. Newly recruited to MGM in the 1930s, the young writer/producer Sam Marx found that he depended upon a score of women heading the various departments to do with 'stories and writers':

They were the best I would ever know in any motion picture studio anywhere. Dorothy Pratt ran the reading department, in which a dozen readers recorded and synopsized an unending flow of picture material. Natalie Bucknall, a stalwart Russian, reputed to have ridden with the Cossacks in the World War, headed the research department. Edith Farrell, a stern task mistress, was in charge of the secretarial workers. My position as a story editor made me boss of them all, but I chose for a long time to maintain this sovereignty in name only, knowing far less than they did about their work.[5]

The most important woman in this invisible army was Kate Corbaley, script reader for Irving Thalberg and studio head Louis B. Mayer. Corbaley was the sombre-suited, no-nonsense Scheherazade of the studio who started out as a silent scenarist for the Triangle Film Company, then joined MGM as a reader in 1926. A 1930s newspaper profile comments in sentimental style that she embarked on her career when her husband died and she was left to support four daughters. The widow earning her mite – it was the kind of story that MGM would sell. It was, in fact, a divorce that prompted the new direction, revealing just how taboo a failed marriage was for a professional woman. Dependable and invisible (her name never appeared on any credit), she sifted through plays, novels and newspaper clippings to find material that could be turned into a good movie, then pitched the ideas to Thalberg and Mayer. Since Mayer was barely literate, he apparently loved to listen to the matronly Corbaley spin the yarns. Hollywood folklore has it that she reminded him of his own mother who used to read him stories when he was a child.

Corbaley's power was extensive; she was relied upon for what the producer Hunt Stromberg once described as her 'down to earth' – implicitly conservative – taste. A profile written in 1938 comments:

Her judgment on scenarios is regarded as unerring. It is estimated that her firm 'No', rising from the usual yea-saying chorus, has saved her studio from many millions of wasted dollars. She is friendly, courteous and warm-hearted – but in business she is a battler and a champion. She has also sold hundreds of stories to producers by her clear, logical presentations.[6]

Corbaley had enough knowledge and experience of the industry to produce films herself, but this 'battler' seemed content to stay anonymous. It was almost as though she didn't approve of career women. Revealingly, in the light of her failed marriage, though she graduated from the prestigious Stanford University she refused to educate her daughters for professional work. As she told her interviewer, her view 'was to prepare them to become good wives and mothers'.[7]

Despite the development of these conservative patterns in which women were seconded to less prestigious posts, Sonya Levien would write positively in Catherine Filene's 1934 edition of *Careers for Women* of employment opportunities for women who wanted to be screenwriters. 'A woman has as good a chance as a man to become a successful screen-writer. Her sex creates no awkwardness or difficulty. She has always been a familiar figure in the screen ranks.'[8] She knew how important it was to encourage young women in their aspirations, even if the reality was tougher than she would publicly admit.

Certainly some studios were more enthusiastic about women writers than others. Filene notes, in the introduction to the section on 'The Motion Picture Industry' in her book, that B. P. 'Ben' Schulberg, head of Paramount, had recently announced a new initiative to promote women in key production and creative positions. '"The purpose will be to accentu-ate the woman's angle and make certain that films appeal both to women and men." Each of his pictures is to be a collaboration of a man and woman writer, each is being edited by a woman.'[9] Schulberg's proposal makes clear that producers believed that women writers were better able to cater for the tastes of a female audience, which were often construed as rather mysterious and something that men could not necessarily recog-nise. Commenting on the work of Zoë Akins, who specialised in stories about the 'female heart … which [are] relished principally by women', one journalist wrote: 'Akins is a master of this subtle psychological woman's stuff. … This feminine angle may partly explain why the New York critics (all men) usually pan her shows … the critics were cool but the ladies saved the day. They bought tickets and dragged their men with them. Word got around. Audiences grew.'[10]

What became of Schulberg's project at Paramount remains unclear, as there is no other record to support Filene's note. Around 1934/35 there was a handful of women writers at Paramount. Of the productions released in 1934, Jane Hinton collaborated with George Marion Jnr to adapt Stephen Bekeffi's stage play, *Kiss and Make Up*. 'Women were putty in his hands,' teased the poster for the comedy about the amorous exploits of a Parisian beautician (played by Cary Grant). The production featured all the lavish costumes and accessories of a woman's magazine spread and was certainly designed to attract female trade. Elsewhere, Gladys Lehman contributed to a supernatural romance, *Death Takes a Holiday* (1934), Shirley Temple's debut *Little Miss Marker* (1934), and a gothic melodrama, *The Double Door* (1934), based on playwright Elizabeth McFadden's Broadway success about a rich heiress who terrorises her feeble half-brother and his new bride. Other women writers credited with films produced at Paramount that year included Sylvia Thalberg (sister of Irving) and Virginia Van Upp, who contributed to the romantic comedies *Now and Forever* (another Shirley Temple vehicle, with Gary Cooper and Carole Lombard providing the love interest) and *The Pursuit of Happiness*. Preoccupied with romance and the family, this selection of films co-scripted by women certainly courted what Schulberg perceived to be the 'woman's angle'.

But during the 30s the link between the 'woman's film' and the woman screenwriter was most obvious at MGM. The roster of women writers was extensive and illustrious, with Zoë Akins, Lenore Coffee, Lillian Hellman, Anita Loos, Frances Marion, Bess Meredyth, Jane Murfin, Dorothy Parker,

Adela Rogers St John and Salka Viertel, among others, all working there at some point in the decade. As representatives of the old guard Marion, Meredyth and Loos found that they were asked for their advice on virtually every script MGM produced during the 1930s. As Marion commented:

> It would have been embarrassing had other writers discovered that the executives asked our opinions about their work and that we were, without credit, making revisions. When we carried the scripts on which we were doing re-writes, we made sure that they were in unmarked, plain covers. But we knew male writers were complaining about the 'tyranny of the woman writer' supposedly prevalent at all studios then, and particularly at MGM.[11]

The actual numbers hardly suggest a 'tyranny', but the power of women writers was evidently noticeable – and possibly perceived as threatening – at MGM. This can be mainly attributed to the Production Head of the studio at the time, Irving Thalberg, who had encouraged women writers since his days as a story editor at Universal. He, like Schulberg, believed that women were better suited to writing material for female stars and that a 'woman's touch' would bring to the script a certain authenticity of feeling. During the 30s, MGM had an impressive line-up of actresses needing star roles to be created for them. Some writers were hired because they were good at writing for certain types. According to Sam Marx, Anita Loos became a valuable asset because the studio had so many 'femme fatales' types, including Joan Crawford, Norma Shearer and Jean Harlow, and Loos could always be relied on for 'shady lady' stories. 'Whenever we had a Jean Harlow picture on the agenda, we always thought of Anita first,' recalled Marx.[12] Other writers found themselves working exclusively for particular actresses. Such was the association between Salka Viertel and Greta Garbo.

Born at the turn of the century into a middle-class Jewish family in Galicia, Viertel came to Hollywood via Vienna and Berlin in 1929. A former actress – she had been discovered by Max Reinhardt – she had been involved in setting up the influential avant-garde theatre group 'Die Truppe', and moved to the United States when her husband, writer/director Berthold Viertel, was invited to work for Fox. Coming from a left-wing intellectual milieu – her friends included Einstein and Eisenstein – Viertel found Hollywood, with its endless whirl of empty-minded lunches and parties, very unsatisfying. Instead she became famous for her own literary salons. Viertel started to write on the suggestion of Garbo, whom she had befriended after they met at one of the many émigré gatherings (it is believed by some that they became lovers). She subsequently worked on four of Garbo's films: *Queen Christina* (1932), *The Painted Veil* (1934), *Anna Karenina* (1935) and the star's swan-song *The Two Faced Woman* (1941). Though it was a happy collaboration, Viertel was all too aware of the limitations of being a 'Garbo specialist' and knew that she was often being courted as a writer on projects because of her friendship with the star. She tried repeatedly to find assignments that would take her in new directions, but her career practically finished with Garbo's. One of her last pieces of work for the cinema, however, was to provide, uncredited, the narration for Jean Renoir's *The River* (1951).

Viertel's first screenplay, *Queen Christina*, is most representative of her work for Garbo. She originated the idea with the encouragement of the actress, who had ideally wanted the film to be produced independently in Europe. Viertel had become fascinated with the seventeenth-century Swedish monarch after reading an obscure biography of her as well as Strindberg's play on the same subject, though she dismissed the latter as misogynous. Strindberg, she believed, had failed to see the real attractions of this bold heroine. 'She was eccentric, brilliant; and her masculine education and complicated sexuality made her an almost contemporary character.'[13] Garbo eventually took the project to an enthusiastic Thalberg, who teamed the novice Viertel with the veteran Bess Meredyth (the British writer Claudine West was also involved at a later stage). Typically, Thalberg had his own ideas about the film, which he outlined in one of their first meetings. As Viertel recalled in her memoirs, *The Kindness of Strangers*:

> He asked if I had seen the German film *Mädchen in Uniform*, a great success in Europe and New York. It had been directed by a woman, my former colleague at the *Neue Wiener Buhne*, Leontine Sagan, and dealt with a lesbian relationship. Thalberg asked: 'Does not Christina's affection for her lady-in-waiting indicate something like that?' He wanted me to 'keep it in mind,' and perhaps if 'handled with taste it would give us very interesting scenes.' Pleasantly surprised by his broadmindedness, I began to like him very much.[14]

The popularity and commercial success of *Mädchen in Uniform* no doubt accounted for Thalberg's interest in the lesbian angle, though *Queen Christina*'s director Rouben Mamoulian was to play it down to the point of almost eradicating it in the final film. Viewed now, the heroine's 'complicated sexuality' – her lesbianism – is buried in the subtext of the film rather than being a manifest concern. *Queen Christina* demonstrates perfectly how the studio system could contain and neutralise a woman writer's attempts to challenge conventional representation of women, even with the star and seemingly also the Head of Production behind the idea. But at least it got made.

Other projects were less successful. Viertel suggested many film ideas for Garbo, including stories based on the lives of George Sand, Marie Curie, St Joan and Sappho. Such proposals, which all had the support of Garbo, demonstrate the writer's commitment to more progressive portrayals of women, but they were all abandoned, often after much time had been put into them.

Viertel started work on *Marie Curie* in 1939, visiting Europe just before war broke out to do some initial research on the scientist. There she found that most of Curie's relatives and associates were initially distrustful about the idea of a biopic, but her thoughtful approach to the subject assuaged their fears about any brash 'Hollywoodisation' of Curie's life. Viertel, however, proved to be over-optimistic about the idea. On her return to California, she had to contend with Sidney Franklin, the less than sympathetic producer who had been assigned to the project at MGM. The first script conference started ominously, with Franklin, who spent the meeting slumped on his office couch, announcing: 'Well, guys, last night, after dinner, I talked to Mrs Franklin about the story and she agreed with me: no pretty girl would ever study chemistry or physics.'[15] Viertel's male colleagues sat silently around the recumbent producer, leaving it up to her to wade in first and protest. She was not helped by another writer in the room, who also made it clear that he hated all 'bluestockings' and intellectual women. Franklin went ahead with the script only after agreeing, much to Viertel's disdain, that the Nobel prize-winner's 'weird' interest in science could be 'motivated' by her being a foreigner. But Viertel didn't have to argue with this since she was taken off the project. The film was finally made as Madame Curie (1944) starring Walter Pidgeon and Greer Garson. 'Mr and Mrs Miniver re-united' ran the publicity. It was soon after this experience that Viertel expressed a keen desire to leave Hollywood.

The Marie Curie fiasco happened a few years after Thalberg's sudden death in 1936. It is worth speculating what might have happened to the project if he had been around still. Thalberg's death shocked all those who knew and worked with him. It seemed like the end of an era. Zoë Akins described in a letter to her agent, Alice Kauser, feelings that were shared by other Hollywood writers:

> While I had Mr Thalberg's protection I was reasonably sure that I was out of the political fires and that what I wrote would reach the screen. But since he is dead, and now that panic has descended on the 'Industry' as a whole, I had rather return to a room in Washington Square and walk to and from the theatre, than go through the onslaught of nerves I have endured for so many years.[16]

Thalberg seemed to have more respect for women writers than others and his attitude to Queen Christina certainly reveals a more liberal approach to the depiction of women, even if it was only the thought of a healthy profit margin that prompted his decision. But his positive influence was also evident in the case of The Redheaded Woman (1932). The comedy was based on Katherine Brush's cause célèbre of a novel which told the picaresque tale of a young arriviste's progress from shop-girl to nobleman's mistress. It was to star the dame of the rumpled boudoir, Jean Harlow, as the heroine Lil Andrews. Scott Fitzgerald was originally hired to adapt the story but he was quickly replaced by Anita Loos, having failed to understand that Thalberg wanted a script that allowed the audience to laugh with rather than at this auburn Lorelei Lee. Loos capitalised on Harlow's mocking sensuality and under her pen the film became a flip meditation on men and sex, with the actress playing her wanton gold-digger role to the hilt. This was a girl who was in control and the audience roared with approval at her antics.

But not everyone was amused. Women's clubs and church groups protested about this depiction of a freewheeling love-style. *The Redheaded Woman* was among a handful of films that highlighted the resurgent issue of censorship in the mid-30s. Cinema in the previous decade indulged in a certain licentiousness that allowed Cecil B. DeMille's risqué bathroom revels and Elinor Glyn's flirtatious 'It' girls. But films like *The Redheaded Woman* proved to be too much, prompting calls from conservatives for more stringent censorship rules, which were finally to be answered with the introduction in 1934 of the Production Code Administration's new prescript. Under the hawkish eye of the 'Hitler of Hollywood', Joseph Breen, the code crusaded for the kind of clean entertainment that the Catholic Legion of Decency could 'A'-grade as morally unobjectionable. If there was a thin line between the 'women's picture', with its traditional fascination with romance, and the 'sex picture', this new censorious climate certainly affected women writers who wanted to portray the kind of female characters, such as the redhead Lil, who could confidently ply their sexuality.[17] No one was more hampered by the code than the writer and performer Mae West, who in 1933 had ruffled Breen's feathers with the ribald sexual innuendo of *She Done Him Wrong* and *I'm No Angel* (both huge box-office successes that contributed towards saving Paramount from financial disaster). But it was the independence of her extravagant and libidinous self-made women, rather than her fruity one-liners, that was really more disconcerting.

But while the censors checked women like West, other writers were held back by their own self-regulated conservatism when it came to the depiction of women on screen. In her best-selling *How to Write and Sell Film Stories* (published in 1937 and dedicated to Irving Thalberg, as a 'tribute to his vision and genius'), Frances Marion expounded on what makes a successful screenplay. 'Women, and do not forget that the majority of movie-goers are women, like to see well-furnished interiors and modes of life among cultured people of more means than their own.'[18] She continues later:

> *Domestic relations*, with their loves, apprehensions, struggles, anxieties and joys, offer a plot pattern that has tremendous interest to women. …
> Women's interest in the problems of married life accounts for much of Ann Harding's success. These plots often skirt immorality, bleached a bit by the insistence that the heroine's motives are pure. They threaten a sex problem rather than portray it.[19]

In her chapter on 'The Theme', Marion suggests two successful storylines: 'The wife who earns more than her husband loses her love', and 'A woman's need for romance makes her an undependable factor in business.'[20] This kind of viewpoint was often echoed by other women in the industry. Zoë Akins' prognosis for storylines was also similar to Marion's. '[Characters] usually have nice manners and leisure and were reared in sheltered upper-middle class homes. Most of the men live for their businesses and women for their feelings or their children. The businesses are successful and the women's feelings are quite subtle.'[21]

Frances Marion found that she was as much subject to the image-making process as the women stars she wrote for.

Akins endorsed such storylines by declaring in one article: 'A woman with a career is a tragedy. Women are not fitted for careers. I, who have one, say it!' Regarding her own life, Marion also professed that husbands and children should come before career. Her friend, the journalist and screenwriter Adela Rogers St John, believed, however, that Marion had put her husband, the Western star Fred Thomson's career too far ahead of hers when he was alive (he died of tetanus poisoning in 1928 when their children were still young). Interestingly she often

Frances Marion found at work with her assistant.

penned scripts for her husband, but under a *nom de plume*. 'You'll find all sorts of men's names listed as Fred's writers. "Frank M. Clifton" was one that I remember, and he's nobody else but me.'[22] Her explanation was simple. 'I didn't want to go on record as the writer of my husband's scripts. Neither Fred nor I thought it wise professionally. Besides, there were times when I couldn't legally write Fred's stories – when I was under exclusive contract elsewhere.'[23] But it might also have been a case of Marion not wanting to eclipse her husband's star, though it was clear to everyone who knew her that Marion's career was the more valuable of the two.

There is a contradiction in Marion's and Akins' traditionalist approach regarding favoured story-lines, given that they proved to be very dependable businesswomen who accrued large incomes often to support their families. Indeed Marion was one of the top salaried writers and was so powerful that the studios allowed her to work at home, a privilege granted to few, which enabled her to care for her children (along with a retinue of nannies) and her career simultaneously. But while Marion seemed happy to endorse conservative story-lines in the 1930s, it was not always the case. Only a decade before, Marion had written an article for *Photoplay* in which she explained why novels are often changed when they are adapted for screen. Her choice of illustration is revealing:

A producer buys a story because it is a 'big seller'. Sometimes it is a splendid story for a man. The woman plays an important role in it, but a passive role. He hands it over to us poor picked-on scribes and says: 'Make this a great vehicle for Norma Talmadge, or Gloria Swanson, or Mae Murray!' When the smelling salts revive us we go to work. What happens to the author's story? !!!!****!!!! – We tear it down, we reconstruct it, we make the woman dominate, and the male character as passive as every woman would like to have her husband. We end up with a splendid vehicle for a woman star – and the cyclone-wrecked story.[24]

Marion's ideas for screenplays were subject to the changing fashions and formulas of the studio around her. Dominant, vampish women may have been fashionable figures in cinema during the pre-code era of Swanson and co, but that was to change. Marion was powerful, but not powerful enough to challenge the producer's ideas. She commented that, during the 30s, 'I was beginning to feel that film writers are like Penelope – knitting their stories all day just to have somebody else unravel their work by night.'[25] It was a situation that left her increasingly disillusioned with the movie business. To her, though, the solution was apparent. 'If a writer wanted to maintain any control over what he [sic] wrote, he would have to become a writer-director or a writer-producer. Writing a screenplay had become like writing on sand with the wind blowing.'[26]

After leaving MGM in 1937 – her last film for them was *Camille* (1937), starring Greta Garbo – Marion spent a short spell working in England on two films. It proved to be an unsatisfactory experience. On returning to Hollywood, she decided that she would only continue screenwriting if she could secure for herself a production or directing deal – or both. She had directed some films in the 20s, including *The Love Light* (1921) for Mary Pickford, which she described as a challenge since Pickford had never been directed by a woman; and the idea still appealed to her. She took a selection of ideas to Harry Cohn, the studio head at Columbia, and he eventually gave her a contract to produce only. But Marion soon found her ambitions thwarted. Her first project was to have been a big-budget Western, but Columbia's finances had recently been put in jeopardy by the epic *Lost Horizon*, a box-office disaster. Marion's Western was consequently shelved. Plans for another film, a Gloria Swanson vehicle, were also jinxed. Rather than returning to her old craft, Marion decided to pursue a career as a fiction writer as well as taking time out to sculpt. These were activities that no one could interfere with. If such a highly regarded writer was unable to achieve the kind of status she desired, what hope did other ambitious women writers have in Hollywood?

One answer for Marion, however, was to channel some of her frustrations about the writer's lot into her work for the Screen Writers Guild. It is indicative of Marion's standing in the Hollywood community that she was voted Vice-President of the SWG in its first year of operation, 1933. Indeed the SWG was one place were women could rise to positions of power. Among the many women activists in the Guild was Mary McCall Jnr, a smart New York journalist who went to Hollywood and won herself a repu-

Frances Marion (centre) on the set with Binnie Hale (left) and Ann Harding (right).

tation as a 'corpse rouger' (the name given to those who could pump some life into moribund scripts) and adapter – even she was amused to be credited for a *A Midsummer Night's Dream* (directed by Max Reinhardt). She was voted the first woman President of the SWG in 1942 and held office for three terms, finally standing down in 1952. Her brief was to fight for employment rights for screenwriters treated by the studios as their property. But unsurprisingly she did not make any formal improvements for women who, it was generally considered, were paid less than male writers (this was more evident at the bottom end of the scale; comparing the salaries for two top MGM writers in 1937, Jules Furthman earned $84,975, while Zoë Akins earned $76,500). That was something for the agents to negotiate on an individual basis. Nor were such issues as maternity leave for women contracted to the studios considered appropriate agenda items, despite the fact that McCall herself had attended script conferences right up to the day before the birth of her twin sons, and returned to work a few weeks later. It is revealing that when the Writers Guild of America (as the union was known later) decided to set up a women's committee in the 1970s, McCall protested that there shouldn't be such a thing. But this was the perpetual contradiction for the small band of career women of the gen-

Mary McCall Junior, the first woman chair of the SWG at a War Activities meeting.
© *Watson Photo Service, Los Angeles.*

eration of McCall, Marion and the rest. Their own lives were testimony to the possibilities for women, but they could not or did not want to inscribe it on to their work to bring about larger changes.

Notes

1. Letter to Chandler Sprague, 20 March 1928, in the Sonya Levien Collection at the Huntington Library, San Marino, California.
2. *The World*, 28 June 1925, p. 6M.
3. Ibid.
4. DeWitt Bodeen, 'Frances Marion', *Films in Review*, March 1969.
5. Sam Marx, *Mayer and Thalberg: The Make Believe Saints* (New York: Random House, 1975), p. 127.
6. Unidentified clipping in Corbaley file at the Margaret Herrick Centre for Motion Picture Studies, *c.* 1938.
7. Ibid.
8. Sonya Levien, 'The Screenwriter', in Catherine Filene (ed.), *Careers for Women* (Boston: Houghton Mifflin, 1934), p. 436.
9. Ibid. Filene received this information from the Association of Motion Picture Producers. I have tried unsuccessfully to research this report further to see exactly what Paramount's initiative entailed.
10. Arthur Millier, 'Business in Ink', *Los Angeles Times*, 11 September 1938.
11. Bodeen, 'Frances Marion'.
12. Gary Carey, *Anita Loos* (New York: Alfred A. Knopf, 1988), p. 150.
13. Ibid., p. 152.
14. Salka Viertel, *The Kindness of Strangers* (New York: Holt, Rinehart and Winston, 1969), p. 175.

15. Ibid., p. 227.
16. Zoë Akins, letter to Alice Kauser, 20 October 1939, Akins collection at the Huntington Library.
17. See Leonard J. Leff and Jerold L. Simmons's *The Dame in the Kimono: Hollywood, Censorship and the Production Code, From the 1920s to 1960s* (London: Weidenfeld and Nicolson, 1990), p. 36. They point out that for Warners' hard-nosed production chief Zanuck, 'women's pictures' did indeed mean 'sex pictures'.
18. Frances Marion, *How to Write and Sell Film Stories* (New York: Corvici Friede, 1937), p. 62. Ann Harding was queen of the early 30s weepies, often playing dutifully self-sacrificing types. A typical Harding film might be *Devotion* (1931), in which she plays a woman who falls in love with a lawyer and takes a job as governess to his son. Or *Gallant Lady* (1933), in which she has to give up her illegitimate son, but years later marries his adoptive father.
19. Ibid., p. 56.
20. Ibid., p. 105.
21. Millier, 'Business in Ink'.
22. Bodeen, 'Frances Marion', p. 86.
23. Ibid.
24. Frances Marion, 'Why Do They Change the Stories on the Screen?', *Photoplay*, March 1926.
25. Bodeen, 'Frances Marion', p. 139.
26. Ibid.

3

Girl Talk

Writing the Women's Picture

> One of the reasons that they hired me is that the men were off at the war, and they had all these big female stars. The stars had to have roles that served them well. They themselves wanted something in which they weren't just sitting around being a simpering nobody.
>
> Catherine Turney, screenwriter for Warner Bros

The advent of World War Two transformed the lives of women in the 40s as they were drafted into the workforce to replace the men away on service. Like any other industry town, Hollywood was affected by the upheaval. Men made up 85 per cent of employed writers, of which 35 per cent were eligible for conscription. It would seem, then, that for the 15 per cent of women writers there were greater opportunities. But the fact that during the war women were making up a large proportion of the audience also impinged on the fortunes of the female writer. The 'woman's angle' was being stressed more than ever. But this was a decade when the women's picture could begin to show some of the stresses and strains of the female experience.

It was at Warner Bros that the changing prospects for women were most evident, both in front of and behind the camera. By the 40s the company that had forged its identity with such hard-hitting crime pictures as *I Am a Fugitive from a Chain Gang*, and had been considered by all those who worked there to be a man's studio, had widened its repertoire and was demonstrating a commitment to melodramas with a woman in the lead. But the turnabout in Warner Bros' interest in the genre had occurred earlier, in 1938, with the critical and commercial success of the Bette Davis picture *Jezebel*. The Civil War story of a wily Southern belle who attempts to trump society's expectations of her was Warners' own *Gone with the Wind*. It won Davis, who had campaigned vehemently for the role, an Oscar and persuaded the studio that the actress' range could be stretched beyond the gamut of supporting ingénue or gangster moll types that had been foisted upon her previously. By the early 40s, Davis had become one of Warner Bros' most valuable assets, starring in a succession of consummate melodramas such as *The Old Maid* (1939), *Dark Victory* (1939), *The Letter* (1940), *The Little Foxes* (1941), and *Now, Voyager* (1942). Having latched onto a profitable formula, the studio started looking round for other versatile and strong Bette Davis types, and gathered for itself a roster of female stars that included Joan Crawford, Barbara Stanwyck and Ida Lupino.

Meanwhile, though men such as old Warner Bros' hand Casey Robinson were relied on to pen films for this new line-up (Robinson in particular was responsible for many of the Davis titles), the studio also started scouting around for women writers to work on long-term contracts with a specific remit to write for the female stars. They found two: Catherine Turney and Lenore Coffee (later a handful of other women were signed up to work at Warner Bros, including the eccentric right-wing novelist Ayn Rand who adapted her best-selling *The Fountainhead*, about a free-enterprising architect, since no one else would touch it).

Coffee was of the old guard, having started out in 1919 and written for such silent era luminaries as the actress Clara Kimball Young and director Cecil B. DeMille. Her 'women's picture' credentials were consolidated during the 30s when she worked intermittently for MGM, writing roles for Joan Crawford and Jean Harlow among others. Indeed Coffee was called upon by Thalberg to give Crawford, who during the 1920s was mostly identified with flapper roles, a 'new personality'. Coffee's script for *Possessed* (1931) saw Crawford playing a factory girl who goes to New York in search of a fortune and ends up the mistress of a politician. The film was a great success. But Coffee, for reasons that were never quite clear to her, was to fall out of favour with Thalberg and Mayer. Consequently she drifted between MGM and Paramount, finally roosting at Warner Bros, where her scripts included such classic Bette Davis melodramas as *The Great Lie* (1942), *Old Acquaintance* (1943) and *Beyond the Forest* (1949).

Turney was relatively new to the game. She had started out in the 30s as a playwright and director, with her work produced in California, New York and London. On the strength of good reviews for *Bitter Harvest*, a play about Lord Byron's relationship with his half-sister, she was given a contract with MGM and was there in 1935 just before the close of the Thalberg era. During her brief stay she was one of the four writers on *The Bride Wore Red*, a whimsical rags to riches story about a chorus girl, played by Joan Crawford, who is wooed by a couple of playboys at an Alpine resort. The only thing that was notable about this formulaic film was that it was directed by Dorothy Arzner, the sole woman to achieve such status from the late 20s through to the 40s. Indeed Arzner frequently collaborated with women writers. Zoë Akins wrote *Sarah and Son* (1930), *Anybody's Woman* (1930), *Working Girls* (1931) and *Christopher Strong*; Mary McCall Jnr wrote *Craig's Wife* (1936); while Arzner's most celebrated film, *Dance, Girl, Dance* (1940), was co-written by the short story writer Tess Slesinger.[1] Turney never met Arzner, but both separately agreed that their film was a forgettable disaster. She left MGM shortly afterwards. It wasn't until she was invited to work for Warner Bros that she made her mark, her most famous script for the studio being *Mildred Pierce*.

Catherine Turney, one of the first women screenwriters to work at Warner Bros. in the 1940s.

Turney was more than happy to be classified as a 'woman's writer'. It meant employment, and besides, she believed women could bring a more authentic dimension to such stories. The studio would seem to have concurred with this. 'They [Warner Bros] recognised the fact that a woman could handle a story about a woman's troubles better than most men could. Anyway, you can rest assured that if the studio didn't think the woman did a better job, she wouldn't have been there for very long,' recalls Turney. But she soon discovered that women were not suffered gladly at the studio. 'Jack Warner didn't really like women writers, in fact he was petrified of them,' Turney remembered, while Coffee thought that the studio was really 'against it [women]'.

The studio, however, could not avoid the fact that women could make money for them (though Turney emphasises that she did not get the same rates of pay as her male peers). 'One of the reasons that they hired me is that the men were off at the war, and they had all these big female stars. The stars had to have roles that served them well. They themselves wanted something in which they weren't just sitting around being a simpering nobody.' Turney reflects that most of her scripts were about women who were 'battling against the odds'.

Lenore Coffee

She was to write for all the key women at Warner Bros during her stint there. She came to be particularly relied upon by Bette Davis and a life-long friendship between the two was cemented by many sessions of what Turney describes as after-hours 'girl talk'. Indeed Davis chose Turney to work for her on *A Stolen Life* (1946), the first film also produced by the actress for the studio, in which she plays identical twins. It was on Davis's orders that Turney was allowed to be on the set during the filming – a practice disapproved of by the studio since they expected Turney, as a contract writer, to be working on other scripts. But the studio respected Davis's wishes. She was taking her producing role far more seriously than other stars, such as Errol Flynn, who had set up similar deals purely for the financial benefits of a producer's credit. Turney was also approached by other actresses at Warner Bros who had found studio-owned properties they wanted her to develop. Barbara Stanwyck first read Clare Jaynes's *Instruct My Sorrows*, which Turney turned into *My Reputation*. Turney found that the women stars at Warner Bros were her most obvious associates.

For when she first arrived at the studio, Turney was the only woman clocking in every morning into the writers' building and lunching at the writers' tables in the studio commissary. The veteran Coffee wrote at home, having managed to excuse herself from the strict rule that all writers worked on studio premises. At Warner Bros, Turney noted, writers clustered together at meal times according to their political beliefs. 'At MGM, they sat according to how much money you made. I think that it was very indicative of the studio itself.' At first Turney found her companions to be a rather cynical pack, contemptuous of the new girl on the block.

> The roster of writers was primarily hard-nosed guys, a lot of newspaper men, sports writers. They were inclined to be condescending with me, at the beginning. They used to say, 'What are you working on?' and then, 'Oh yeah, a woman's picture.' And they dismissed it. But they didn't after some of those pictures went out and made a lot of money.[2]

In such a potentially estranging environment, Turney was lucky to find an ally in one of the studio's top producers, Henry Blanke, who adopted her as his protégée. Blanke had been at the studio since the 20s, but rose to prominence in the late 30s as the producer of a string of bio-pics and then, later, the Bette Davis successes. Blanke proved to be a champion of women writers. Indeed his preference for them was particularly noted by the director King Vidor, who once commented that he felt he had to 'put up' with Lenore Coffee on the Blanke films *Beyond the Forest* (1949) and *Lightning Strikes Twice* (1951).

Turney was pleased to have Blanke's support, though their working relationship did not pass without comment.

> Of course the men in the writers' building thought that there was some hanky-panky going on between me and him. But there was none of that. Blanke apparently took a liking to me and decided to teach me the tricks of the trade. For though I had spent some time at MGM, my theatre background showed through. He would go through my scripts with me and scratch bits out. In many ways the women's problem picture was a very tricky one to do since they depended on emotional scenes that could veer towards the sentimental. It was important to approach these moments obliquely rather than punch them on the nose – give them a hard edge. But the most valuable lesson that I learned from Blanke was that it is best to let the camera do as much as possible.

Turney came to be relied on as a highly skilled adapter of other material, whether novels, plays or even existing films. Her first assignment at the studio came from Jerry Wald, an ambitious young producer who asked her to work on James M. Cain's *Mildred Pierce*, a novel he had wanted to bring to the screen since its publication in 1941. The story is a complex and compelling account of a dowdy Glendale housewife who is so devoted to her daughters, especially the eldest, the impetuous Veda, that her husband leaves her. Forced to make a living of her own, she turns her cookery skills to advantage and finally becomes a successful restaurateur, only to have her life and happiness sabotaged by Veda. Turney was fascinated by the premise. But even with Wald behind the project, the studio did not see the immediate appeal in a film version. 'Their attitude was who cares about a woman who knows how to bake pies. It was hardly a very glamorous proposition,' recalls Turney. Studio head Jack Warner also anticipated problems with the Hays Office. In the story Veda has an affair with her mother's second husband; and adultery and incest by proxy were high on the Production Code's list of taboos. Indeed when the novel was first published, Hays Office head Joseph Breen had gone out of his way to describe it as a 'sordid and repellent' work.

In order to appease Breen, Wald decided that a murder mystery twist should be added to what was essentially a melodrama. Such a framework would allow for a resolution in which the despicable Veda – who in the film version kills her lover – could be punished for her transgressive act of loving him in the first place. Wald also struck on the idea that the story could be told in flashback. Curiously the same narrative device was being used in Paramount's adaptation of another Cain novel, *Double Indemnity*, which was released just before *Mildred Pierce* started filming. *Double Indemnity*'s dark story of homicide and adultery marked not only a stylistic breakthrough for film-makers but also signalled some relaxation in the Hays Office's moral patrol of the screens. It was encouraging news to Wald and other producers who wanted to take more risks. Murder could make money, murder spiked with love and lust could make twice as much. With such ingredients added to *Mildred Pierce*, Wald deduced that he would have a hot property on his hands since the film would appeal to more than just the women's audience. He first approached Cain to write a story outline with this new ending in mind, which the writer agreed to do, though he gave up after a couple of months. Then one of Warners' script analysts, Thames Williamson, was brought in to complete the treatment and on the strength of that the studio gave the project the go-ahead.

It was at this point that Turney started working on the script, though she had reservations about the proposed changes:

I felt that the introduction of the flashback idea was a pure gimmick. But when he then said that the story should be told from Mildred's point of view, I began to see how it could work. But I was still unsure about the murder. I worried that it would detract from the core of the story – which is essentially about a housewife's desire to make something of herself, and also her conflict with her daughter Veda. In the novel, there is a younger daughter Kay; she's still there in the film but her role is cut down. I thought it was so sad that Mildred preferred Veda over her and wanted to explore that in the film. But the thing that Jerry [Wald] could never see and that really interested me in the book was that Veda really did have a beautiful voice and ended up singing at the Hollywood Bowl. So in a way, Mildred's worship of this seemingly unworthy daughter was vindicated. But Jerry just wouldn't go for that. He wanted her [Veda] to wind up crooning in some honky tonk – just a big nothing. I can see that the censorship question called for that. But I would have liked to see how it could have worked without the murder business, the relationships between the women in the book are so strange and I think that would have been powerful enough.

Turney's approach married uncomfortably with what Wald wanted and the association between writer and producer was cool. She worked on the script for three months, concentrating on developing the characters' relationships, and was then taken off it while Albert Maltz, a specialist in the thriller genre, honed the murder angle. Turney then returned to the project but under Wald's strict instructions that she should stick to Maltz's narrative blueprint. Eventually she left *Mildred Pierce* when Davis asked her to work on *A Stolen Life*, though she was kept up to date about the latest script revisions on the production and is one of the two credited writers on the film (along with Ranald MacDougall, a favoured Wald writer, who came on to the project after Turney), which went on to receive an Oscar nomination for best script.

Mildred Pierce overhauled the women's movie and gave it a much darker finish. If it was Warner Bros' patented style, it was one that Turney adapted to in subsequent projects. In *The Man I Love* (1947), Ida Lupino stars as an independently minded cabaret singer who ends up performing at a club owned by the Mob when she returns to her home town. She wisely spurns the affections of her dubious boss only to fall hopelessly in and out of love with a jazz pianist, who just happens to be still hooked on his first wife. Raoul Walsh took time off from his action films to direct, and Turney recalls that since this 'wasn't the kind of thing they generally gave him', she was allowed more input. It proved to be a happy collaborative experience for her and Walsh. The film – dismissed by Leslie Halliwell as a 'dreary little melodrama'[3] but which director Martin Scorsese cites as one of the key inspirations behind his *New York, New York* – pays as much attention to the domestic as to the gangland milieu. In particular, Turney touchingly foregrounds Lupino's loyalty to her sisters and extended family with some well judged scenes full of robust 'girl talk'. But perhaps what is most surprising about the film is its ending, in which Lupino, unable to have and hold the man she loves, takes leave of him and walks away, her head held high.

During the 40s, and through to the early 50s, this hybrid of melodrama and film noir proved to be a staple genre for female screenwriters who, like Turney, found that they were hired for projects ostensibly because they were deemed to work well with women's material. The new wave of stories offered a more psychologically complex perspective on the traditional woman's realm of domestic concerns, with the once hallowed sanctuaries of home and marriage now proving to be rather unsettling places. The woman's weepie was replaced by the woman's shocker. The legacy of the Gothic novel, a literary genre with which women writers have had a strong association, had found its way into the movies. Indeed the first glimmer of this cinematic trend came with Hitchcock's *Rebecca* (1940), co-scripted by Joan Harrison (Hitchcock's script editor) from Daphne Du Maurier's novel.

Rebecca set a pattern for films about women caught up in dubious relationships who find themselves engaged in struggles to hold on to their sanity, their identity, even their lives. These include *Suspicion* (1941), Hitchcock's follow-up to *Rebecca*, which was also scripted by Joan Harrison but this time in collaboration with Hitchcock's wife, Alma Reville.[4] The film follows a newly-wed who suspects that her seemingly charming husband might be trying to murder her. In the chilling ghost story *The Uninvited* (Lewis Allen, 1944), written by Dodie Smith in her one brief fling with Hollywood, a young woman begins to believe that she is being haunted by the malevolent spirit of her mother. Muriel Roy Bolton scripted *My Name is Julia Ross* (Joseph H. Lewis, 1945), in which a lonely secretary is kidnapped and forced to play an heiress with a psychopathic husband. In *The Accused* (William Dieterle, 1949), written by Ketti Frings, a female professor of psychology stumbles into her own private nightmare after accidentally killing a student who has attempted to rape her. If the cue for these films came mostly from the studios rather than the writers themselves, it is still fascinating to see how women screenwriters fared with the potent themes on offer.

The work of one writer, Silvia Richards, deserves some scrutiny, particularly in the light of certain biographical details. Richards had been working as a writer on a succession of radio shows, including Bill Spier's highly regarded 'Suspense' programme. She received her first break in films in 1946 when Jerry Wald, anxious to repeat the success of *Mildred Pierce*, hired her to adapt a *Cosmopolitan* magazine novelette, *One Man's Secret* by Rita Weiman. This became *Possessed* (1947), which provided another angst-ridden role for Joan Crawford. It opens with Crawford wandering the Los Angeles streets in a semi-comatose state and repeating the name 'David' like some unholy mantra. She is taken to hospital, where the doctors put her under hypnosis. 'We're just helping you to tell us what we want' is the rather creepy line which implies more a process of interrogation than cure as the doctors give Crawford permission to speak. As her story unfolds, we discover that she had been driven mad with love for David, a young engineer, only to kill him. The film is packed with all the classic Gothic ingredients, with the female characters being sent insane as their desires are strangled by those around them. The love-lorn Crawford is employed by a wealthy industrialist to look after his sick (and also mentally disturbed) wife, who eventually commits suicide. As the poor woman's children are told: 'You know your mother was unhappy – it was part of her illness.'

Possessed was one of the films that made manifest Hollywood's burgeoning obsession with psychological conundrums. The affair started in earnest in the 30s when producer Sam Goldwyn invited Sigmund Freud to write a script for him on the subject (Freud declined). As the practice of psychoanalysis became more fashionable, film-makers flocked for their sessions on the couch. Meanwhile Freud's ideas filtered through into their movies, often in the most laughably obvious ways. Richards went into analysis in the mid-40s with Phil Cohen, who was then regarded as being one of the leading practitioners among Hollywood's intellectual left. She had just split up with her husband, the writer Bob Richards, and was struggling to support her two young children and her mother on her own. This had been emotionally exhausting and Richards claims that the first two months of sessions with Cohen saved her life. But it later proved to be a revealing experience in a different way, particularly when Cohen informed Richards that as a woman her first priority was to remarry.

Richards's second screenplay, *Secret Beyond the Door* (1948), might have been a rebuttal of such advice. Written for producer Walter Wanger and director Fritz Lang, it is filled with obvious Freudian allusion but is no less fascinating for that. The story updates the Bluebeard myth, with a young woman embarking on a marriage with a disturbed architect who has an unusual fancy for collecting rooms in which murders have been committed. 'This is not the time to think of danger, this is my wedding day,' the bride reflects ominously at the opening of the film. Installed in her husband's macabre house, she makes it her mission to discover what is kept in the one chamber that remains locked. In this compelling fantasy home was never such a perilous place to be.

It seems horribly poignant that five years later Richards would find herself caught up in a very real nightmare of secrets, locked rooms and dominating patriarchal types. As a former member of the Communist party, she was called to testify in front of the House Un-American Activities Committee. Interestingly, she explained to the historian Victor S. Navasky in his excellent study of the turbulent period, *Naming Names*, that her decisions about HUAC 'were passive – those of a woman'. She was under pressure from various influential men around her – including her writing partner Richard Collins, who was already cooperating with the Committee, her lawyer Martin Gang, who thought it was better to inform than to be blacklisted, and indirectly her therapist Cohen, who many subsequently suspected had been collaborating with the FBI about the political persuasions of his patients. When, finally, she was subpoenaed, it was family worries that were foremost in her mind. 'My ex-husband was not helping to support the kids. Gang said, "If you answer one question you are obliged to answer all of them." I was young and scared of going to jail and I knew Bob couldn't take care of the boys.'[5] But despite her cooperative testimony, Richards, who had by now also co-written the scripts for *Rancho Notorious* (Fritz Lang, 1952) and *Ruby Gentry* (King Vidor, 1952) and was beginning to carve for herself a distinguished career, didn't get to work much again and finally chose to close the door on Hollywood and become a nursery school teacher instead. During her harrowing ordeal in front of the Committee, one wonders if the anguished Richards might have been reminded of one of her more chillingly resonant lines: 'We're just helping you to tell us what we want.' It's a line that might also sum up the predicament of the powerless screenwriter, eternally subject to the behest of her producer.

Notes

1. Unless credited otherwise this and all subsequent quotes are from an interview conducted with Catherine Turney in December 1990.
2. See Claire Johnston (ed.), *The Work of Dorothy Arzner – Towards a Feminist Cinema* (London: British Film Institute, 1975) for an invaluable critical survey of Arzner's work. Though Arzner would make additions to the scripts, she had the highest regard for the writer. Akins, who became a good friend of Arzner's, and McCall both commented on how pleasurable it was to work with the director. McCall was even invited on to the set of *Craig's Wife* for the duration of the shoot and consulted on the script changes on a daily basis.
3. Interview with Catherine Turney in Lee Server's *Screenwriter* (New Jersey: The Main Street Press, 1987), p. 241.
4. Leslie Halliwell, *Halliwell's Film Guide* (London: Grafton, 1977), p. 621.
5. Reville's creative contribution – credited or uncredited – to the Hitchcock oeuvre cannot be overstated. She met the director at the outset of her own career as a cutter at the London Film Company. When Hitchcock directed his first film *The Pleasure Garden*, Reville, who was by then engaged to him, was the script supervisor and assistant director. After each shot, Hitchcock said, 'I'd turn back to my fiancée, asking, "Was it all right?".' He relied on her astute nods and comments for the rest of his career. The *Los Angeles Times* film critic Charles Champlin wrote on the occasion of her death that 'the Hitchcock touch had four hands, and two were Alma's'. Perhaps it would be more appropriate to talk of the Hitchcocks' pictures.
6. Victor S. Navasky, *Naming Names* (New York: Viking, 1980), p. 267.

4

Taking More Control

The front office attitude resents a woman in authority and it probably always will – they recognise women writers but prefer to keep us in prescribed groves. Some day they will have to admit that a woman can function successfully as an executive, too.

Joan Harrison, 1944

A small change in the fortunes of women screenwriters during the 40s is marked by the fact that two of them – Joan Harrison and Virginia Van Upp – managed to beat the studio system and become writer-producers (or 'hyphenates', as they were to become known in the industry). Such a move was a privilege that was granted to few in the writing community, which makes these women's achievements the more remarkable. For Hitchcock's former associate Joan Harrison it was a necessary step to acquiring the desired control over her scripts. 'You see before you a thwarted writer,' she explained to a *Los Angeles Times* journalist in 1944 regarding her career after leaving Hitchcock. 'Everything I wrote either was shelved or turned out so badly I asked to have my name taken off it.'[1] Consequently, she fought to be an associate producer on the thriller *Dark Waters* (André De Toth, 1944). Later that year, when Universal offered her a writing assignment which would eventually become the film noir *Phantom Lady*, she agreed only on condition that she could produce the movie as well. Her new status was now confirmed.

Undoubtedly the Hitchcock connection gave Harrison the requisite bargaining power. Universal was employing a servant of the master of suspense who could pass on some of the tricks of his trade. Harrison was sensibly capitalising on eight years of hard work for the director, most of it during the British phase of his career, which culminated in her co-scripting five of his films. But if it was an association that Harrison could exploit to her advantage, it was also one that would cast a shadow over the films that she made independently. She would always be known as Hitchcock's former secretary, with the implication that she would have been nothing without him. Conversely, when her films were successes, they would be complimented for being in the Hitchcock tradition.

For some it would be all too easy to assume that she contributed nothing to the Hitchcock oeuvre during her time with him. In François
Truffaut's extensive interviews with the director, the film-maker and former *Cahiers du Cinéma* critic notes that Harrison's name appears on the
credits of *Rebecca* and other screenplays and then asks Hitchcock: 'Did
she actually work on the screenplay or was that simply a way of represent-
ing you on the credits?' It is a revealing question but not so surprising
given *Cahiers du Cinéma*'s then fashionable 'auteur' theory. Hitchcock
admits that Harrison was a secretary who took notes on the scripts, then
'Gradually she learned, became more articulate, and she became a
writer.'[2] Charles Bennett, who worked on the scripts of many of
Hitchcock's films, including *Foreign Correspondent* (1940), which is also
credited to Harrison, is entirely dismissive of her involvement:

> As regards Joan, Joan was our secretary, but she happened to be
> Hitchcock's protégée at the time, and he asked me as a favour if I would
> mind letting her name be on the picture. She had only been his secre-
> tary. She had never come up with a solitary idea or a solitary thought. I
> thought, 'I'm so bloody important, what the hell does it matter?' So I
> said yes.[3]

By this point in her career, Harrison had worked on the screenplays for
Jamaica Inn (1939) and *Rebecca* (1939). The latter was a particular
favourite, which she had recommended to Hitchcock as a possible project
on reading the proofs of the Du Maurier novel. Indeed Harrison had been
promoted to working on scripts soon after she joined Hitchcock because
she had proved to be a bad secretary but perceptive about film stories. At
first she acted in a development capacity for Hitchcock, reading material
and advising him on its cinema potential; the writing came next. By the
time she left the director, she had been working with him on all aspects of
production from casting to set design. It was a perfect training, and one
that she recognised it would not have been possible to acquire in the
Hollywood studio system. 'It was because I started where the industry is
smaller and less specialised that I was given the opportunity to learn all
the things I know to be a producer.'[4]

It is a vindication of her abilities that Harrison's move was viewed by
Hitchcock as a tremendous loss (though she was to go back to work with
him in the 1950s as the producer of the TV series *Alfred Hitchcock
Presents*). But with attitudes like those of Bennett it is small wonder that
Harrison decided she needed to prove that she could go her own way. She
was an exceptionally bright and articulate woman. Born in Guildford, the
daughter of an affluent newspaper publisher, she might just as easily have
grown up to become part of the county set. But after graduating with a
degree in 'Modern Greats' (modern philosophy) from Oxford, where she
wrote film reviews for a student paper, and then spending some time at the
Sorbonne, she decided she wanted to pursue a career in the arts. When
Harrison was later interviewed by the redoubtable Hollywood journalist
Hedda Hopper, she referred to her need as a young woman to find some

Joan Harrison and Alma Reville, the women behind Alfred Hitchcock.

form of employment in order to elude the social expectations put upon her. 'The boy next door was very nice. His father was a barrister. My people and his thought we'd be married one day. I think that I was subconsciously seeking an escape.'[5] She worked briefly as a copy editor before answering Hitchcock's advertisement for a 'producer's assistant'. She was given the job after impressing him with her knowledge of the cinema, as well as criminal law. The latter was gleaned from days spent attending trials at the Old Bailey, a pastime facilitated by her uncle, who was Keeper there.

Working independently from Hitchcock, Harrison would pursue her interest in psychologically driven crime stories. 'I am a specialist. I am proud of being a specialist. I don't want to make pictures with the Andrews Sisters,' she told *Time* magazine in 1944, at the outset of her new career. In the same article she outlined two intriguing ideas for films that indicated the direction that she wanted to go in. One was to be made entirely by women while the other was a murder story involving only children. Unfortunately these projects went no further. Meanwhile, in another interview, she explained that she wanted to concentrate on producing thrillers with a 'woman's angle – as women must have something to pull for, you know, whether it's a dog, a horse, an old beggar – or even another woman!'[6]

Certainly the first two films that Harrison produced fulfil this desire, both being prime examples of the melodrama/film noir hybrid discussed earlier. In particular *Dark Waters* (1944) subscribes to the gothic woman-in-peril scenario of *Rebecca*, with its young heroine, a traumatised victim of the war, sent to convalesce with her uncle and aunt in their Bayou mansion. This balmy setting is soon overcast as she finds that she has to muster all her energies to foil her relatives' schemes to certify her so that they can inherit her fortune. Harrison's second film, *Phantom Lady* (1944), adapted from a Cornell Woolrich novel, is a more typical example of urban film noir and features an intrepid heroine by the name of Kansas.

Joan Harrison, who left Hitchcock to become a writer-producer. ©Universal Pictures Co., Inc.

Believing that her boss has been wrongly accused of murdering his wife, the bright and determined woman sets out to prove his innocence, fearlessly putting herself in potentially dangerous situations in order to obtain information. Harrison was particularly proud of this female private eye story, the 'woman's angle' par excellence.

Despite her pedigree, however, Harrison's interest in crime was still presented as a novelty. A press release from Universal studios neatly sums up the Harrison package:

> A girl with wavy blonde hair, dimples and a 24-inch waistline could entertain people with something besides crime stories. But not Joan Harrison. She lives and breathes crime – in her imagination, of course – and then tells it to others via the motion picture screen. Miss Harrison is a woman movie producer, one of the few in Hollywood. Her feminine slant has added freshness to 'cops and robbers' plots.

Harrison would find herself written about in everything from *Cosmopolitan* to *Time*. But most of the profiles followed the press release's cue and paid particular attention to her physical allure. There was as much interest in, as one scribe put it, the producer's 'ah-inspiring legs' as in her films. *Parade* magazine even ran a photo story entitled 'Joan produces thrillers' in which the fashionably dressed Harrison is depicted in a variety of poses. The accompanying captions make entertaining reading: 'Joan leaves a book shop with her usual load of mystery stories'; 'Comfortably abed in her rambling hillside home, Joan becomes engrossed in book, selects it as her next production.' Though such coverage ensured that Harrison had a higher profile than her male peers, it was double-edged. As were the writers in previous decades, the producer was being marketed as a film star and that put extra strains onto an already pressurised job.

It is revealing that when Virginia Van Upp was appointed Executive Producer at Columbia Studios a memo was sent out by the publicity department to newspaper photo libraries asking for all previous pictures of her to be withdrawn. Earlier photographs depict the bespectacled Van Upp sitting by a film camera. But the new 'official' portrait is of Van Upp without glasses and with a flower tucked behind her ear. The writer/producer of the Rita Hayworth vehicles *Cover Girl* and *Gilda* had an image to live up to.

One can only speculate how Van Upp and Harrison felt about their portrayal. In 1944 Harrison contributed a light-hearted article, promisingly entitled 'Why I Envy Men Producers', to *Hollywood Reporter*'s fourteenth anniversary issue. Her initial litany of complaints is revealing.

> They [male producers] don't have to worry about their appearance. They can spend Saturday afternoon playing golf, instead of wasting endless hours at the hairdresser's. They can report to the office looking like the shadow of a roaring evening without giving it a second's thought – or others tossing them a second glance. The absence of a long needed

shave only gives them a certain carefree dash, hollows under the eyes suggest that they've been working hard, and rumpled clothes stamp them as intellectual, rugged individualists.

Tartly written, the article points to the then prevailing attitudes about what was deemed acceptable behaviour in men but not in women. But halfway through the piece the sense of irony and grievance disappears as Harrison retreats into a giddy celebration of all that is 'feminine'. Men producers 'don't know the delights of buying three hats at one time. They can't try a new hairdo if they get tired of the old one.' And finally, she quips, 'They are not allowed the woman's privilege of changing her mind.'

One may question the wisdom of such an article, however frivolous it was meant to be. Harrison was fighting to be accepted as an equal in a tough profession but seems quite happy to perpetuate a few female stereotypes. Harrison knew too well that a belief in the difference between the genders stalled the progress of a woman's career. 'Men have an inborn distrust of our ability to handle money, she once concluded. But in order to secure the little power that she had, Harrison had to play a particular game and that no doubt confused matters for her. Later in life, she would advise those young women who wanted to work in film that their femininity was an asset that should not be lost as they pursued their careers. Women could be writers and producers and still remain feminine. 'But I don't think that women can be directors. It doesn't make for a happy woman … to be a director you have to be a s.o.b. It is much harder for a woman to be this.'[7] It is worth noting that at the beginning of her independent career Harrison had expressed an interest in directing. One must assume that such aspirations were quickly cut down to size.

Harrison learnt how far a woman could go in Hollywood. In a particularly candid interview with Myrtle Gebhart of the *Boston Sunday Post*, Harrison commented on the difficulties of getting anywhere in the industry 'except as an actress or, much down the scale, as a writer'. She explained that in her new role as a producer she found that there was never the 'slightest friction' with any member of the cast or crew; rather the problem was with those above her as she hit what would now be described as the glass ceiling. Indeed her criticisms ring uncomfortably true half a century on:

> The objection comes from higher up, the front office. They – those ultimate 'they' who have the say-so on such decisions – simply do not want to give a woman authority. That's their objection. They recognise our capabilities, but it goes against the grain of the male ego to place a woman in a position of responsibility. … The front office attitude resents a woman in authority and it probably always will – they recognise women writers but prefer to keep us in prescribed groves. Some day they will have to admit that a woman can function successfully as an executive, too.[8]

Meanwhile at Columbia, the writer-turned-producer Virginia Van Upp was deemed worthy of such authoritative status and was promoted to the role of executive, in which capacity she supervised the studio's output from 1945 to 1947. But ironically it was a post that she had to be pushed into accepting, so concerned was she about how the new work pressures might infringe on her family life (she was married to radio producer Ralph Nelson, who was then away on military service, and had a young daughter by a previous marriage). The appointment meant many changes for Van Upp, not least that initially she found herself alienated from her male peers. When the studio head Harry Cohn announced her appointment at a lunch meeting in the presence of Van Upp and ten men who believed they were in the running for the post, no one could bring themselves to wish her well. Later in the day, Cohn rang Van Upp to enquire whether any of her colleagues had come round to congratulating her. It transpired that only one had. By the time Van Upp started work in her new capacity, the other begrudging fellows had been fired.

Cohn chose Van Upp for the role partly because he admired the fact that she would stand up to him in arguments and hold her ground. He respected her knowledge of scripts and had been particularly impressed with the way she had handled two films that had fashioned a star for the studio out of Rita Hayworth – *Cover Girl* and *Gilda*. But as one contemporary film industry commentator noted, the appointment also reflected the studio's desire to court the women who made up a major proportion of audiences during the war.

> [Van Upp] will select stories, okay casting, and generally keep an eye on the biggest attractions the company will make. Needless to say the 'woman's angle' will be kept in mind, and this will undoubtedly please exhibitors everywhere when they start counting the take. Women have long edited some of the nation's most popular magazines, and their policy, in most instances, has upped circulation and profits.[9]

According to Cohn's biographer Bob Thomas, the studio head also appreciated Van Upp for her 'ability to survive in a man's world without losing her femininity'. Indeed Van Upp's daughter, Gay Hayden, describes her mother as being 'very tough, very funny and very feminine'. Van Upp's relationship with Cohn was reputedly flirtatious but ultimately wholly professional. Van Upp recalled for Thomas that Cohn would make jokey advances towards her which she would brush off, taunting him that she might demand a clause in her contract prohibiting verbal rape. When Cohn began to believe her threats, however, the game came to an abrupt end.

Cohn played the rather over-protective, even possessive, patrician with Van Upp. If anyone swore in front of her, Cohn would chide them severely. If she went out to dinner with any of her male colleagues, he would be none too happy. But perhaps this was more to do with the fact that the atmosphere in the executive suite at Columbia was generally one of paranoia. Nobody could be seen to be too friendly with anyone else, which was anathema to the congenially disposed Van Upp. Meanwhile she endeared herself to her crews by being an inveterate gambler who could

Virginia Van Upp, the writer-producer of Cover Girl *and* Gilda.
© *Columbia Pictures, photo by St. Hilaire.*

shoot craps with the best of them. She could be tough indeed, but as the publicity photograph incident suggests she had to prove that underneath it all she could still be lovably – and unthreateningly – feminine.

Van Upp had been born into and grown up with the industry and that helped her to be immune to its demands. Her mother, Helen Van Upp, even provided her with a career model since she herself had been an editor and subsequently a title writer for the Ince Company. Virginia Van Upp's own involvement with Hollywood started at an early age. She was a modestly successful child actress, but as she grew older switched to working behind the scenes, first as an assistant casting director and then as an assistant agent. Later, in order to further her own screenwriting ambitions, she took a job as secretary to the writer Horace Jackson, working with him at Pathé and then at Paramount. Soon she was filling in for Jackson, finishing his scripts when his predilection for drink had finished him. It could have been another tinsel-town tale of thwarted talent, but fortunately Van Upp's gifts were swiftly recognised by Paramount. She was given a writing contract of her own and eventually paired up with the director E. H. Griffith, with whom she worked for almost her entire time at the studio. The most intriguing exception to this partnership is that Van Upp wrote the script for *You and Me* (1938), a musical about a couple of ex-cons who fall in love, directed by Fritz Lang, with songs by Kurt Weill.

At Paramount, Van Upp established a sure reputation for herself creating snappy roles for such female leads as Carole Lombard and Madeleine Carroll. Indeed Cohn enticed Van Upp to Columbia specifically because he needed a writer to come up with some star material for Rita Hayworth. Van Upp's first screenplay at Columbia was for the musical *Cover Girl* (1944), which teamed Hayworth with Gene Kelly in a standard 'girl makes good' story about a young model's rise to fame. Van Upp's involvement in the project extended beyond tailoring a role for Hayworth on the page: she paid attention to the grooming of the actress into top-line material right down to organising her costumes. During the production a bond developed between the writer and the actress. Subsequently when Van Upp wrote the beguiling *Gilda*, Hayworth would only agree to take the title role if Van Upp also produced the film. The studio not only agreed to Van Upp producing *Gilda*, but also granted her similar status on other projects she was working on.

In *Gilda*, Hayworth plays a former singer/dancer caught in a bizarre *ménage à trois* with her husband Mundson, a German casino owner, and her ex-lover Johnny, who is on Mundson's payroll in order to take care of 'all the things that belong to him'. This includes Gilda, whom he loves like a bauble. The film seethes with the most sadistic of emotions, with many of its most cutting lines thrown like poisoned darts towards Gilda. 'You haven't much faith in the stability of women,' says Gilda of the misogynist Johnny after one particularly cruel exchange. Later he tells her that she is nothing more than the laundry to him. 'Any psychiatrist would be able to tell you that means something,' she retorts. *Gilda* fathoms the contemptuous relationships the characters are embroiled in and looks at the way that misogynist attitudes erupt. It 'washes the men's dirty linen', since the repressed feelings that ricochet between Mundson and Johnny have much to do with their desire to destroy the wilful Gilda. Van Upp's heroine is all too woefully aware of her damned situation, toasting 'disaster to the wench' at the outset of the film. But finally she rattles the cage that the men have erected around her in an unabashedly provocative sexual display as she sings and dances to 'Put the Blame on Mame', a song that sums up the Eve-old plight of women who are faulted for all the world's woes.

Perhaps it is because the film treads such a delicate line between being about misogyny and being construed as misogynist that Hayworth wanted Van Upp on board as producer as well. In Van Upp, Hayworth, who had grown to be quite circumspect about her scripts, had found an ally she could trust and that was something she needed at the time. Her marriage to Orson Welles was beginning to fray and the emotional rancour that permeated *Gilda* was becoming uncomfortably familiar to her. Hayworth finally separated from Welles during the shooting of the film and it is a measure of her friendship with Van Upp that she found refuge at the producer's house.

Van Upp became Hayworth's unofficial writer-in-residence and counsellor. She even made uncredited additions to Welles's *The Lady from*

Shanghai when the film did not pass muster with Cohn. She also bailed out Hayworth in subsequent emotional crises, flying down to Acapulco to counsel her when Hayworth's second attempt at married life with Welles broke down during the shooting of *The Lady from Shanghai*. Later, when Hayworth was having an affair with the playboy Aly Khan and hiding out from the prurient press in Mexico City, Cohn despatched Van Upp to persuade the actress to come back and resume work at Columbia. There, a poignant exchange between the two friends took place as Hayworth, who did not feel secure about Khan's affections for her, playfully berated Van Upp for her emotional quandary. 'It was the writer's fault,' she declared. Van Upp asked why. 'Because you wrote *Gilda*, and every man I've known has fallen in love with Gilda and wakened with me.'[10] In the anecdote, which Van Upp recalled for Harry Cohn's biographer Bob Thomas, the writer acknowledges the discrepancy between the fantasy female figures she invented for the screen and the reality of a woman's lot.

Gilda was the most glamorous of Van Upp's creations and one of cinema's most fascinating and powerful femme fatales. But the writer's other heroines include prime examples of another type that briefly surfaced in Hollywood films of the late 30s and the 40s: the career woman. Two romantic comedies which Van Upp wrote and produced for Columbia merit particular attention: *Together Again* (1944) and *She Wouldn't Say Yes* (1945). In each case a professional woman's determined attachment to her single status is turned into a conundrum. The career woman might be presented as a comic novelty, but the jokes are in her favour as she knocks the men down a notch or two. These films are comparable to other comedies of the time relying on boisterous banter between the sexes (for example, *His Girl Friday* and *The Lady Eve*), but they spelled out a more troubled view of romance and marriage on the way to the happy conclusion required of the genre. The provocative question at the heart of each film is: 'Are husbands necessary?' (This particular line of inquiry was even intended to provide the title to one of Van Upp's Paramount films in which Madeleine Carroll plays a judge, but it had to be hastily changed to *Honeymoon in Bali* since Carroll was then involved in divorce proceedings.)

In *Together Again*, Irene Dunne plays a widowed mayor who is being hounded by her former father-in-law to marry again since he doesn't consider it 'normal' for a woman to be 'a big shot in your office and a nonentity in your own home'. But this is his problem, Dunne retorts, as he can't 'bear to see a woman alone and liking it. No man can. Instinctively, it terrifies them.' Meanwhile in *She Wouldn't Say Yes*, Rosalind Russell plays Dr Lane, an eminent psychiatrist who just says no to all marriage offers. Her reason is simple: too many women who visit her office are there because of their problems with men. At one point Lane sighs sadly: 'Sometimes I think that it would be easier to be a man.' As a play on assumptions about appropriate behaviour for each of the sexes, the film finally resolves itself with a little twist on convention as Dr Lane takes the lead and proposes to a suitor she has fallen in love with. And while this might seem a small concession as the story ends with Dr Lane choosing a domestic life rather than a career, the film has raised enough questions to make it seem quite progressive for its day.

As a producer/writer Van Upp had more power to influence the content and outcome of her films, and it is difficult not to surmise that she had some hidden agenda. Was she a proto-feminist who finally had to capitulate to convention as she married her career girls off to live happily ever after, again all too aware of the discrepancy between the lives on screen and the lives on the street? According to her daughter Gay Hayden, Van Upp was of the opinion that her women should always find a happy ending in romance. 'I think she believed that was the way it should be.'¹¹ Her own life, however, was not to have such a neat finale. Her relationship with her husband Ralph Nelson would seem to have suffered precisely because of her career. She resigned from her duties as executive producer in 1947, reputedly to 'resume her marriage' with Nelson, who was now attempting to build his own career as a producer. Two years later the couple were divorced. Asked by a reporter whether professional jealousy was the cause of the break-up, Van Upp replied: 'I suppose so. How can you ever explain these things?' She explained to another journalist: 'I am going to marry my work – I think that's safer.'

But unhappily for her, Van Upp's career shifted gear just at the time when she needed it most. She returned to writing for Columbia but only two of her scripts were produced. One of them, *An Affair in Trinidad* (1952), was a tired attempt to capitalise on the *Gilda* formula, with Rita Hayworth playing a nightclub singer who goes undercover to help the police investigate the murder of her husband. Neither this nor her other film, *Here Comes the Groom* (1951), were particularly successful. Subsequently Van Upp went to West Berlin, where she became involved in the production of propaganda films for the US government. During her time in Germany, Van Upp negotiated a deal with Republic Pictures, in which she was to produce, direct and write the script for a contemporary story set in Germany, *The Big Whisper*. But unfortunately during pre-production Van Upp was taken ill and the film never got made. Though she was only 52, Van Upp decided when she recovered to quit movie-making.

Poor health was the immediate reason for Van Upp's early retirement. But it also coincided with a period of upheaval as the film industry adjusted to the postwar world, the divisions brought about by HUAC and the emergence of television as a serious rival to cinema. The all-important audience demographics were changing as the men returned from war service and the women returned from the workforce back to their homes. And while there was a brief boom in cinema attendance immediately after the war as courting couples went to the movies, it was followed by a rapid decline – marked particularly in city centre movie houses – as those couples married, settled down in the newly expanding suburbs and looked to home or locally based forms of entertainment.

By the beginning of the 1950s, the studio system was starting to crack up under such pressures and, rather than putting producers, directors, stars and screenwriters under contract, there was a move to hire creative personnel on a project by project basis. Job security vanished, but that was traded for a degree of creative independence. For those such as Van Upp who had been nurtured within the system, it might have seemed like an appropriate time to leave. The old-style Hollywood may have been chauvinistic but there operated a benevolent and protective paternalism that was positively encouraging for some women. Men like Irving Thalberg, Harry Cohn and Henry Blanke, who had been particularly instrumental in the advancement of certain women's careers, were described as gentlemanly in their attitudes towards them. The women would reciprocate by being 'ladylike' and thus everyone stayed happy.

Of course, there were those who thrived through the changes. For writers such as Catherine Turney, the arrival of television provided a new lease of life, particularly since the 'woman's angle' was deemed perfect for the new medium. For women working in film, it was mostly those in writing teams such as Phoebe Ephron (with Henry Ephron), Betty Comden (with Adolph Green), Fay Kanin (with Michael Kanin), Frances Goodrich (with Albert Hackett), Ruth Gordon (with Garson Kanin) who had an easier ride. This was the era of the light comedy and the musical, in which these partnerships excelled. But there were women who worked individually, again mostly in musicals and comedies. Dorothy Kingsley was the only woman during that period to come to Hollywood via radio comedy gag writing. Persuading the executives to overcome their reservations ('They had never seen any women gag writers'[12]), and with the help of her friend, the actress Constance Bennett, she arrived at MGM. There she specialised in the swimming star. Esther Williams's aqua-stravaganzas, such as *Bathing Beauty* (1944), *Neptune's Daughters* (1949) and *Dangerous When Wet* (1953). She also contributed to the movie versions of such musicals as *Seven Brides for Seven Brothers* (1954), *Pal Joey* (1957) and *Can-Can* (1960).

Isobel Lennart also started writing for MGM in the early 40s, having worked her way up from the typing pool, and continued to script for the studio's films through the 50s, with the occasional sortie to 20th-Century Fox. Her metier was also light comedies and musicals, such as *Anchors Aweigh* (1944) and *Meet Me in Las Vegas* (1956). One of her most interesting works is *Love Me or Leave Me* (1955), which she co-wrote with Daniel Fuchs, and which was based on the life of the singer Ruth Etting, who eventually married her manager, the sadistic ex-mobster Martin Snyder. Set against a showbiz background, the film depicts the troubled partnership, with Etting reluctantly under Snyder's thumb and compromised because she needs him for her career. As a biopic about a strong female performer, it was a precursor to her better known film about the life of Fanny Brice, *Funny Girl* (1968), which Lennart first created as a stage piece in 1961. *Funny Girl* was Lennart's last film (she died in a car crash in January 1971). Produced for Columbia by Ray Stark, a former agent who became one of the key industry players during the 60s and 70s, it was very much part of the new Hollywood, yet as one of the last musicals its traditions were rooted in that of the old.

The crumbling of the studio system was also significant in that it allowed room for the smaller, independent companies, some who would feed the film chains, others who would later feed the television networks. Not that they had not been there previously; Howard Hawks's H. B. Productions, for example, had operated under the auspices of Warner Bros during the 40s. Such a model of independence was the prerogative of a director who had established himself as a financial asset to the studio. But soon others would set themselves up with their own production bases, and relish a certain level of autonomy. It is significant that as the studio era came to a close one woman was able to make a significant career breakthrough. Fed up with being typed as a second division Bette Davis at Warner Bros, the actress Ida Lupino decided, along with her husband Collier Young, who had previously worked for Harry Cohn, to establish their own company (first bank-rolling their films themselves but later striking a deal with Howard Hughes at RKO). This gave Lupino the opportunity not only to produce and co-write films, but to become the first woman since the era of Lois Weber to direct them as well (Dorothy Arzner did not quite enjoy the same level of control).

Lupino, who had sold one script to RKO earlier in her acting career, was continuing in the tradition of the silent stars who had made the switch to working behind the camera (intriguingly, one of Lupino's contemporaries, Rosalind Russell, also made the cross-over and wrote scripts for two movies under the pseudonym C. A. Mcknight). During the 40s Lupino had established a salty 'tough broad' persona for herself on screen in such film noirs as *They Drive By Night*, *High Sierra* and *The Man I Love*. There was immense respect for her on-screen persona, which helped her work behind the camera. It seems that the crews, who rarely gave her trouble, were in awe of their glamorous star director, while later in her career she delighted in their nickname for her, 'mother'.

The first production for Lupino and her husband Collier Young's company Emerald Films (later renamed The Filmakers) was *Not Wanted* (1949). A story of an unmarried mother who has to give up her child, it is typical of Lupino's prolific output for the years 1949–1954. Lupino became renowned for her 'problem' pictures, all made for less than $160,000 and mostly without star names. She proved the raw, low-budget ethos, that to work outside the mainstream meant one could maintain one's integrity on the most difficult of subjects. *Outrage* (1950) dealt with rape and its after-effects; *Hard, Fast and Beautiful* is about a sadly ambitious mother who thrusts her daughter on to the competitive tennis circuit; *The Bigamist* (1953) follows the story of a forlorn travelling salesman who juggles two lives and two wives. These films were marked by a concern for ordinary people – book-keepers, diner waitresses, gas station attendants – the world depicted by the painter Edward Hopper. And Lupino examined her subjects without resorting to conventional, easy resolutions.

Not Wanted is a good example of the Lupino approach. The young heroine, Sally Forrest, has an affair with a charming piano-player and finds herself pregnant. Rather than marrying the local gas station owner, Keefe Brasselle, who is devoted to her, she chooses to leave town and ends up at a home for unmarried mothers. Only weeks after reluctantly relinquishing her baby she is arrested on kidnapping charges after cradling another

Ida Lupino

infant. At the pre-trial hearing, however, a judge who is sympathetic to her predicament persuades the child's parents to drop the case. Lupino liked to bring the law into her films: hence similar courtroom scenes in *Outrage* and *The Bigamist*, demonstrating how society regulates the 'problem'. Returning home, Forrest finds Brasselle still waiting for her but she succumbs to him only after an exhausting struggle. This is certainly not a happily resolved ending to a film which throughout requires the audience to question the prevailing moral judgments about single parents.

But Lupino's films were not restricted to 'women's issues'. Indeed, in interviews, Lupino would insist that she chose these subjects not because they were women's stories but because they were based on 'true stories', again emphasising the social document angle. Even *Hard, Fast and Beautiful*, she claimed, was founded on a true case. Her interest in true stories propelled her into more masculine terrain. *The Hitch-hiker* (1953), is a dark road movie in which two fishing buddies give a lift to a mass murderer and find themselves on a ride for their lives; while *Private Hell 36* (1954), directed by Don Siegel with Lupino producing and co-scripting, investigates police corruption. Character-driven, both these films concentrate on a psychological exegesis of the crisis at hand, sharply focused but bleak portraits of men under pressure.

During the five years of Filmakers, Lupino revitalised the social conscience film (like Lois Weber before her). A testimony to what she stood for in Hollywood was a 1950 *Negro Digest* interview on the subject of 'race prejudice': Lupino was then advocating integrated casting.

In our latest film, *Outrage*, we have a routine scene of a lineup of criminals at a police headquarters. The girl comes and identifies one of the men as her attacker. The policeman who takes the girl through the station is Negro. I know that's a switch. Usually films don't show Negro cops – especially in authority at station houses. But we don't handle stereotypes in our outfit ... what we plan to do is integrate Negro actors in all our productions. We'll show Negro college students, gas station attendants, cops, business men, housewives.[13]

In the interview Lupino reveals plans for a film about 'Mexican-Americans':

I want to go into a city block and photograph the conflicts between the American and Mexican groups on the street, the lack of human feeling among them. ... This picture and all those I make will say the same thing and show the same thing dramatically. This lack of feeling for one another is terrible. People must learn to love and respect each other. The movies are a good place to begin.

But Lupino's progressive dreams would be stopped short in 1954, when Filmakers disbanded (she and Young had by now divorced). Against her better judgment, Lupino's partners had elected to go into film distribution. In an interview with Debra Weiner published in 1977, she expressed strong feelings of regret about the decision:

Filmakers was a family group. We all contributed ideas, we threw them in the pot. ... I'm very sorry that my partners chose to go into film distribution. If they hadn't, I think we still would be going today. We should have stayed an independent company, with distribution coming from whichever high-level outfit gave us the best break. I thought it was wrong, but I was outvoted. And sure enough the Filmakers didn't make it distributing their own pictures. We didn't get the right playing dates in the right house. We weren't very wise to step into a field which we didn't know too much about.[14]

Without her company, Lupino was stranded. But as an issue-oriented director she found work for herself in television. Typically, her first project was a dramatisation of a true incident: the trial of Mary Seurat, who was hanged as a suspect after the assassination of President Lincoln. Soon, however, Lupino was inundated with television offers for very different programmes. On the strength of *The Hitch-hiker*, she was asked by producer Richard Boone to direct for the Western series, *Have Gun Will Travel*. Work on similar action or suspense dramas followed, including

The Fugitive, The Untouchables and *Twilight Zone*. The irony of type-casting was not lost on Lupino. 'Here I'd always done women's stories and now I couldn't get a woman's story to direct'.[15] But Lupino would be assigned to stories in these series that did have a more feminine angle. Frank Price, executive producer of *The Virginian*, explained that he hired her for 'her ability to handle sentimental stories with great "taste"', citing one episode about a teenage girl who develops a crush on the hero James Dury.[16] Producer Norman Macdonnell, who was responsible for *Gunsmoke* and *The Road West*, commented: 'You use Ida when you have a story about a woman with some dimension, and you really want it hard-hitting.'[17]

From the movies she selected to make at Filmakers it is clear that Lupino liked variety in her work. In television, she no longer enjoyed the same degree of control over her material, though she did work once again with Collier Young. They set up Bridget Productions, modelled on Lucille Ball and Desi Arnaz' successful Desilu Productions, and devised a series for Lupino and her new husband, Howard Duff. The comedy show *Mr Adams and Eve* (1956–7) was a parodic take on the *I Love Lucy* formula, featuring Lupino and Duff as a hapless showbiz couple. It was fun, but for Lupino nothing could top the experience and the freedom that she had had during the four years with The Filmakers. Lupino had discovered the rewards of independence in Hollywood.

Notes

1. Philip K. Scheuer, 'Producer's Spurs Won by Woman', *Los Angeles Times*, 23 February 1944.
2. François Truffaut, *Hitchcock* (revised edition, London: Paladin, 1984), p. 176.
3. Interview with Charles Bennett by Pat McGilligan, *Backstory: Interviews with Screenwriters of Hollywood's Golden Age* (Los Angeles: University of California Press, 1986), p. 36.
4. Ann Daggett, 'It's a Woman's World Too', *Modern Screen*, February 1945.
5. Hedda Hopper, 'Wrath Made Joan a Producer', *Los Angeles Times*, 14 October 1945.
6. Barbara Berch, 'A Hitchcock Alumna', *New York Sunday Times*, June 1943.
7. Gilbert Millstein, 'Harrison Horror Story', *New York Times Magazine*, 21 July 1957.
8. Myrtle Gebhart, 'Her Film Hits Open the Way for More Women Producers', *Boston Sunday Post*, 13 August 1944.
9. W. R. Wilkerson, *Tradeviews* (undated clipping in Van Upp file at the Margaret Herrick Library, Los Angeles).
10. Bob Thomas, *King Cohn* (New York: McGraw-Hill, 1990), p. 279.
11. Gay Hayden, interview with author, 11 March 1992.
12. Pat McGilligan, *Backstory 2* (Berkeley: University of California Press, 1991), p. 117.
13. Robert Ellis, 'Ida Lupino Brings New Hope to Hollywood', *Negro Digest*, August 1950.
14. Debra Weiner, 'Interview with Ida Lupino', in Karyn Kay and Gerald Peary (eds.), *Women and the Cinema* (New York: E. P. Dutton, 1977), p. 176.
15. Ibid., p. 177.
16. Dwight Whitney, 'Mother Knows Best', *TV Guide*, 8 October 1966.
17. Ibid.

5

Writing it Like a Man

I have always worked with men, I have always written exclusively for men. I haven't written for many women – I wrote for
Gable, for Tracy, Heston, Robert Taylor, Mitchum, Wayne, Lee
Marvin, Peck; the only big name that I didn't write for of that
era was Gary Cooper. … I like men, they amuse me very much.

Marguerite Roberts[1]

Since so many female screenwriters were roped in on the 'woman's
angle' during the studio period, it would be easy to surmise that they were
only interested in or capable of writing material aimed at their own
gender. Women writers became closely identified with the 'woman's
film', but they did not have exclusive rights to it. Plenty of men were wom-
en's specialists too (it is revealing that women wrote just under half of the
fifty-odd films directed by the women's movie specialist George Cukor).
More often women writers who had established themselves in the wom-
en's picture genre might be summoned to flesh out the female roles in
otherwise male-centred stories. When she was at Warner Bros, Lenore
Coffee made uncredited additions to Raoul Walsh's story of General
Custer and his demise at Little Big Horn, *They Died With Their Boots On*
(1941). Her brief was to bring a little feminine authenticity to the character
of Mrs Custer.

Meanwhile there were a few women who crossed the genre boundaries to write scripts that had a strong male bias. Frances Marion won her
first Oscar for *The Big House* (1930), which told the story of an attempted
escape at a maximum security prison. Disquieting in its gritty portrayal of
penitentiary life, *The Big House* was a far cry from Marion's staple diet of
Fannie Hurst adaptations (though closer to the films she penned for Fred
Thomson under a pseudonym). But the film fulfilled a very specific purpose in that it highlighted grim prison conditions. Marion had spent some
time researching the penal system and had visited San Quentin several
times. As a document on prison life, *The Big House* was perhaps not such
an unusual subject for a former protégée of Lois Weber, who had made a
speciality of social issue films. It is also no coincidence that the film was

the first of three that Marion collaborated on with the director George Hill, to whom she was married at the time.

Marion's second film with Hill, *The Secret Six* (1931), was her one foray into the gangster genre. Even she was surprised when MGM asked her to write it. But Warner Bros's *Little Caesar* had just shot onto the scene and all the studios were anxious to emulate its success. It was perhaps not so strange for MGM to want their Oscar-winning writer to have a stab at the formula. Marion was duly despatched to view the film and then to Chicago, where she was ordered to 'see the places where the gangsters holed in, like Big Jim Colosimo's restaurant, and we'll have you meet the offspring of some of the mob they haven't bumped off yet.'[2] The former war correspondent was not the least bit perturbed and managed to tap some Mafia tales during her stay there. The resulting screenplay followed the rise of a hoodlum from stockyard slaughterer to Capone-like leader. Marion had come up with what the studio wanted. *The Secret Six* was a standard issue genre piece which 'received fairly good reviews, along with the other gangster pictures that took their bows at the time.'[3]

Newspaperwoman Virginia Kellogg also came up with reportage-style material with a tough social bent that formed the basis of various screenplays. In the early 30s she wrote a novel about a young woman doctor who decides to have a baby before getting married, which Warner Bros filmed as *Mary Stevens M.D.* (1933). *Variety* described this B-movie as 'exceptionally good adult entertainment with a pronounced feminine appeal'. In the late 40s she was to renew her association with Warner Bros (where her brother Phil Kellogg was now a producer), but with rather different fare. After observing the work of Treasury operatives and consulting previous research material on the subject, she drafted the story that would ultimately form the basis for *White Heat* (1949), the explosive last film in the Warners gangster cycle.

Previously Kellogg had sold a treatment to Eagle Lion productions based on the same research, which eventually became the thriller *T-Men* (1947). Though Kellogg did not contribute to the final script and was written out of the credits, *T-Men* can be more obviously traced back to her time at the Treasury through its story of a pair of undercover agents trying to infiltrate a Detroit counterfeiting gang. Differing from the final film, though containing many of its basic elements, her first draft of *White Heat* was also devoted to the field investigations of two agents. Kellogg sold the story rights to Warner Bros in 1948 for $2,000, and although she was eventually taken off the script, she was given an original story credit (for which she received an Academy Award nomination) and landed a five-week contract to come up with other proposals for the studio.

There is nothing sinister about the fact that Kellogg had no involvement in the final drafts of either *T-Men* or *White Heat* (in the case of the latter, Warner Bros assigned the script to Ivan Goff and Ben Roberts, who the studio considered to be good action writers, though the writers themselves thought their metier was comedy). She had no experience in the construction of screenplays and was principally an ideas woman. But intriguingly, when producer Jerry Wald decided that he wanted to do a film about women's prisons, he approached Kellogg with a view to researching and co-writing the screenplay. It was commonly considered that the Warner Bros film *I Am a Fugitive from a Chain Gang* (1932) had proved to be such an indictment of the penal system that it had brought about changes in the prison laws of six states. Wald wanted to create the same impact with a women's prison picture. The scrupulous Kellogg characteristically spent several months visiting women's prisons throughout the United States, even managing to swing a stay in one for a two-week period. For Kellogg this was not meant as some Hollywood publicity stunt. Her write-up of the experience in *Collier's* magazine is an exhaustive and disturbing exposé.

> Out of my prison observations, the most frightening thing of all was the realisation that the conditions that I saw exist even in our most enlightened states, and that few Americans have any idea of what is going on in their own back yards. Club women often visit the women's penitentiaries in their states (on carefully guided tours). Invariably they come away impressed with the clean, modern buildings and the superintendents, most of whom are the capable officials recommended by penal-reform organisations. But the club women cannot see the *rot* inside the buildings.[4]

The screenplay for *Caged* (1950) remains faithful to Kellogg's concerns. The film follows Marie Allen, a young and naive woman who is convicted for aiding her husband in a small-time robbery. Prison proves to be less a punishment than a toughening experience, but not with the best of results, as Marie descends into a cycle of crime. A depressingly realistic account of prison life framed in a film noir style, *Caged* proved to be the provocative movie that Wald required. It was in the best of the studio's social realist traditions, unsentimental in its presentation and discerning about the facts.

With the success of *Caged* (it received three Academy Award nominations, including one for the script) Kellogg became pegged as a women's issues writer, but her career wavered just as she had established some success for herself. In 1950 she worked on two projects: *Badge 23*, based on the life of Mary Ross, the first woman member of the Los Angeles vice squad, and *Night is So Deep*, about women veterans in a mental ward. But neither film was made. She finished her career writing for the veteran actress Ethel Barrymore's TV anthology series. Nothing could be further from the exploits of the *T-Men*.

Some women were to by-pass the 'woman's angle' right through their careers. Oddly, the one genre with which women writers had developed strong links since the silent era was the Western and this was an association that was to continue. This phenomenon is perhaps surprising since, more than any other genre, Western films were presented from a male perspective and were not thought to appeal to female audiences. The canon of Western literature includes the work of women novelists such as Willa Cather and Laura Ingalls Wilder, who chronicled the fortunes of the pioneering families as they eked out a living on the great plains and established the new American frontiers. But such homestead preoccupations do not provide the classical narrative drive of the true Western film. The audience for these films was considered to be predominantly male and working-class.

If, however, one looks at the credits of the many B–Westerns that were churned out by such studios as Republic during the 1930s, when the practice of double-billing films at the cinemas created a new demand for cheap and shorter features, one discovers that many were written by women. Silent scenarist Adele Buffington continued to write in the 1930s and was still writing TV Western serials in the 1950s. Other exponents of the genre during the 1930s and the 1940s included Elizabeth Beecher, Betty Burbridge and Olive Cooper, who wrote for Republic for most of their careers, and Luci Ward, who worked for both Republic and Warner Bros.

While there were more than a handful of women working in the genre, these Western writers were still considered to be something of a novelty by the press, attracting some curious, almost comical, attention. A short profile of Betty Burbridge in the January 1940 issue of *American Magazine* is accompanied by a picture of the writer dressed in check shirt, kerchief and cowboy boots and sitting with her typewriter astride a 'galloping platform', the device used to simulate horse movement in films. 'When moviegoers are held breathless on the edge of their seats while the cowboy hero gallops against death to save his heroine from the bandit's villainous clutches, chances are they are seeing a Western thriller by Betty Burbridge, Hollywood's ace writer of Westerns. ... She writes from hearsay, not from experience. No horsewoman, she hates the back of a nag.' The article dresses up Burbridge in Western tack but then reminds us that she is not really a hardened frontiers-woman. It implies that though she may be able to rustle with the best of them, underneath the plaid shirt she is all woman. An interview conducted the previous year also points out: 'Miss Burbridge played in the movies when she was 17, but that was at the old Thomas Ince Studio, and she wouldn't say just how far past 30 she is now. Anyway she's attractive.'[5]

Burbridge is perhaps typical of the women who ended up in the B–Western stable since she found herself writing for them by default rather than through a particular passion for the genre. She started her career as an actress but soon switched to journalism, becoming a syndicated columnist specialising in the traditional woman's page subjects of home economics, etiquette and child training. From this to Westerns seems a bit of a leap, but Burbridge made the transition in the early 1930s when she was asked by a producer friend at Republic to work as a story doctor on a 'cow epic'. The producer liked her ideas and hired her to work on subsequent projects. Unsurprisingly, she decided that Westerns would be more fun to write about than 'cheese soufflés and chintz curtains'. And knowing very little about the genre, she set out to brush up on the lore:

I read pulp Westerns until I was bored to tears. But that's how I learned the story racket – that and talking to the movie cowboys on the set. When I began doing these things I'd take my plots from New York stage plays that I had seen. I'd simply change the setting to the wide-open spaces, put the characters on horses, work in a couple of chases with a sheriff and a posse – and there would be a screen story.[6]

Burbridge wrote many films for Gene Autry, the singing cowboy. She also contributed to some of John Wayne's Republic pictures. Reminiscing years later about her work, she recalled that the directors would always remind her not to write lines that were too difficult for the young and at the time rather hammy Wayne.[7]

Boasting such titles as *Come On, Cowboys* (1937) and *Pals of the Saddle* (1938), Burbridge's films may be forgotten now and no doubt for good reason. But as a writer she proved to be dependable at her swiftly learnt craft, adhering to the formula and notching up during her career nearly a hundred film credits. For Burbridge it was purely a job; she even admitted that when she went to the cinema Westerns were not favourite viewing, certainly not the kind of Westerns she was writing, which were considered even then to be rather low-grade stuff. Indeed this might explain why there was a concentration of women working on these B films. There was no status attached to them – industry hacks derisively called them 'Giddyuppers' or 'horse operas' – and the pay reflected this thinking. So while Burbridge and her contemporaries at Republic escaped being stereotyped as 'women's picture' writers, they were ghettoised in another way.

There were women, however, who were able to make respectable careers for themselves by writing against type. Starting out in the 1930s, Marguerite Roberts was one of the handful of women in the studios' 'A' league who made her reputation with what could be typed as 'men's films'. Clark Gable once said of her while she was at MGM that she 'writes men with more balls than any other guy on this lot.' Typically, for *Sailor's Luck*, her first original script written in 1933 for Fox, the studio teamed her up with the hardened director Raoul Walsh. Interviewed in the early 1980s, Roberts recalled that Walsh turned what she considered to be a silly comedy into a respectably 'rough and rowdy' movie. From then on her taste for a robust style was confirmed and would run through her career right up to *True Grit* (1969). In fact, it was with the Western that Roberts made her mark, but as with Burbridge this was not necessarily a speciality of choice. As Roberts delivered one successful Western, another would be suggested: 'They kind of cast you, the writer, and I didn't say no.'[8]

A tough and stalwart spirit, Roberts ingratiated herself with the studio's male culture. Reputedly Clark Gable favoured her partly because she didn't blush when he told his risqué stories. With her passion for jazz and horse racing, she was accepted as one of the boys. When she built her own stables, MGM studio boss Louis B. Mayer even gave her mares from his prize stud farm and would invite Roberts and her second husband (the novelist John Sanford) over to his ranch for breakfast. She fitted in. 'I

Marguerite Roberts on her first day of work as a screenwriter being welcomed abroad by Frank Craven.

enjoyed MGM, it was like a club. If you produced for them they treated you magnificently. They would throw you right out of the window if you didn't.'[9] Conversely Roberts wasn't afraid of causing trouble and took to task the directors of her scripts if they made changes of which she disapproved. Her concerns were serious – she rattled Sam Wood for reducing the American Indian characters in *Ambush* (1949) to 'worm-eating fellas'. In Roberts's version of the story about a young white woman kidnapped by a band of American Indians, the woman wants to stay with her new-found family rather than return to the white settlers' life. The curmudgeonly Wood, however, did not favour the writer's ideas.

Roberts's mettle was moulded in the harsh west. Unlike Burbridge, she could make legitimate claim to a western background. Born in Nebraska, brought up in Colorado, Roberts was a true daughter of the pioneering times, an inveterate horsewoman who thrived on the outdoor life. She told a reporter in 1968 while writing the murder-mystery Western *Five Card Stud*:

I was weaned on stories about gunfighters and their doings, and I know all the lingo too. My grandfather came West as far as Colorado by cov-

76

ered wagon. He was a sheriff in the state's wildest days. And my father was a town marshal. He never carried a gun, but all the bad men were afraid of him. He was short and stocky, but some people said he was the strongest man in Colorado, and nothing scared him.[10]

Such fond details helped create a mythology around the writer, authenticating her claim to the genre. Roberts also recalled that to help make ends meet at a time of considerable poverty her mother took in the local laundry, and as she grew up it became her ambition to find herself a good job so that her mother could give up the washing rounds (much of Roberts's income from her Hollywood career went home to her family). She decided upon a career in education and attended Colorado State Teaching College. But these plans were put aside when she left her small home town and hit the road with her first husband, a travelling salesman. Together they roamed from state to state selling fake pearls, with the diminutive Roberts often playing the role of mannequin and modelling the goods in store windows. She tired both of this life and her husband when they reached California.

Roberts chose to roost there for a while and found herself a job as a correspondent for the local Imperial Valley Press. But while most cub reporters tend to be delegated to births, marriages and the most ordinary of deaths, Roberts was despatched on her first assignment to follow up a particularly gruesome murder. It gave her a taste for action. In her spare time she turned her attention to crime fiction (though nothing was ever published), but then developed an interest in a screenwriting career. With this in mind, she was happy to demote herself when she heard through a friend that there was a vacant secretarial post in the script department at Fox. Toiling over speculative scripts at the weekends, she proved to her boss that she was worth taking seriously and was eventually hired as a writer after an apprenticeship of answering phones and taking dictation.

Roberts's early writing career ranged over an assortment of screenplays from *Peck's Bad Boy* (1934), a Jackie Cooper vehicle that followed the misadventures of a clumsy but well-meaning youth living in a small Midwestern town, to *Hollywood Boulevard* (1936), a melodramatic and somewhat cautionary tale about the tarnished allures of the film business. Roberts flitted from genre to genre but it wasn't until *Honky Tonk* (1941), a ribald Western in which Clark Gable and Lana Turner starred as two con artists set on out-fleecing each other, that she found a style for herself. By now she was one of the MGM stable, having moved there from Fox via Paramount, and was working for the producer Pandro S. Berman, with whom she would stay for her run at the studio. Knowing that she was writing for Gable, she originated the idea for *Honky Tonk* and co-scripted it with Sanford (it was the only script they worked on together – Sanford said he only contributed three per cent of it). Gable liked her flippant turn of phrase and asked her to work on his next film, *Somewhere I'll Find You* (1942), a story about two war correspondents, designed to prepare America for battle after Pearl Harbor.

In her later recollections Roberts claimed that she wrote mainly for male stars while she was at MGM during the 1940s. But she also worked – mostly doing rewrites – on such pictures as *Ziegfeld Girl* (1942), which followed the professional and emotional dilemmas of the famous chorines, and *Undercurrent* (1946), a noirish melodrama in the *Gaslight* mould starring Katharine Hepburn and directed by Vincente Minnelli. But apart from these titles, women usually took secondary roles in her scripts. Although Roberts claimed that she didn't care for women's pictures, the one film she would like to have scripted for Berman was *Madame Bovary* (the assignment went to Robert Ardrey) as Flaubert's analysis of bourgeois society interested her. But she also realised that the complex nature of his heroine would never reach the screen intact. Her fears about the film, which was eventually directed by Vincente Minnelli in 1949, proved to be well founded. The adaptation seemed to have little to do with the book; indeed, in Roberts's opinion it was impossible at the studio to write the kind of female roles which interested her.

> At Metro it was very difficult to write for women since they [the studio] had such old-fashioned ideas. There were two kinds of women – whores and angels – and they didn't make for interesting people. That is the thing that turned me off from writing for women – they just weren't interesting, they were so clichéd. There were prescriptions about what they could do or not do – a lady couldn't do this and a whore couldn't do that. I think that women are a mixture and that is what drew me to men. You could do anything with a man.[11]

This conviction was confirmed for her when she attempted to embellish Katharine Hepburn's character in Elia Kazan's Western, *Sea of Grass* (1947). Hepburn played the wife of a cattle tycoon (Spencer Tracy) who is so involved in his work that he almost loses his family. Roberts wanted the Hepburn character to resolve to leave him, but the director wouldn't have it. 'Kazan's politics were very liberal at the time, but he was a chauvinist and politics, for him, didn't enter into that.'[12]

In the end it was Roberts's steadfast political views that divided her from Hollywood. She was an esteemed member of the MGM writing team – her films made money which gave her clout in the eyes of the finance men, while she was also critically respected. Her screenplay for *Dragonseed* was included, alongside *Mr Smith Goes to Washington* and *Casablanca*, in John Gassner and Dudley Nichols's highly regarded anthology *Best Film Plays of 1943–1944* (New York: Crown Publishers, 1945). It seemed as though her place at MGM was guaranteed; she was even honoured with a prized monthly invitation to the hallowed dominions of the executive dining room. But apart from her horses, Roberts didn't care too much for the Hollywood trimmings. Her interests were more ideological.

By the late 1930s Hollywood had undergone a politicisation, its screenwriters at the forefront of the process. Founded in 1933, the Screen Writers Guild had become the most politically active union in the industry.

Meanwhile the Communist Party had established itself in town and was finding many of its recruits among the intellectuals in the writing community. For those who joined – particularly after 1935 when the Communist International announced Soviet support for a People's Front against fascism – the Party had become the attractive and acceptable left-wing alternative in post-Depression America, committed to anti-fascism and providing a source of social idealism that married more with traditional notions of American radicalism. Evening meetings for the screenwriters' branch would include screenings of Soviet and other progressive European films followed by discussions of their radical content and technique. But the fruits of such a progressive and stimulating education could never be harvested since the writers would find that they had to erase all this good work from their minds when they returned to their sorry lot at the studios the following day.

Roberts, who joined the Party with Sanford (Sanford was very much the bohemian radical: before his brief stint at MGM, where he met Roberts, he had shared a mountain hut with Nathanael West), was typical of the new 'soft' membership, believing in social reform rather than revolution. But as a member of the Screen Writers Guild – she was voted on to the council in 1945 – she supported a militant Guild with every 'active member really active'. Standing for Vice-President in 1948, she stated in her electoral address: 'I am against blacklists in any form, either on the part of the employees or in the Guild itself. I believe that such blacklists exist in both places, and I intend to expose them.' These were contentious views that did not get her voted in.[13]

If her politics were allowed to surface anywhere in her films, they are most evident in *Escape* (1940), her adaptation of an Ethel Vance novel in which an American rescues his mother from a Nazi concentration camp on the eve of World War Two. The *New York Times* film critic Bosley Crowther ordained it 'far and away the most dramatic and hair-raising picture yet made on the sinister subject of persecution in a totalitarian land.' Hardly surprising, then, that the film was one of the twenty-five features investigated by the Senate Subcommittee on War Propaganda, set up in Washington in response to the isolationist lobby's accusations. They maintained that the movie industry was in cahoots with the Roosevelt administration in promoting America's entry into the war. In this instance the America First senators were seen off by the persuasive arguments of both the Producers' Association, which represented the studio management, and the Screen Writers Guild.

Roberts would not be so lucky when Washington clashed with Hollywood again. Her principles would finally see her banished from the studios for over a decade when she was blacklisted during the dark era of the House Un-American Activities Committee's inquisitions. Named by one of the chief witnesses, Martin Berkeley, Roberts was hauled up in front of the Committee in September 1951. Taking the Fifth Amendment, she refused to co-operate. MGM was alarmed at the prospect of losing one of their valuable writers and tried to convince Roberts to name a few names so that she could vindicate herself as far as HUAC was concerned. They even offered to provide her with a lawyer. But Roberts refused. Consequently her contract with MGM was terminated and her name wiped from the credits of *Ivanhoe*, the film she was working on at the time. She was sent into the wilderness for over a decade. Later, she was to relish the irony that her most celebrated screenplay, *True Grit*, starred the most famous reactionary of them all, John Wayne. Roberts, however, was to be pleasantly surprised by the man: 'In his biography, he wrote that *True Grit* was the best script that he had ever read. That is pretty generous for someone who knew that a woman had written his Oscar picture and who was banned from the pictures for her political views.'[14]

For Roberts and her radical contemporaries, the political agenda was dominated by a concern with class and, in the years before and during the war, with challenging fascism. In the 1930s and 1940s gender politics were not a significant concern for Hollywood's left wing. But at the Writers Clinic, set up by the Communist Party to discuss both formal and thematic aspects of screenwriting, the 'woman question', as it was described, was referred to. In these sessions clinic participants did have to ask themselves whether, for instance, a story about a man could be deemed successful if there was no attempt to integrate women characters into it. It was also agreed that screenplays about working women should be encouraged in order to challenge 'male chauvinism'.

The debates about the 'woman question' interested Roberts, but few of the conclusions could filter through into her studio work. So as an obviously principled writer, Roberts stuck to her guns and believed that it was more rewarding – and more fun – to write about men because she didn't want to be party to perpetuating what she considered to be female stereotypes.

Leigh Brackett is another female writer who went against the grain in the material she wrote, starting with *The Big Sleep* (1946) for Howard Hawks and stretching to *The Empire Strikes Back* (1980) for George Lucas. But Brackett is considered to have been in a league of her own. She wasn't a hired studio hand. She may have made her screenwriting debut at Republic with a ten-day wonder, *The Vampire's Ghost*, a monster picture which she later described as 'terrible'; but her film career was really anchored by her extensive collaboration with Hawks, for whom she wrote five films, three of which were Westerns. She also established a reputation for herself outside Hollywood as a prolific and much respected writer of science-fiction and crime novels. In science-fiction circles she was to become best known for the creation of the swashbuckling hero Eric John Stark, whose Odyssean adventures were featured in the *Planet Stories* magazine during the 1940s and were reintroduced in the 1970s for a series of novels she wrote for Ballantine Books. Her detour into crime started with the 1944 novel *No Good for a Corpse*. Her other crime fiction includes *The Tiger Among Us* (1957), about a vicious teenage gang from the middle-class suburbs, which was typically both a compelling narrative and a provocative treatise on violence and evil. She even ghost-wrote a thriller for the actor George Sanders. But it was *No Good for a Corpse* that brought her to the attention of Hawks. Its classic hard-boiled prose style, in a tale of a private dick on the case of a murdered femme fatale, convinced Hawks that its writer was the 'man' for the job of adapting (along with William Faulkner) Raymond Chandler's terse and bewildering thriller *The Big Sleep*. Completing the script in a frenzied five days – she and Faulkner worked on different parts of the book, in separate offices – Brackett demonstrated that she could match the chief correspondent for the 'mean streets' style.

The story of how Hawks came to hire Brackett is as infamous as it is revealing: 'Hawks liked my dialogue and called my agent. He was somewhat shaken when he discovered that it was Miss and not Mister Brackett, but he rallied bravely and signed me on anyway, for which I have always been extremely grateful.'[15] Hawks commented on their first meeting at his offices on the Warner Bros lot: 'In walked a rather attractive girl who looked like she had just come in from a tennis match. She looked as if she wrote poetry. But she wrote like a man.' Hawks was not averse to women writers. When he optioned a *Collier's* short story about a havoc-causing panther called Baby, he was so impressed by its wit that he invited its young author, Hagar Wilde, who had never worked in movies, to work on the script with the experienced Dudley Nichols. The skeleton of *Bringing Up Baby* had only to be fleshed out a little. 'It was such a funny story, it

Leigh Brackett with Howard Hawks on the set of El Dorado.

was easy to be funny in it. ... I wanted to keep the same thought, that method of treating it. She had the characters for both Hepburn and Grant so well.'[16] Subsequently Hawks invited Wilde to co-write the cross-dressing comedy that also starred Grant, *I Was a Male War Bride* (1949).

Comedies were different, though. Hawks was surprised to find a woman interested in tough thrillers. But it wasn't just the fact that Brackett was a woman, but that she was the kind of woman who looked as though she played tennis rather than 'drive a truck' that seemed to amaze him. And not just Hawks. When Bogart was asked to comment on the completed script, he directed criticisms to Brackett about some of the lines he considered to be far too genteel. It transpired, however, that these were Faulkner's contributions. Consequently, Bogart nicknamed Brackett 'Butch' and went to her with any dialogue that he felt needed a roughing up.

Coincidentally, it was after watching Bogart in *The Maltese Falcon* in 1942 that Brackett 'conceived a mad passion for detective stories'. Setting out to write one of her own, she put herself through 'an intensive course of studying Steinbeck, Hemingway, Kipling, Chandler and Dashiell Hammett because they got so much into so little'.[17] Her interest in reading and writing adventure stories, though, had started much earlier than that: 'I grew up a tomboy. Never read any of the books for girls. I devoured Edgar Rice Burroughs, the Tom Swift series, and every book about Indians I could get my hands on. I started writing at the age of 13 and wrote for ten years before I sold anything.'[18] As a budding novelist who was encouraged and subsidised by her grandfather, her preferred genre had always been science fiction. This alarmed the female members of her middle-class family:

> Everyone warned me, 'You'll starve to death. It's not a very respectable field, you know. I mean, only nut cases write for it and only nut cases read it.' ... My aunt used to say, 'Why don't you write nice stories for the *Ladies Home Journal*?' I used to say, 'I wish I could, because they pay well, but I can't read the *Ladies Home Journal* and I'm sure that I couldn't write for it.'[19]

Brackett worked hard to elude the traps that were laid out for women writers. Her reading provided a vision of other possible pursuits, while her background gave her the fortitude to chase them.

> I guess that I was liberated on the day I was born, because my mother was a feminine, helpless little person and all the women of my family were professional ladies with a capital 'L'. A lady never did anything for herself; somebody always did it for her. They looked down on me a great deal because I was big and husky and active, running up and down the beach, playing with the boys and doing things. Oh, goodness, I got so many lectures. I think I was just the opposite type, that's all, and possibly became even more opposite because I so despised their attitude. I thought it was so ridiculous. ... I don't believe that you are supposed to sit around waiting for a man to come along and want you and

provide you with this, that, and the other. I don't need anybody to provide anything for me. I'll provide for myself. My father and mother dearly loved each other and they were wonderful people and they got married and he died. So where was she? I always prefer to have a little of something in my own hands that I have control of.[20]

Like most of her screenwriting contemporaries, Brackett was a tough and independent woman. She had without any difficulty found a respected place for herself in a male-dominated genre that interested her. But importantly, and this makes her unusual, she was able to put female characters like herself into the scripts she wrote for Hawks. Take Vivian Regan (Lauren Bacall) in *The Big Sleep*, or Feathers (Angie Dickinson) in the classic Western *Rio Bravo* (1959), and you'll find cynical, wise-cracking heroines who are in control of their sexuality and who are essential to the plot. These aren't secondary, love-interest roles of the kind found in so many male-driven stories. But then one would have to search hard for such female characters in a film by Howard Hawks. 'The Hawksian woman' was a marvel unto herself. She was first given critical attention in the early 1970s when the feminist writer Naomi Wise identified the phenomenon.[21] Surveying Hawks's films, Wise argued that they collapsed the paradigm of good girl and bad girl beloved of Hollywood films and created a bold new type: 'In fact, the heroines are, if anything, superior to the heroes.' It is a supposition that Wise found particularly in the Hawks films written by Brackett.

Conventional heroines and domestic stories bored Brackett and certainly could not be found in her crime and science-fiction writing. The critic Tom Milne comments of her 'sword and sorcery' stories:

> Her heroines never melt, simper, faint or whimper. On the contrary they usually start out (and often remain) as the villainesses, thirsting for power and domination, and only tempering their instinct to sadistic cruelties (as in *The Sword of Rhiannon*) when matched against a man who can respect the masculine drive, respond to the feminine need, and envisage a future as equals.[22]

Brackett had found a soul-mate in her director. Writing in response to Wise's article, Brackett stated: 'I've been working with Howard Hawks, off and on, since 1944, but I never really stopped to think what exactly he was doing with his women, I only knew that I liked them and was comfortable with them.'[23] The creation of strong female characters was not something that had to be put on the agenda by Brackett: it was already there. Indeed, it was sometimes something to be played down. 'More than once I've argued with Hawks that the girl was getting too pushy, and couldn't we let the poor boob of a hero make just one decision all by himself? I was always overruled, and I guess Hawks knew what he was doing, because it came out right in the end.'[24]

One only has to look at other Hawks heroines such as punchy star reporter Hildy Johnson in *His Girl Friday*, written by Charles Lederer, to appreciate how important the director's stand on women was. In the play *The Front Page*, on which the film was based, Hildy was a man. Hawks was hardly a proto-feminist – he commented in the 1970s that he didn't think much of the newly established women's movement because 'the people who seem to be doing most of the talking are so unattractive that I don't think it's fun.' But the sexual politics of his films are fascinating. Asked why such exceptionally strong-willed female characters appeared in his films, he replied: 'That happens to be the kind of girl I like, so it's fun to be with 'em. I know 'em better. You might term them honest and direct.' Romance in a Hawks film was encapsulated in the sparring of two equals, not kissing in the moonlight, while love and marriage were banished words. Hawks was an anomaly for his times in his appreciation of bolder women characters. It is important, then, that he was one of the few directors working during the studio era who also produced his own films. In that respect he enjoyed a level of autonomy over his work which permitted his – and Brackett's – particular vision to remain intact.

Brackett's screenwriting work has received, and merited, considerable critical attention. Interviews with her have been anthologised and she is the only woman contributor to a discussion on screenwriting in Donald Chase's book *Filmmaking – the Collaborative Art*.[25] With only nine credits to her name, her work still has a cohesion to it that invites such scrutiny. Undoubtedly her association with Hawks is partly responsible for this. But Brackett later fashioned the cynical and clever *The Long Goodbye* (1973), another Chandler adaptation, directed by Robert Altman, which allowed Marlowe to be more battered than his 1940s Bogart manifestation; in the bitter end he murders the friend who betrayed him (something, Brackett commented, the 1940s Marlowe would never have been allowed to do). Her last script was for *The Empire Strikes Back* (1980), the sequel to *Star Wars*, a fitting finale to the career of a woman who 'looked like she wrote poetry, but wrote like a man'.

Notes

1. Unpublished interview with Tina Daniell, 1983.
2. Frances Marion, *Off With Their Heads* (New York: Macmillan, 1972), pp. 214–15.
3. Ibid., p. 216.
4. Virginia Kellogg, 'Inside Women's Prison', *Collier's*, 3 June 1950.
5. 'She Writes Westerns for Films', *New York World Telegraph*, 27 July 1939.
6. Ibid.
7. This recollection is courtesy of Mary C. George, a friend of Burbridge's.
8. Ibid.
9. Ibid.
10. Interview with Marguerite Roberts, *Citizen News*, 5 April 1968.
11. Unpublished interview with Marguerite Roberts by Tina Daniell, 1983.
12. Ibid.
13. Marguerite Roberts, *The Screenwriter*, October 1948.
14. Unpublished interview with Marguerite Roberts by Tina Daniell, 1983.
15. Leigh Brackett, 'From *The Big Sleep* to *The Long Goodbye* and More or Less How We Got There', *Take One*, vol. 4 no. 1., 1972.

16. Howard Hawks, in Joseph MacBride, *Hawks on Hawks* (Berkeley: University of California Press, 1982), p. 70.
17. Hedda Hopper, 'They Call Her for Salty Dialogue', *Los Angeles Times*, 28 December 1965.
18. Ibid.
19. Interview with Leigh Brackett by Juanita Roderick and Hugh G. Earnhart, part of the Youngstown State University Oral History Programme, 7 October 1975.
20. Ibid.
21. Naomi Wise, 'The Hawksian Woman'. *Take One*, vol. 3 no. 3, 1972, pp. 17–20.
22. Tom Milne, 'Leigh Brackett: A Man's Woman', *Monthly Film Bulletin*, vol. 47 no. 588, July 1980.
23. Leigh Brackett, 'A Comment on the Hawksian Woman', *Take One*, vol. 3 no. 3, 1972, pp. 17–20.
24. Ibid.
25. Donald Chase, *Filmmaking – the Collaborative Art* (Boston: Little Brown & Co., 1975).

6

Feminism Comes to Hollywood

For the screenwriter the shake-up of the studio system and the arrival of TV had inevitable repercussions on their profession. But by the 1960s other forces were coming into play that would potentially reshape the outlook for women screenwriters. In 1963 Betty Friedan's *The Feminine Mystique* was published, and with that the first sounds of an American feminist movement clamoured to be heard. As its idea took root over the next decade, women in creative professions would find themselves and their work perused as feminist or not. 'Feminism', with its multifold meanings, became something that women writers could espouse, distance themselves from, or claim to have never come across. It was a knot in the background fabric, there to be unravelled or ignored.

For women in film, the publication in 1973 of both Marjorie Rosen's *Pop Corn Venus – Women, Movies and the American Dream* and Molly Haskell's *From Reverence to Rape – The Treatment of Women in the Movies* marked a turning point in the illumination of issues about the history of the representation of women in American film. The previous year various members of the Writers Guild of America (West) had decided to set up a women's committee. A statement of intent outlined their central concern: to 'provide the means of ending discrimination against women writers in the industry and to work to improve the image of women in film, television and radio, and to sponsor events designed to increase knowledge of the craft and the market place.' To be a woman screenwriter, it was implied, was to have a responsibility regarding the depiction of women in films.

Also in 1972 the Canadian film journal *Take One* devoted an entire edition to women in cinema, with one feature looking at the results of a questionnaire sent to a variety of women working in the industry throughout the world, whether as screenwriters, editors, critics or the few who had made it by now as directors and producers. The magazine solicited thoughts on such questions as whether they thought that their work had been affected by the fact that they were women; what difficulties they had experienced; whether the reviews of their work mentioned or dealt with their films in terms of their sex. It was mentioned that 'the majority of responses came from women who seemed interested in the concerns of women in the profession and in society as a whole.' Those respondents who were working in the American industry included the screenwriter Eleanor Perry and the writer-director Stephanie Rothman. In tracking the careers of Perry and Rothman it is possible to explore the various options open to those who in the 60s and 70s were overtly interested in challenging the then prevailing image of women in film.

Eleanor Perry came to screenwriting when she was in her late forties and in the second phase of her life, having run to New York from a failed first marriage, a self-confessed 'refugee from Cleveland and suburbia'. Perry, who was brought up and educated in the Mid-western city (apart from a stint at the Sarah Lawrence College for women), trained as a psychiatric case-worker, writing educational plays on the subject which were produced and published by the Cleveland Mental Hygiene Association. She also co-wrote plays and mystery novels with her first husband, Leo G. Bayer, a lawyer, under the pseudonym Oliver Weld Bayer.

Her interest in mental health issues would be manifest in her film career. Her first script, *David and Lisa* (1962), was based on a case history about two disturbed adolescents. The film was directed by her new husband, Frank Perry, who had previously worked in theatre. The two had met in the late 50s on the occasion of the New York production of one of Perry's plays. Dispirited by the state of contemporary drama, they decided to turn to cinema, heartened by the French New Wave which was hitting the New York shores at the time. 'Serious European films like *Hiroshima, mon amour* had a great impact on us. We decided we'd have a go at films too,' explained Eleanor Perry in an early interview.[1]

Spare in style, the low-budget *David and Lisa*, which the Perrys made by scraping together their own funds, was heralded as part of the American new wave. 'Tact, taste, insight and forthrightness make this one of the most incisive and original films treating mental problems,' said *Variety* of the film. The Perrys, who were even nominated for an Academy award, immediately won themselves a serious art house reputation. But this did not stop Eleanor Perry being courted by Hollywood, and finding that she would be niched as a woman's picture writer. 'I was offered several [adaptation] jobs. The novels all dealt with retarded or mentally ill adolescents or were sappy, soapy stories which the producers called "women's pictures". The term really infuriated me.'[2]

Keen to maintain their integrity, the Perrys kept on the independent path. Their next film, *Ladybug, Ladybug* (1963), also dealt with the psychology of adolescents and also took its cue from a real incident. Eleanor Perry had come across a news article about a nuclear alarm that had gone off in a school in California during the Cuban missile crisis. She decided to use this as a starting point to investigate how children were dealing with the fears of the nuclear age. The Perrys' convictions that civil defence was a futile business ensured that the film had a forceful anti-war stance. This provoked strong feelings among audiences and critics, and comment in the *New York Times*. 'I've had such a mixed bag of comments, ranging from the wildly enthusiastic to unbelievably hostile. ... It's as if we have put our fingers on a sore spot, made people face things they would rather not think about,' commented Eleanor Perry at the time.[3] The film even elicited a response from Dr Benjamin Spock, who praised it for airing a crucial concern:

> Studies have shown that 25 to 50 per cent of our children believe that nuclear attack will come. This is hard for us adults to believe because we have such a capacity to deny what we cannot face. But *Ladybug, Ladybug* shows us very poignantly how vulnerable our children are to anxiety about war. It reminds us how much we must do to secure for them a more peaceful world.[4]

But even with controversy and Dr Spock's sanction, the film was a box-office failure.

The Perrys did not make another film until 1968. Again it was Eleanor who initiated the idea to adapt John Cheever's short story, *The Swimmer*. The premise – a middle-aged suburbanite discovers that his family have left him and decides to cross New England via the swimming pools of the state's elite – was again hardly commercial. But they eventually interested Hollywood producer Sam Spiegel, who was willing to work on it as long as he had the say on the male lead and the final cut. This meant that Sydney Pollack came on board to direct some scenes as well. With Burt Lancaster cast as the flabby hero in trunks who has to face up to some unpleasant home truths, the film is a bizarre and compelling odyssey that signalled the beginning of the end of the American Dream.

The Swimmer is typical of the Perrys' liberal humanist approach to both the choice and the treatment of their subjects. With mental health care and nuclear war already on their agenda, it might have seemed obvious for them to move on to questions of sexual politics. But Eleanor Perry wouldn't admit to becoming interested in feminist ideas until the early 70s, after the break-up of her marriage with Frank. Ironically, their last film together was an adaptation of the Sue Kaufmann novel *Diary of a Mad Housewife* (1970), for Universal, the Perrys by now having been drawn into the Hollywood web. The film is a bleak portrait of marital breakdown Manhattan-style, memorable for the performances of Carrie Snodgress as the put-upon wife and Richard Benjamin as her vindictive and ambitious lawyer husband. Perry later acknowledged that the film exorcised a few of her feelings about her first marriage. She would do the same for her second marriage in her novel *Blue Pages* (1979), which recounts the painful estrangement of a screenwriter wife and her film director husband.

After the Perrys went their separate ways, Eleanor only wrote three more screenplays. The first two were modest thrillers, *The Lady in the Car with Glasses and a Gun* (1970) and *The Deadly Trap* (1972). But it was her final screenplay, *The Man Who Loved Cat Dancing*, which saw her divorced from Hollywood. Perry was already beginning to demonstrate her anger and despair about the prospects for women in the industry. She had joined a consciousness-raising group led by the feminist theorist Susan Brownmiller. This, she told one interviewer, 'opened up my eyes to the way women have been treated. Especially in films. I hope to do some-thing very positive to change this image. It's usually a man's point of view anyway.'[5] On a discussion panel at the 1971 New York Film Festival, Perry commented that she was 'tired of seeing women portrayed as prostitutes or merely love objects' and 'that women can be prolific in the field of liter-ature because it is a monastic effort, but the collaborative nature of film-making allows for exclusion of women as undesirable members of the team, or relegation to assignments dealing only with female subjects.'[6] The following year, at the Cannes Film Festival, she led a group of women pro-testers who sprayed red paint over a poster advertising Fellini's *Roma* (it depicted a woman with three breasts). They also picketed screenings of the film, waving placards inscribed 'Women are People, not Dirty Jokes'. Such activities followed in the fashion of Robin Morgan's recent publicity stunt at the Miss America pageant and no doubt branded the writer as a trouble-maker.

Perry's experience with *The Man Who Loved Cat Dancing* only confirmed for her how dire was the situation for women in film. It was the first of her scripts to have an overtly feminist agenda and in her opinion it was to suffer because of that. In various interviews conducted in 1972, Perry was full of ideas, even expressing hopes for an eventual move into directing. But an immediate project was to script *The Man Who Loved Cat Dancing*, the 'first Women's Lib Western', based on Marilyn Durham's novel. Perry sum-marised the film's story: 'The hero is a tough westerner who is haunted by the fact that he killed his Indian wife. In his search for their children, he teams up with an amazingly liberated housewife who is running away from her husband. And they have an abrasive, absolutely marvellous love affair.'[7] If this storyline does not constitute the most obvious of feminist agendas, it was Perry's attempt to provide a more positive heroine for the mainstream. Meanwhile she explained that *The Man Who Loved Cat Dancing* was the first 'Women's Lib Western' because 'it's the first one where the leading lady isn't a hooker'. Perry may have overlooked the feminist potential of such previous films as the Doris Day vehicles *Calamity Jane* (written by James O'Hanlon, 1953), in which Day plays the gun-toting tomboy, and *The Ballad of Josie* (written by Harold Swanton, 1967), in which she plays a western widow holding out on her own in the prairies. But the writer was on a mis-sion to make her feminist mark, so much so that she decided to act as associate producer on her dream project.

The Man Who Loved Cat Dancing, however, soon turned into a night-mare, demonstrating to Perry that the industry could not accommodate independent women either on or off the screen. She had teamed up with the producer Martin Poll, who had secured a deal for the film at MGM and who had promised her equal control and input on it. But as soon as Perry turned up at the Thalberg building on the Metro lot, she realised that she had been put in her place. 'My associate's office had rugs, leather furniture, leaded glass windows, and a secretary sitting outside. My office was down the hall next to the john, full of cracks, with a broken air-condi-tioner and a tiny desk'.[8] If Perry could deal with Poll's gestures of one-upmanship, she was less happy about his approach to more important aspects of the deal. She found that she wasn't consulted about the casting of Burt Reynolds and Sarah Miles in the lead roles but, more importantly, neither was she consulted when changes were made to her original script.

> There was talk that Burt Reynolds was dissatisfied with the script. I said, 'I'm the writer, why don't I meet him?' My associate said, 'He doesn't want to work with you. He wants to work with a man.' My associate kept on implying that I didn't know about westerns, as though there was something mystical about the westerns, that only jocks can write westerns. I can write this sagebrush crap; I know the proper curse words. Finally one night after a long drink, I called Burt and he said, 'What do you mean? I wondered why you weren't here.'[9]

Various male writers were assigned to the script, including William Norton and Sarah Miles's husband Robert Bolt. In the rewrite Perry found that the Sarah Miles character had been softened and, worse still, that a crudely handled rape scene had been added. According to Perry, Poll's reason for this addition was that 'it turned men on'.[10] Despite her vehement protest at the final cut, Perry still retained a solo credit, even though Norton had gone to the Writers Guild of America (West) arbitration committee to ask for a review. There are financial advantages in retaining solo credit, but even so it is odd that Perry should have clung on to a film that she so clearly despised. It was also despised by the critics, though not necessarily for ideological reasons, and soon disappeared from the screens.

Perry would never see another of her scripts produced. Various projects were mooted, such as *Clout*, which was to star Cicely Tyson as a black congresswoman opposite George C. Scott in a Hepburn/Tracy-style love-story, and a screen adaptation of Joyce Carol Oates's novel *Expensive People*. The film composer Michel Legrand also approached her to write the script for his projected directorial debut. But nothing came of these ideas, nor did Perry fulfil her own plan to direct.

Instead, she remained vociferous on the subject of women in the film industry and was involved in schemes to bring young women into films at a writing and directing level. This included setting up workshops at the American Film Institute and being sent as an envoy to Washington to give evidence before a Senate educational committee. Perry even made the headlines in 1977 when she interviewed the former actress Grace Kelly, then Princess of Monaco, and decided to abandon protocol and the pre-planned questions about her children and her interest in pressed flower collages. Instead, she elicited a few comments about her thoughts on such topics as the image of women in Hollywood and feminism. Perry was unimpressed but unsurprised to find that her royal subject's attitudes were still 'stuck in the 50s'.[11]

A tireless campaigner to bring women into the 70s, Perry was not afraid of being provocative. But as soon as she was labelled as a feminist screenwriter, she courted trouble. She also found herself typecast again. In one of her last interviews before her death from cancer, she commented that she still felt stereotyped as a female writer; she had always wanted to write a war film but 'instead, I get scripts about marriages, divorces, abortions and suffragettes'. Despite the feminist potential of such subjects, Perry was disenchanted. She found that as a feminist she was assumed to have an overriding concern to deal with women rather than to bring a feminist perspective to all subjects, including war. She might have been better off sticking with the New York 'independent' mentality and continuing to write scripts for low-budget films over which she had control. But that culture was also very director-oriented; this worked for Perry when she was in partnership with Frank, but she lost her foothold when she went solo.

The answer, again, was to become a director of one's scripts. The 60s and 70s saw a handful of women make that transition – notably Elaine May, who was one of the first women to direct as well as write for a major studio.[12] It was more likely, however, that writer/directors would find work in the independent sector, as Lupino had done before them. For those committed to narrative cinema, the low-budget 'exploitation' genre, as typified by the output of the producer Roger Corman, was one possible route. The term exploitation had, and still has, a double edge. The low pay and swift turnover of the films left those involved in making them tired and poor. Conversely the deal was not so hard for those film-makers who wanted to exploit a genre to investigate ideas that the big-budget commercial imperative would usually not allow. For a film-maker such as Stephanie Rothman, who was interested in pursuing certain ideals, this had a definite appeal.

Rothman graduated in film from the University of Southern California, where she became the first woman to be awarded a Director's Guild Fellowship. By the mid-60s she had joined the 'Roger Corman School of Filmmaking', and began her feature film apprenticeship recycling East European material into fodder for the drive-ins. Typical of this Corman cut-price approach is *Blood Bath* (1966), a beatnik vampire movie culled from a Yugoslav horror film; Rothman revamped the material, shooting scenes in Venice, California, as a match for the original's Dubrovnik locations.

It's a Bikini World (1966) was the first film Rothman co-wrote and directed from scratch. The beach picture genre was not her own choice but it afforded her a chance to direct. 'Corman told me he wanted lots of nudity and that everyone should look very attractive. Beyond that I was allowed to do what I wanted to do.'[13] Consequently Rothman devised an entertaining twist on the Samson and Delilah story that begs a few questions about the appeal of 'macho' men. Samson is a beach bum who believes that Delilah will just swoon for his over-toned flesh. But when he discovers that Delilah prefers boys with specs rather than pecs, he masquerades as his nerdish brother Herbie and successfully wins her over. Meanwhile Delilah challenges Samson to a series of sporting feats, finally beating him up when she discovers that he has been letting her win. Delilah knocks Samson into shape as he finally realises that his Herbie persona is more appealing.

Such a revision of a well-oiled formula set the pattern of Rothman's future work for both Corman and later Dimension Pictures, the company she set up in 1972 with her husband, the writer and producer Charles Swartz. *Student Nurses* (1970), *The Velvet Vampire* (1971), *Group Marriage* (1972), *Terminal Island* (1973) and *Working Girls* (1974) all took popular formats (whether the vampire or prison movie) and rehabilitated them, often with comic effect. 'I was eager to try every genre offered to me.' In each instance she would be given certain story parameters and, as long as there were the requisite scenes of sex and violence, she could push the film in whichever direction she liked, low budget permitting.

> I was told that there were certain things that I had to do, but once I took those things into account I was allowed the freedom to do what I wanted to do, as long as I could make a coherent piece that the people who had put up the money felt would not offend their audience. I had to make certain assumptions about what would and would not offend. Perhaps the difference between me and other directors was that I was less timid in terms of what I thought audiences would accept.

Certainly, Rothman was concerned about how she represented her female characters.

> I knew that anything I did would have women in certain active roles. I knew that I wouldn't treat the female characters the way that men did. ... The way that women were being treated in films reinforced the idea that men were all-powerful and that women were powerless. I certainly did not have sympathy for that view, nor did I observe it to be particularly true.

But she was most interested in exploring the wider social context that determined what roles women were allowed to play. '[My films] took up issues that were concerned with that very year and that very decade.' She attempted an ideological critique of American society, demonstrating an interest in the social contract as much as anything else. Thus *Terminal Island*, her version of the 'Devil's Island' action picture about convicted 'lifers' sent to a island penitentiary set up by a dictatorship, was more psychological exploration:

> The primary reason for making that film was to look at what might happen if the death penalty was no longer legal and you had to do something to these people who were sentenced to a lifetime of incarceration. Considering the attitudes of most tax-paying citizens to the people (which is that they resent the idea of having to support them for the rest of their lives), I thought that it would be an interesting idea to explore what would happen to them if you banished them with very little resources to a place where they could survive depending on their own ingenuity and what kind of society they would establish, and if they continued to be the same people that they were prior to sentencing.

Rothman injected *Terminal Island* with the required dosage of violence, though this was something that she viewed with ambivalence.

I don't think that anybody making a violent film should deny the fact that while you may not inspire [audiences] to commit violent [acts], you are providing them a blueprint of how to do it. On the other hand, violence and its consequences are a part of our lives. In addition to that they are the very essence of drama. You have no drama without conflict, whether it be a clash of ideas or otherwise. I don't think that you can avoid dealing with violence. And if you are going to deal with violence, you should deal with it as realistically as possible, and by that I mean I don't think that you should deny its awful consequences.

This pungent brew of ideas and action ensured that Rothman's films were as popular in the art-house cinemas as in the drive-ins. They also elicited interest from feminist critics writing in such journals as *Film Comment* and *Screen*,[14] both of which published articles about the writer/director's work in 1976. With such critical attention Rothman might have looked forward to the progress of her career, perhaps following other Corman graduates like Joe Dante and Jonathan Demme into the mainstream, but sadly she never made another film. After dissolving Dimension Pictures, she decided to concentrate on scripting and had developed a number of stories in the science-fiction and action genres, but found that she could not sell any of her work. By the late 70s she felt that the industry had 'turned its back' on her, and she was forced to earn her living outside it. When interviewed in the early 90s, she was writing for a undisclosed political organisation. For someone who once won a prestigious Directors' Guild fellowship it must have been particularly galling to relinquish a career in her chosen medium. 'I have thought about this at great length, discussed it with close personal friends in the industry too, but I just can't find an answer.'

It is too easy to say that Perry's and Rothman's careers suffered because they were women who wanted to revise attitudes to women on screen. Hollywood soon caught up with feminism when it realised that there was an audience to be catered for. The studios backed such chamber-works as *Alice Doesn't Live Here Anymore* (directed by Martin Scorsese and written by Robert Getchell, 1974) and *An Unmarried Woman* (written and directed by Paul Mazursky, 1978), though the feminism of these undoubtedly important films did not extend to employing women writers to work on them.

But then there were women writers who did not make a conscious or obvious stand for feminist ideas, but rather let them gently filter into their work. Joan Tewkesbury and Carole Eastman are two of the key writers to emerge out of the period, though neither really fulfilled the promise of their early careers in cinema. Tewkesbury, who once stated, 'People think I am a feminist. I'm not a feminist. I'm for folks',[15] won acclaim with the screenplays for *Thieves Like Us* (1974) and *Nashville* (1975), both for director Robert Altman, before pursuing a career as a writer/director in television.[16] Later Altman commented to his former protégée (he had seen one of her theatre plays and hired her as a script supervisor on *McCabe and*

Mrs Miller) that he had noticed that it was only the women in *Nashville* who go through any changes. To which Tewkesbury replied, 'Obviously I know women better, so I wrote about each of them going through a particular stage of something'.[17]

Meanwhile Eastman (who used the pseudonym Adrien Joyce) scripted, among other films, *The Shooting* (directed by Monty Hellman, 1967), which was described as the first existential Western, and the seminal 70s film *Five Easy Pieces* (directed by Bob Rafelson, 1970). The latter was written at the request of Jack Nicholson, an old friend she met at acting school. Trailing in the American new wave of films such as *Easy Rider*, the film is an intense and provocative portrait of Bobby, a disillusioned drifter from a fragile middle-class family of musicians, and those he collects around him. According to Eastman, he was a character to be neither condemned nor celebrated: 'In any situation of pressure Bobby is only capable of reacting at the level of what is easiest – he explodes and turns away. He has lots of artistic temperament, but his ability and discipline are not equal to it. … His harsh treatment of others has to be seen in relationship to his own pain.'[18] For the critic Molly Haskell, he was just another in the parade of angry young men in films. Only men, it seemed, had *angst*, and that was usually reflected in their attitude towards the women around them. In *Five Easy Pieces*, Bobby's girls are Rayette (Karen Black), whom he dumps at a petrol station, and Catherine (Susan Anspach). Interestingly, Eastman wanted the two female characters to be the opposite of each other, but Rafelson imposed changes on the script:

> I had originally conceived Catherine as a European woman, capable of having an affair with a man like Bobby without it altering the course of her life. She is not swept off her feet; she has the capacity only men in our society are supposed to have. Their relationship was a reversal of that between Bobby and Rayette, who is dependent and vulnerable, and the relationship affects Bobby, not Catherine.[19]

Eastman had also intended another ending for Bobby and Rayette. Bobby was to have been killed as his car swerves off a bridge (a reference to the then recent Chappaquiddick case), while Rayette, who survives, believes that he intended to kill himself – the manic loose cannon who can only auto-destruct.

The writer, who won an Academy Award nomination for the screenplay, certainly had reservations about the director's approach and soon after expressed a 'basic dissatisfaction with writing which is not at the same time made complete by directing'. A project with Jeanne Moreau and Jack Nicholson was announced, but her directing ambitions were never fulfilled. Nor were her screenwriting ambitions fully realised. Though there are several other scripts to her credit, including *Puzzle of a Downfall Child* (Jerry Schatzberg, 1970), about a model suffering from a nervous breakdown, *Five Easy Pieces* remains the high note of her career.

One critic has suggested that Eastman's career was marred by bad business decisions and guidance.[20] It is perhaps illuminating, then, that the one writer to sustain her career through the 60s and 70s (and who still works now, mostly doing rewrites) is Jay Presson Allen, who had the support of her husband, the movie and theatre producer Lewis Allen, before becoming powerful enough a player to produce her own films. Her scripts for such celebrated films as *Marnie* (Alfred Hitchcock, 1964), *Cabaret* (Bob Fosse, 1972), *Funny Lady* (Herbert Ross, 1975) and *Prince of the City* (Sidney Lumet, 1981) have won her critical and financial success. Though for someone who is also both a novelist and playwright, it seems that it is the financial success that most motivates her when it comes to film: 'I was never writing for fame and fortune. I was writing for fortune. If you are going to write for fame, you certainly don't write for the movies.'[21]

Presson Allen came to cinema from the theatre. She got her first break in film when Hitchcock approached her to work on *Marnie*, based on Winston Graham's novel, after seeing an advance script of her stage adaptation of Muriel Spark's *The Prime of Miss Jean Brodie* (which she later transposed to screen as well). Evan Hunter, who had recently adapted *The Birds* for Hitchcock, had already worked on two drafts of *Marnie* but was not happy about including a rape scene in the film. The director, seeking a 'fresh mind' to approach the 'stale material', consequently turned to the novice Allen. 'I think that he wanted a woman's point of view on *Marnie*, and that's why he asked me.'[22] Presson Allen had not considered writing for film until then: 'It seemed something so exotic and alien.' She remembers Hitchcock as a generous teacher, bent on demystifying the process of scripting. She scripted *Marnie* following his strict instructions, including those scenes which Hunter had demurred over. It is a screenplay, however, that she claims to be not particularly happy with for technical reasons. 'He taught me as fast as he could. But I couldn't learn fast enough.'

Marnie, however, would set a precedent for Presson Allen's future screenplays. She found a niche for herself as an adapter of others' work, seeing her sex as an asset in this respect. 'I don't think that women are as likely to throw the baby out with the bath-water as men on adaptations.' But while she might be typecasting herself here, it would seem that others typecast her regarding the kind of material she was offered. One writer has pointed out that *The Prime of Miss Jean Brodie*, *Cabaret* and *Funny Lady*, as well as her adaptation of *Travels With My Aunt* for George Cukor (1972), are all 'dealing with women whose control of their lives is not as total as they would have others believe'.[23]

Presson Allen, however, claims to take little political interest in the representation of women in her films. 'I don't concern myself with it. It is not an issue that I think about.' But certainly she was considering how she could acquire more control in the film industry. By 1979 she had secured herself a six-picture deal with Warner Bros. It was to produce, not necessarily write, though she scripted four of the projects, including *Prince of the City*, which finally took her into new territory.

Presson Allen initiated the production after reading Robert Daley's book based on a true case of corruption in the New York Police Department. She decided that it would be perfect material for the director Sidney Lumet, whom she had recently worked with (as producer on *It's*

My Turn), seeing it as a follow-up to the similarly themed *Serpico* (also directed by Lumet). *Prince of the City* proved to be the more intriguing film. It is a brilliant investigation that bustles with complex questions about the nature of authority and loyalty. Presson Allen and Lumet create a world where law and disorder blur, closely examining how that affects the young detective turned informer (memorably played by Treat Williams) and those around him both at work and at home. The plotting is intricate, the relationships between the men, in a department about to fall apart, keenly observed. It is Presson Allen's most arresting film, and if one compares it to the less psychologically interesting *Serpico*, it certainly suggests that a woman can bring a new dimension to the representation of the world of men. Feminism might have meant nothing to the writer. But in *Prince of the City* there is certainly powerful feminist potential in the idea of a 'fresh mind' working on 'stale material'. One would hope that might be the legacy inherited by women writers working today.

Notes

1. Faye Hammel, 'Film Makers at Home', *Cue*, 21 December 1963.
2. Kay Loveland, interview with Eleanor Perry, *Film Comment*, Spring 1971.
3. Joan Cook, 'Reactions to Film on Children Varied', *New York Times*, 9 January 1964.
4. Ibid.
5. Rosemary Armmia Kent, 'Admirable Perry', *Women's Wear Daily*, 14 February 1972.
6. Reported in *Variety*, 8 December 1971, p. 4.
7. *New York Times*, 2 January 1972.
8. From interview with Judy Klemesrud, 'The Woman Who Hated Cat Dancing', *New York Times*, 29 July 1973.
9. Ibid.
10. Marion Weiss, 'Interview with Eleanor Perry', *Women and Film*, vol. 2 no. 7, Summer 1975.
11. *New York Daily News*, 13 April 1977.
12. May established her credentials as a writer/performer and a brilliant satirist in the late 50s/early 60s, working in partnership with Mike Nichols on the New York review circuit. Hollywood first summoned Nichols in 1963, to direct *The Graduate* and *Who's Afraid of Virginia Woolf?*, among other films. May first worked in film in 1964, when she was asked to adapt Evelyn Waugh's *The Loved One*, though later the project was taken over by Terry Southern and Christopher Isherwood. Her first produced screenplay was *Such Good Friends* (1971), directed by Otto Preminger, but she is credited under the pseudonym Esther Dale since she was unhappy with the production. The same year, however, saw her debut as writer/director as well as female lead in *A New Leaf*, a wry comedy about a gold-digging bachelor (Walter Matthau) who pursues an eccentric rich botanist (May). The film was both a critical and a financial success, but again May attempted to take her name off it since she did not approve of the version that the studio (Paramount) released. May has continued to have an uncomfortable relationship with Hollywood. Her film *Mickey and Nicky* (1975) became a *cause célèbre* when she went over budget and then into lengthy court battles with Paramount to secure artistic control. Though she has done respected work as screenwriter on *Heaven Can Wait* as well as uncredited contributions to *Reds* and *Tootsie*, her insistence on such directorial control has given her a difficult reputation. This was not helped by *Ishtar* (1987), which was a monumental failure and a likely reason why she hasn't worked behind the camera since.

13. Interview with Rothman by the author, December 1990. Unless stated, all other quotes are from this interview.
14. See Terry Curtis Fox, 'Fully Female', *Film Comment*, November/December 1976, and Pam Cook, *Screen*, vol. 17 no. 2, 1976. See also Danni Peary, 'Stephanie Rothman: R-Rated Feminist', in Karyn Kay and Gerald Peary (eds.), *Women and the Cinema: A Critical Anthology* (New York: E. P. Dutton, 1977).
15. Jack Slater, 'Out of the Doll's House', *Emmy Magazine*, May–June 1982, p. 21.
16. Tewkesbury's directorial debut was *Old Boyfriends* (which was scripted by Paul Schrader). The rest of her work has been as a writer/director for television, though she did do an uncredited rewrite on the film *The Accused*.
17. Slater, 'Out of the Doll's House', p. 22.
18. Estelle Changas, '"Easy" Author on Cutting Edge of Lib in Films', *Los Angeles Times*, 2 May 1971.
19. Ibid.
20. Joel Bellman on Carole Eastman in the *Dictionary of Literary Biography, Volume 26, American Screenwriters* (Detroit: Gale, 1984), pp. 117–19.
21. Interview with Jay Presson Allen, conducted by the author in January 1991. Unless cited otherwise all quotes with Presson Allen are from this interview.
22. Donald Spoto, *The Dark Side of Genius: The Life of Alfred Hitchcock* (New York: Little, Brown and Company, 1983), p. 499 in Ballantine edition.
23. Nick Roddick on Jay Presson Allen, *Dictionary of Literary Biography, Volume 26, American Screenwriters*, p. 15.

7

Chipping Away in the Blockbuster Era

> On a Tom Cruise racing movie, there is not so much room for
> us even with the best will in the world. It is like those women
> who try to interview in the sports locker rooms. But then we
> are stuck with films like *Steel Magnolias* and we don't want to
> be relegated to that side of the fence, do we?
>
> Alice Arlen[1]

In November 1990 the *Los Angeles Times* ran a cover story: 'Women and
Hollywood: It's Still a Lousy Relationship.'[2] In the article the journalists
Elaine Dutka and Sharon Bernstein solicited thoughts from actors and
movie executives regarding the status of women on the big screen. They
had been prompted by an industry rumour, albeit unsubstantiated, that
during the previous summer a major studio had been circulating a memo
suggesting that all female-driven projects should be put on hold. And
while Hollywood breeds industry gossip and rumours as substantial as the
outpourings of its fiction factory, this particular piece of hearsay was
depressingly plausible. Statistics released that year by the Screen Actors
Guild seemed to prove a trend. The SAG report confirmed that men had
nearly 71 per cent of all feature film acting roles, with women meriting
just over a quarter. 'If the trend continues … by the year 2010 we may be
eliminated from the movies altogether,' retorted Meryl Streep at SAG's
first National Women's Conference, held soon after the report's publication.[3]

Indeed the prognosis was gloomy. The *Times* feature verified that
female actors currently working did not even enjoy some small share of
the kind of pull at the box office that their antecedents in the 1930s–50s
had known. And, depressingly, the situation had worsened rapidly in the
last decade. According to the 1989 Quigley poll of US theatre owners, only
one woman – Kathleen Turner – was in the top ten list of box-office
money-makers, and she had just scraped in at tenth place. This compared
to the 1981 results when four women were in the charts (Bo Derek, Jane
Fonda, Goldie Hawn and Dolly Parton). Those interviewed expanded on
the statistics, stating that women did not have the box-office clout to lead

films and studios were therefore relegating them to the usual array of stereotyped subsidiary roles such as wife or girlfriend.

The much discussed article reflected accurately the exasperated mood among women in Hollywood at the time. Indeed the type of product that the film industry was peddling seemed increasingly dictated by the desires and tastes of what the marketing departments identified as the core consumer: the twenty-five year-old male. Nine out of ten of these young John Does preferred action adventure stories and thus would not only trot along to the local multiplex to see *Total Recall* or *Die Hard 2* but, just as importantly, buy the T-shirt and play the computer game, the lucrative spin-off merchandising which helps keep the film industry buoyant. Marcy Kelly, president of the Los Angeles branch of the campaigning organisation Women in Film, summed up the overall situation: 'If you look at the make-up of the hierarchy in Hollywood, you see that it is a very white, male-oriented structure. So the people who are commissioning scripts, finding scripts, then directing the scripts and writing the scripts are men. Men are telling their stories from their perspective. And women's voices are not being heard, period.'

In this boys' club milieu, the question of opportunities for women on screen runs tangentially to that of opportunities for the woman screenwriter (interestingly the *Los Angeles Times* journalists only canvassed opinions from one member of the screenwriting profession, William Goldman). Only the year before, the Writers' Guild of America (West) had published *The 1989 Hollywood Writers' Report – Unequal Access, Unequal Pay*, which stated that the percentage of feature film scripting work going to women at the major studios had dropped from just over 17 in 1982 to 15.5 in 1987. But more revealingly, women screenwriters were not part of the much publicised phenomenon of the 'feeding frenzy' (auctioning of scripts which sent fees escalating into the millions around 1989/90). Such a phenomenon has more to do with the skill and power of the agents negotiating the deals than with the quality of material on offer, but only men were muscling in on the beano. Shane Black's *The Last Boy Scout* and Joe Eszterhas' *Basic Instinct*, with their 'high concept' sting-in-the-tale stories containing the magic box-office ingredients of sex and violence, were scripts that reportedly fetched two and three million dollars respectively.

But Hollywood is a very contradictory place. Tastes can turn on a cent overnight as movies dictated by one trend flop at the box office and another fad rises out of the rubble. While the *Los Angeles Times* article contended that women had never had it so bad, various factors were coming into play which seemed to promise change. By the end of 1990 the importance of what the marketing departments identified as a woman's audience was beginning to be revalued. The remarkable success of *Ghost* and *Pretty Woman* had roused the pundits to acknowledge that alongside the dollar-spinning action adventure stories there existed once again a profitable niche for 'feelings' movies, stereotyped as appealing most to a female audience. It was not that these films had ever gone away but that in recent years they had been regarded as not having the same box-office stamina as films in the action-adventure genre. Once upon a time these 'feelings' films would have been called women's pictures, their stories character-centred and emotionally driven rather than action-oriented.

Such a notion of what a female audience wants panders to regressively old-fashioned Hollywood values, with women as slaves to sentimentality and warped visions of themselves – as in *Pretty Woman*. But at least it recognised the power of the female consumer, and that undoubtedly began to shift the thinking of studio executives. Meanwhile, the following year heralded far more progressive change. With the release of *The Silence of the Lambs* and *Thelma and Louise* in 1991, new kinds of screen heroines took audiences by storm as well as receiving the Oscar stamp of approval. The 1992 award for best original screenplay to first-time writer Callie Khouri for her script of *Thelma and Louise* seemed to signify that Hollywood was beginning to hear the woman's voice which Marcy Kelly talked of.

But was this renewed interest in the women's audience and the genres traditionally associated with it likely to change the situation for women screen writers as a group? Women screenwriters had hardly cornered the market for even that type of film. The fact that *Ghost* and *Pretty Woman* were both written by men – Bruce Joel Rubin and Jonathan F. Lawton respectively – demonstrates how male screenwriters will always be protected against the changing genre trends since they have always written across the spectrum of genres.

The evidence, however, indicates that women writers do profit most when Hollywood favours these 'feelings' films. The end of 1990 saw the first script by a woman being sold for an exorbitant 'feeding-frenzy' figure when first-time writer Kathy McWorter's screenplay, *The Cheese Stands Alone*, was bought for a reported one million dollars by Paramount Pictures. A romantic comedy, the story is a perfect specimen of the 'feelings' genre. Certainly, McWorter has been rewarded by the renewed interest in more emotionally driven films, though three years after it was bought her script had yet to be filmed. Surveying writers' credits of films released in the US and the UK in 1991 reveals quite a healthy list of women's names, but more often than not those names were attached to small, romantic comedies and domestic dramas like *Once Around* (Malia Scotch Marmo), *The Man in the Moon* (Jenny Wingfield), *Mermaids* (June Roberts), *Fried Green Tomatoes at the Whistle Stop Cafe* (Carol Sobieski and Fannie Flagg), *For the Boys* (Lindy Laub with Neal Jimenez and Marshall Brickman), *The Prince of Tides* (Becky Johnston with Pat Conroy from his novel), or *Men Don't Leave* (Barbara Benedek).

Most women screenwriters would appear to be choosing to write scripts that have a greater chance of being made when the climate in Hollywood inclines to nurturing material that falls under the 'feelings' heading. The majority of the late 1990/91 crop of films with contributions from women screenwriters focused on such stories, often with female protagonists, providing central roles for the roster of underused female stars, the more powerful among whom are adopting an active role in order to readdress their employment situation. And some of them are turning to women writers to create those roles. Such films as *For the Boys* and *Mermaids* were developed by their stars' (Bette Midler and Cher respectively) own companies.

Representation in numbers might have improved for actresses on the screen, but the quality of representation in the types of roles they play has not necessarily improved as well. *Pretty Woman* hardly challenged the stereotypes, but it is difficult to imagine that a woman could be interested in writing such a film. Though even in the 1990s it would be naive to believe that just because more films are being made from screenplays written by women, the female experience is being reflected in a more varied fashion on the big screen. The Hollywood homogenisation process from script to screen is one which affects scripts written by men as much as by women. (Indeed *Pretty Woman* was radically altered – Lawton's original script more realistically saw the prostitute heroine dumped in the gutter after she had secured a winning deal for her apparent champion, rather than sailing off in a limo with him as in the finished film's Cinderella-like ending.)

Survey the subject matter of the films to which women writers have recently contributed, however, and there is a sense of *déjà vu*. From the list of films for 1990/91, one might deduce that many of the women screenwriters are following the same brief: a female protagonist's relationship to her family. Some of these stories, however, do offer more perceptive accounts of the familial ties being explored, and obviously benefited from a female writer's perspective.

Take *My Girl* (directed by Howard Zieff). Rarely in recent years has a rite of passage story centred on a young girl in shorts rather than the usual young boy. But Laurice Elehwany's script for *My Girl* championed a thirteen-year-old heroine, Vada, who aspires to be a writer in what initially seems like a companion piece to *Stand By Me*. Set in the early 1970s, with all the appropriate allusions to *The Partridge Family*, Watergate, hippy culture and women's lib, the story follows Vada as she struggles with the often painful process of growing up. This includes the usual pre-adolescent preoccupations, such as crushes on teacher, as well as the more offbeat: she is a self-confessed hypochondriac. Vada's mother died giving birth to her, so she has been brought up by Harry, her undertaker father, who houses his family over the shop, and her grandmother, who is mostly comatose. All their lives are to change with the arrival of free-wheeling Shelly, a mortuary beautician, who breathes some life into the moribund household.

If the casting of Macaulay Culkin (the biggest child star since Shirley Temple) as Vada's best friend, Thomas J., guaranteed a box-office success, it also framed *My Girl* as mushy kids' fare. But the film had more going for it than most critics allowed. The setting suggests that the film might offer more to the adults who can identify with this portrait of a 1970s childhood: Vada is, after all, a motherless daughter growing up during the sexual revolution. But *My Girl*'s themes are as much gothic as nostalgic, as they tease out the heroine's anxieties. Vada believes that she killed her mother, while she is neglected by her father, who lavishes more attention on his corpses than his daughter. Shelly might seem like the good fairy but her true colours can only be revealed after a combative challenge. Vada first adores this new woman (Shelly is a hip divorcee, more liberated single woman than obvious feminist), then resents her as she becomes the object of Harry's affection. Ultimately Shelly proves to be integral to Vada's adolescent individualism. As Vada comes to the end of her childhood her tomboy days seem to be over – symbolised in the traumatic death of Thomas J. – and she becomes more aware of her female destiny. It is a spirited and more emotionally mature Vada, who has learnt to express herself in her writing, who bicycles into the distance with her new-found female friend at the end of the film.

The same subject matter handled by another woman screenwriter can go awry, proof that women will not necessarily champion women and create stories for their female characters that differ from the more conservative Hollywood formulas. *Welcome Home Roxy Carmichael* (1990, written by Karen Leigh Hopkins and directed by Jim Abrahams) also follows the tribulations of a young girl on the verge of womanhood. It too echoes the theme of daughters trying to establish their own identity in the ghostly shadows of absentee mothers. The protagonist is another tomboyish figure, Dinky Bossetti, dressed in the *de rigueur* black apparel of the angst-ridden teenager. She's adopted but becomes increasingly convinced that her real mother is the home town's minor celebrity, Roxy Carmichael, and obsessively pursues this idea. And while the final film hints at a more considered handling of its subject (and one may wonder exactly what remained of Hopkins's original script), it fails to offer anything very different from the usual teen movie fare with its disappointing resolution where Dinky just becomes another girl who discovers that she's prettier in pink and finds true love with her school chum, the sensitive Gerald.

The years 1990 and 1991 also saw two films that investigated the neglected theme of fathers' relations with their daughters. But comparing *Class Action* and *Father of the Bride* also proves that just because a woman is involved in the writing of a script doesn't mean the subject matter is going to be treated any differently. *Class Action* borrowed the format of *Adam's Rib* and pitted an advocate daughter against her advocate father as they take opposite sides in an industrial damages dispute. Lawyer/writer Samantha Shad's first script (which was later to be worked on by the husband and wife writing team of Carolyn Shelby and Christopher Ames, whose previous work had been for such TV shows as *Growing Pains* and *Dirty Dancing*) reverses the generational stereotypes – he is the comfortable old liberal and civil rights expert who espouses 60s-style radicalism, while she is the glittering protégée of a prestigious corporate law firm. The film is as much an examination of their emotional alienation as of their differing political ideas. With industrial espionage and corruption supplying the requisite intrigue to the courtroom drama, it is ultimately the skilled and generous characterisations – which provided striking roles for Mary Elizabeth Mastrantonio and Gene Hackman – that make the film so compelling. The daughter and father's perspectives are equally weighted and honestly accounted for. *Class Action* is old-school Hollywood at its progressive best and manages to be moving without being overly sentimental.

In contrast, the mawkish comedy *Father of the Bride* (Charles Shyer and Nancy Meyers' remake of the Vincente Minnelli/Frances Goodrich and Albert Hackett original of 1950) offers a folksy account of the same family ties, with Dad – a role written for Steve Martin – the central focus of attention. Reputedly Meyers and Shyer wanted to investigate the relationship between fathers and daughters, but it is revealing that they decided to explore the theme within the confines of a remake that already dictated how the story would be angled. Here, they seem to have strayed far from such previous work as *Baby Boom* and *Private Benjamin*, in which the sharply drawn female protagonists were the focus. While Meyers and Shyer update the 50s version with the mother and daughter exchanging domesticity for careers, the blandness of the characters makes them wholly forgettable. Diane Keaton, who was so hilarious as the roaring career girl encumbered with a foundling in *Baby Boom*, is indeed short-changed as the rather insipid wife.

The screenwriters responsible for *Class Action* and *My Girl* prove that 'feelings' movies need not be fatuous and that a woman writer who wants to present a different perspective within the terms of the genre may find that this ends up on the screen. But the fact that so many women writers are writing for a particular genre does not of course mean that they can only write about certain themes. During 1990/91 a handful of women screenwriters contributed to screenplays that were less easy to categorise: Nora Ephron's *My Blue Heaven* (directed by Herbert Ross) was a Steve Martin comedy vehicle of the mismatched buddy-partner variety, about a Mafia hoodlum who is sent to suburban nowheresville as part of a government witness protection programme; old hand Jay Presson Allen was called upon to polish the political thriller *Year of the Gun* as well as a second adaptation of *Lord of the Flies*; Judith Rascoe's script for *Havana* (directed by Sydney Pollack) was conceived as a historical epic; Caroline Thompson made her debut with two American gothic comedies – *Edward Scissorhands* and *The Addams Family*.

Undoubtedly, however, women writers are still more often associated with female-oriented material that keeps within the prescribed genres. This may not necessarily be of their own volition. As the Los Angeles literary agent Bettye McCartt comments:

> When we get a call [from a producer] for a writer, they'll say, 'Who do you have who can write an action adventure piece?' If I suggest a woman, well, they laugh at me. There are certain genres where a woman won't even be considered. By that same token, they'll call and say, 'What woman writers do you have for a piece on so-and-so.'[4]

Screenwriter Alice Arlen (whose credits include *Alamo Bay* and *Silkwood*) believes that such a commissioning process can lead to writers like herself being regarded as no more than 'little dressmakers'. This is most crassly manifest when they are approached to tailor an issue to an actor.

Disney keep writing to me – Meg Ryan wants to do a thing about abortion. There it is and it just hits you on the nose. It's an issue and it would be a dog if it came out. Of course it would be great to work with Meg Ryan and it would be great to write a story in which an abortion takes place but I don't want to have to come at it like a freight train. I've been talking to a director about doing a script around the true story of the jazz player Billy Tipton. Everyone presumed that he was a man, but he turned out to be a woman when 'he' died. Now if Tipton were to have an abortion, then the story would be going somewhere!

While a writer like Arlen admits that she feels 'more at home' with material about women and their experiences, she is pessimistic about the chances of more sophisticated stories reaching the screen. She is not convinced that Hollywood shares her interest in 'grown women' characters. 'But then I don't think that this country is interested in grown women.' This, she believes, is the great 'catch 22' for women screenwriters.

As Mary Agnes Donoghue concurs, regarding her experience on *Beaches* (1988), the story of two women friends that was criticised for overdosing on the saccharine, there is a real problem with fine-tuning emotionally driven material. 'The script that I wrote wasn't that sentimental. And sentimental and emotional aren't the same thing.' She was even fired from the project at one point because she refused to write all 'this terrible stuff' that the director Garry Marshall (also of *Pretty Woman*) wanted. The 1988 writers' strike, among other things, ensured that the script was eventually given back to her. 'But it's amazing how much a director can change a script. You don't need to alter the words for the whole thing to be destroyed. If I had made the movie my way, it would have been a little more honest, a little tougher. And maybe then it wouldn't have been as successful.'[5]

Notes

1. Interview with author, 1990.
2. Elaine Dutka and Sharon Bernstein, 'Women in Hollywood: It's Still a Lousy Relationship', *Los Angeles Times*, 11 November 1990.
3. Ibid.
4. *WGAW Journal*, February 1990.
5. Interview with author, 1993.

8

Some Current Case-studies

'I am drawn to domestic things. Even *Silkwood* is written as a domestic story because I believe that even people who do amazing, heroic things have to put their socks on in the morning,' comments Nora Ephron.[1] Of the women screen writers currently working, Ephron is the only one who had established a modicum of status for herself before turning to a career in film. This has undoubtedly helped to give her more prominence as a screenwriter, with her name often dropped in reviews of her films. When I mentioned to people that I was writing this book, it was invariably the names of Ephron and Anita Loos that cropped up. In the critics' discussion of *When Harry Met Sally*, Ephron (and her script) even became the star of the film, eclipsing the director. An article in *The Times* dubbed her the 'author' of the film, a rare appellation these days for the members of her profession. Rarer still, 1991 saw her joining the slim ranks of women writer/directors with her directorial debut *This is My Life*.

The eldest daughter of the 1940s/1950s screenwriting team Phoebe and Henry Ephron, who named her after the heroine of Ibsen's *Doll's House*, Ephron was blessed with a silver-tongued wit and seemed destined to be a writer from an early age. The vibrant Phoebe Ephron's oft-quoted maxim, 'Everything is copy', particularly life's most grievous experiences, was taken to heart by mother and daughter alike. After graduating from Wellesley College, Nora Ephron swiftly found success as a journalist in New York. Her pithily written articles for the *New York Times* and *Esquire* won her a reputation as a purveyor of a cutting and dry wit. But while some called her the new Dorothy Parker, her detractors criticised her for a smug, trivialising approach to her subject. Certainly Ephron was not a banner-waving feminist. During the birth pangs of the women's movement in America, Ephron was entertaining her readership with articles about being flat-chested. But her postbag belied her critics. Her confessional pieces brought humour to subjects that until then had been rarely broached.

Ephron's return to the family profession was in fittingly novel circumstances. In the early 70s Ephron was going out with – and later married – the *Washington Post* writer Carl Bernstein, who was then flush with the success of the Watergate scoop:

They were doing *All the President's Men* as a movie. William Goldman had delivered the first draft. Carl and Bob [Woodward] were very unhappy with it and they asked me if I would help them rewrite it. I now realise that this is something that we should have not done professionally but then we thought, let's take a crack at it. And essentially Carl and I went through and changed a lot of the things that bothered them, and in the course of doing this I essentially ended up retyping about half of William Goldman's screenplay. Goldman then stopped speaking to me, not to them [Bernstein and Woodward], which I thought was very interesting. In any case we have patched things up and I have told Bill [Goldman] that typing up one of his screenplays is a great way to learn to write them. He writes very, very economical scenes. You learn an enormous amount by going through a script by a writer like that, especially about how quickly you can get things done in a movie.

While only one of the Ephron/Bernstein scenes appeared in the final film – Goldman describes it in his *Adventures in the Screen Trade* as 'a really nifty move by Bernstein where he out-fakes a secretary to get in to see someone' – the experience proved to be more than just an exacting lesson for Ephron. The Ephron/Bernstein draft of the script did the Hollywood rounds and Ephron was soon being hired to work on various projects. Though at that point none of her scripts was made, an Ephron draft of *Compromising Positions*, adapted from Susan Isaacs's comic novel (Ephron's script was not used for the final film), came to the attention of Arlene Donovan, an agent at International Creative Management (ICM). This was at the beginning of the 80s, when agents were starting to play a more integral role in the production of films by putting together talent 'packages'. Donovan was looking for a writer to work on a film which interested Meryl Streep, based on the life of anti-nuclear martyr Karen Silkwood. Streep was by then a highly popular actress and her attachment to a potential film project should have been enough to guarantee a major studio's interest in getting it made.

Meryl wanted to do it and then Mike Nichols wanted to do it because Meryl wanted to do it. But even then the studio did not want to make the movie, they were dragged kicking and screaming into making this movie, because they realised that if they didn't make it some other studio would obviously make it with those two elements attached to it. Someone was going to get nominated for Academy Awards and they were going to look like schmucks if it wasn't theirs.

The subject matter was considered contentious in Hollywood, particularly after the Three Mile Island disaster (though another Hollywood film – *The China Syndrome*, 1978 – had previously touched on the same issues). Silkwood had worked at a nuclear power component plant and had died in 1974 at the age of 28 in a mysterious car accident just as she was about to pass information to a reporter about the dangerous practices that she had uncovered at her plant. Donovan felt that Ephron's background in

106

journalism made her a suitable candidate for the task, though the story's gritty nature hardly seemed to marry with Ephron's droll style. But there were also the parallels between the Silkwood case and *All the President's Men* – true stories of individuals daring to air the shrouded sins of publicly accountable corporations. Ephron subsequently hooked up with a friend from New York, Alice Arlen, to write the script. At the time, Arlen's film experience extended to working on an unproduced script for Robert Redford, but she had known the lawyer involved in the Silkwood case and that, she believes, was crucial to her involvement.

Ephron claims of *Silkwood* that 'it taught me about the dark side of American capitalism'.[2] Indeed it found the writer in an unusually solemn mood. The film is an affecting account of Silkwood's endeavours to expose the nuclear industry's perilous secrets, despite concentrating rather more on Karen's dilemmas at home than the politics of the business she was daring to investigate. Ephron argues that she and Arlen chose to elaborate on Silkwood's domestic life since 'even heroes have to put their socks on'. But as the *Time Out* critic John Gill caustically commented of *Silkwood* when it was released in Britain, 'Ultimately it's rather akin to making a film about Joan of Arc and concentrating on her period pains.' Would *All the President's Men* have spent half the film's running time with scenes around Bernstein and Woodward's respective kitchen tables at the expense of their delve down the murky corridors of power?

Silkwood can be criticised for lingering on the soap opera elements of its persevering protagonist's story at the expense of its political gist. But are Karen Silkwood's actions any less heroic in *Silkwood* because she is seen in the context of her home life as well as the factory? The hazards of the nuclear industry are still driven home in liberal Hollywood fashion. And by focusing on the details of Silkwood's blue-collar lifestyle, the film emphasises her ordinariness in a way that contributes to making her deeds more exceptional. It is Silkwood's concerns for the friends with whom she lives and works that initially motivates her investigation. Bernstein and Woodward were only doing the job they were trained for.

Silkwood won Ephron and Arlen an Academy Award nomination in 1984. Ephron has since established herself as a screenwriter with a reputation for covering the familial battlegrounds of kitchen and bedroom rather than the political arena. Her next produced script was *Heartburn* (1985), adapted from her own novel and also directed by Mike Nichols. It was a cautionary tale of the break-up of a glittering marriage between an esteemed New York food writer and her celebrated Washington columnist husband – a thinly disguised account of events leading up to Ephron's own divorce from Bernstein after he unceremoniously ditched her for Margaret Jay, wife of the then British Ambassador to Washington. Ephron was back to turning her elegant, but at that moment chipped, life into copy. The novel was hilarious but the translation to the screen – a vapid account of divorce Manhattan-style, when it should have had the high-voltage emotional sting of the original novel – was less successful. But then Ephron had her tongue tied over the screenplay when Bernstein went to court to try to stop the film being made. He failed to do that, but the script was severely compromised in the dispute and as a consequence lost much of its bite.

After the sour experience of *Heartburn*, *When Harry Met Sally* found Ephron in a sweeter mode. Her most celebrated screenplay leisurely teases out that old question of 'Will they, won't they?' as Harry and Sally, two platonic friends, agonise over love, sex, marriage and the whole damn thing in a lonely New York. Ephron seems to be in her element with conventionally female-oriented material. 'I don't mind the calls that I get about doing things about marriage or love, or any of that. I don't think that they are just calling me because I am a woman, but because I have written about all that stuff and it is interesting to me. But I don't feel that I have been pigeon-holed at all and I feel that I have done a certain amount of work to keep that from happening.' This includes the two fluffy Mafia comedies, *Cookie* (Susan Seidelman, 1987) and *My Blue Heaven* (Herb Ross, 1990), both critical and financial failures which Ephron prefers to draw a veil over, other than commenting that Herb Ross 'could drive anyone to directing. … The experience made me know that there was no point in turning my work over to other people if I didn't have to.'[3] Though Ephron's scripts are hardly entirely to blame, it would seem that she is more comfortable and successful with material for which she has a more immediate affinity.

> I always like to look for some personal response. You get to a certain point where you say that given there is so much that I can do, is this the best use of the extremely limited talent that I have? You get a sense of what you can do and what you can bring the most to. I saw a very good scary movie the other night and realised that I could never write one because I don't like scary movies. I can't imagine a cop movie ringing that bell for me.

Unsurprisingly, then, for her directorial debut in 1991 she chose to adapt (along with her sister Delia Ephron) the Meg Wolitzer novel *This is Your Life*, which was produced by Linda Obst at Fox for a relatively modest budget of $10 million. Ephron was not daunted by the move from behind the word processor to behind the camera.

> I don't feel that I have a training as a director, but Mike Nichols was unbelievably generous – we were allowed to be there for every bit of those two movies [*Heartburn* and *Silkwood*] – including the casting. After watching him work on those I do feel that I know a teeny bit about talking to actors. And when you write a screenplay you do have pictures in your head of what you want it to look like. *This is My Life* is not a very hard movie to direct as first movies go. It's a very intimate movie, it takes place inside, it is about characters. There are no takes rolling over the hills of Korea or shoot-outs in Brooklyn or anything like that. Those I would be genuinely mystified to know how to film.

This is My Life is a comedy about Dottie Ingels, a divorcee from New Jersey who makes it to the comedy big time after years of working at Macy's cosmetic counter, dispensing wisecracks along with face packs to her customers. Much to her two young daughters' chagrin, she makes a habit of rummaging through their lives to find new material for her stand-up routine. This, according to Ephron, closely parallels her own family history. 'I started thinking about my parents, who had written a stream of things about all of us' (Ephron has three sisters including Delia). Indeed, as a child Ephron often found herself incorporated into her parents' scripts. (Their play *Three's a Family*, about a couple learning to live with their new baby, was written soon after Nora was born, while *Take Her, She's Mine* borrowed extensively from the letters she wrote home while at Wellesley College.)

'This is a movie entirely about women, it's a completely personal movie, it's based on someone else's novel, but it's completely about my life. It's about my childhood, my parents, it's about my life as a mother and it's about my children.' (With playful irony the title of the film has even been changed from that of the Wolitzer novel, *This is Your Life*, to *This is My Life*.) Ephron has taken the material and made a refreshingly honest and individual film that asks questions relevant to many women's lives as it follows the crazy family conflicts that success brings to Dottie when her daughters in turn prey on her life and want her at home rather than happy in her new-found career. It is wisely less a film about stand-up comics than about the cabaret that family life can be. But choosing an open ending, *This is My Life* cannot offer a neat resolution to Dottie's dilemmas about how to balance parenthood with career. In order to safeguard the story's integrity Ephron was adamant that she should be the director. 'I thought, who is going to direct this movie? Well, someone might and then they would say, this isn't how I feel, I feel this way. You know, I don't want to bend this script to fit how someone else feels.' Particularly if that someone else is more likely to be a man.

Ephron agrees that Hollywood is 'a very male town'. In such an environment it has become important for her as a writer to be dealing with what she believes to be a more honest version of the female experience, though she is quick to add that she writes about men as well. But she is apparently more interested in women. Projects waiting to be made include *Maggie* (co-written with Arlen), about the American war correspondent Marguerite Higgens, the first woman to report from the front during the Korean War. Ephron and Arlen consider Higgens to be their perfect subject, a woman with the kind of character complexities that cannot easily be washed over. That is precisely why Alice Arlen believes the film has yet to be made.

> It's a pungent story about a strong, difficult woman. But the male directors don't seem to like her. They say this is a great script but they have difficulty with the fact that she did everything she could to get where she was going. It puts them off, but that is exactly what interested us. Perhaps now that Nora is directing, the film finally has a chance of being made.

As a director of her own scripts, Ephron will be allowed to stick to her word:

I do think sometimes that it's a good thing that people like me are drawn to and want to write complicated women characters because everything that happens to the script thereon attempts to uncomplicate them and make their parts less important, by taking away their best lines and the rest of it. There is no question that everyone who complains about how little Hollywood cares about women characters is telling the truth. For instance, though I had a great experience with Rob [Reiner] on *When Harry Met Sally*, it was a big shock to him that the movie was as much Sally's as Harry's. Harry had more jokes but he was a less complex character. I knew this when I wrote it but he [Reiner] didn't know it, so when Meg [Ryan, who played Sally] began to work in the movie they were all stunned since she kept stealing scenes. But those scenes were all there in the script ready to be stolen by the right actress.

With another romantic comedy, *Sleepless in Seattle*, her second film as a writer/director, released in 1993 and a box-office success, Ephron has established herself as one of the more powerful women in a creative position in Hollywood. But what is interesting about *Sleepless in Seattle* (which Ephron co-wrote with David S. Ward and Jeff Arch) is that it self-consciously maps out the pleasures of the romantic comedy genre, drawing attention to what differing responses it might elicit from male and female audiences. The story follows Annie, who falls in love long-distance with Sam, a man she first actually meets in the last five minutes of the film. 'You don't want to be in love, you want to be in love in a movie,' quips Annie's best friend. For Annie is heeding the plot of the bitter-sweet romance *An Affair to Remember* (1957), in which two estranged lovers arrange a rendezvous atop the Empire State Building. 'That's a chick's movie,' contends one of Sam's male friends. Indeed, the women in *Sleepless in Seattle* all weep while watching or even thinking about this 50s classic, much to the bemusement of the men. They in turn pretend to get churned up while talking about the explosive war film *The Dirty Dozen*. Wryly stereotyping how men and women are affected by the movies, Ephron might enjoy the irony of being described as a 'chick's movie' director. While the chick's movie is in, she will undoubtedly rule the roost.

☆   ☆   ☆

The men in my scripts and stories are more metaphors. I don't know much about the world that men perpetrate, never having been in that world. I come from a world of women. I don't have a 'proper' job or anything, so I don't know what they do out there. I am from a neighbourhood emotionally very much like the neighbourhood in *Edward Scissorhands*, an American suburban vision of the world run by women into which the men are invited as guests for overnight stays every night.

Caroline Thompson tackles questions of gender in her scripts obliquely, and there are some extraordinary undercurrents in her work which she does not necessarily admit to. In her first produced script, the comedy *Edward Scissorhands* (directed by Tim Burton), the hero is an outlandish boy cursed with a bristling bunch of assorted blades for hands. When his inventor-'father' dies, he is left to rust alone in his crumbling castle. That is until the local Avon lady arrives and whisks him back to her pastel-coloured housing estate. Burton's direction accentuates the garish clash of styles. In both theme and vision it is as if MGM had decided to make a horror film with the Grimm-style story dragged into an America preoccupied with shopping malls, make-overs and Bar-B-Qs.

For Thompson, however, it is a lighter and much sweeter version of a theme she explored in her first novel *FirstBorn*, a bizarre story about a woman who has an abortion but in a horrific turn the foetus lives and is taken to be raised in a research laboratory among animals. Then at the age of seven he is reunited with his mother.

> It wasn't meant to be an anti-abortion story by any means – rather the story of the ultimate outsider, the child who is disposed of. Like *Edward* it is about any of us kids who find themselves in a world with rules that they don't understand, that can turn around and bite. I and several other people that I knew as children felt as though we were on the outside trying to look in and we just didn't get it. Some of us have carried that through to our adult lives. There is a lot of the *L'Enfant Sauvage* in it, a lot of *Kaspar Hauser* and *The Elephant Man*. Any of those tales of deprivation.

The novel was optioned by director Penelope Spheeris in 1985. Spheeris had just made her mark with the low-budget features *Suburbia*, *The Boys Next Door* and *The Decline of Western Civilization*. 'An agent sent me the book, and I was immediately fascinated by it because of the mother-child relationship – and also by the fact that it was the story of an ugly and pitiful creature that still needed to be loved.'[4] Spheeris, who was attempting to raise money for the project, unsurprisingly found that the story was one that Hollywood couldn't easily grapple with. The script was shelved. 'The people with money are men and men don't like this movie. For one thing, the father in the script comes off as a real jerk. Both I and Thompson were going through divorces at the time we wrote the script and it really shows.'

For Thompson, the experience of writing the *FirstBorn* screenplay had its benefits. Her agent set up a meeting with Tim Burton, who was also a client. She was sent a tape of Burton's first feature, *PeeWee's Big Adventure*, he was sent a copy of *FirstBorn*. These singular imaginations were teamed together to brainstorm. 'Tim told me about an image that he had of a boy with scissors for hands. We never talked about him as a creation – that's all he said. But I was really struck by the power of that image and what it meant, the thought of someone who can't feel with their hands and can't touch anything without harming it.' Thompson had not then read Heinrich Hoffmann's classic cautionary tales for children, *Struwwelpeter*, though she subsequently recognised the similarities between Edward and Hoffmann's boy with straw hair and elongated claw-like nails. Instead she saw parallels with her own neglected creation in *FirstBorn*. 'I write about these isolated individuals. They are always metaphors. Abortions don't come back, boys with scissors don't exist but for me the metaphor gets to the reality in such a cleaner way and is so much more direct.' Continuing the theme, she has subsequently completed a screenplay about a man who thinks he's a chicken:

> Everyone wants to rehabilitate him and he goes along with it for a while, but ultimately he reverses because he knows what he is doing. The story comes from the same place as Edward but it is the next phase. As an adolescent everyone tells you what to do all the time, but usually you know better. This is a story about someone who chooses to see the world through the eyes of a chicken rather than a person.

Thompson's preoccupations with the gothic and the fantastical have won her a particular niche which she revels in.

> I am much happier when things are pushed to the extreme, whereas the darkness seems to frighten most people off. I am interested in the humour that can erupt out of those sorts of situations – it's much more fun than the earnest, noble type of stories. I don't think that there is a place more repressed than America. I love the way that it leaks out: it has to.

After the happy experience of *Edward Scissorhands*, she was hired to co-write *The Addams Family* (with Larry Wilson, who had written *Beetlejuice* for Burton). It proved to be a writer's nightmare, however, since both were dumped by the studio three weeks before the production. 'It was hard, but since it was an assignment I didn't feel as if there were bits of my blood in that film.' Indeed she found that her perceptions of the Charles Addams drawings differed from the studio's. 'To me they were such witty allusions to the decaying WASP culture of New England – all those American aristocrats.'

Interestingly most of Thompson's protagonists are male, yet women loom large in her scripts.

> I don't pay particular attention to the women characters over any of the others. I am a feminist but in the sense that it never occurred to me that I couldn't do what I wanted to do with my life. On the other hand I think that I must be a terrible sister since I don't think that I go at things in a political way, with a political perspective. But conversely while I don't have a particular agenda I know what politics I am engaging with, I am not blind to the impact. My major characters tend to be male but the real characters in all these stories are the women. I was flattered when a development person commented that what struck her

most about *Edward* was the range of roles for women. Indeed there are an awful lot of parts. It's a fairy tale, so they are all functional roles and they may not be the kind of characters that actresses take seriously. But then I look at an actress like Sissy Spacek. When she did *Carrie* and *Badlands* she was brilliant, but when she started picking those so-called serious roles like *Marie – A True Story*, it was so boring – nothing more than an earnest TV movie.

Women feature more obviously in another speculative Thompson project. The genesis of the piece is typically offbeat:

Part of it takes place in the 1920s since it is a period that fascinates me so much. I read this statistic that between 1910 and 1922 women shed 80 per cent of their underclothing. That's about twelve pounds of underwear, imagine what it must have felt like – all those stays and corsets abandoned. My script partly explores that.

Such a story might more overtly explore the female experience but Thompson's preoccupation with outsiders could be construed as an expression of female anxiety. Choosing the gothic genre, she follows in the tradition of the literary women (such as Mary Shelley with *Frankenstein*) who have explored the repressed and unspoken in their writings. As one of the few women screenwriters working in the genre cinematically, it will be interesting to see whether Thompson's darker and more disturbing visions reach the screen or whether, like *First Born*, they will be put aside.

Meanwhile other Thompson projects have included an adaptation of the classic children's novel by the nineteenth-century writer Frances Hodgson Burnett, *The Secret Garden*. The film was produced by Francis Ford Coppola's American Zoetrope company with Agnieszka Holland directing. Thompson, who is an avid reader of all things fantastical for both children and adults, was delighted to have worked on the script. *The Secret Garden* is the second in Coppola's planned series of classic children's films, the first being *Black Stallion* (written by Melissa Mathison) which, along with *Carrie*, Thompson cites as her two biggest influences from contemporary cinema.

Children's cinema continues to be an area in which women screenwriters can flourish (from the 40s through to the 60s Lillie Hayward was one of the key exponents of the genre). But it is only after sixty years in the business that the paternalist Walt Disney Pictures have recruited women to write their animated features. Once again collaborating on a Tim Burton project, Thompson has now written the bizarre children's fantasy *The Nightmare Before Christmas* for the studio. The first woman to get a break at Disney was Linda Woolverton, who had previously written both teenage fiction and TV cartoon shows. The studio approached her when they decided they wanted to make a *Beauty and the Beast* for the 90s, giving her the brief that the heroine should be a positive role model for little girls. Reputedly, Woolverton drew her inspiration from the Katharine Hepburn character in the film version of *Little Women* to come up with

Belle, a bookish type whose life, unlike her Disney predecessors, does not seem to revolve around waiting for her prince to come. When the film was released in 1992 it became the highest grossing animated feature ever made. Subsequently Woolverton was rewarded with a long-term deal at Disney and has since collaborated with Thompson on the live-action film *Homeward Bound: The Incredible Journey*, a remake of the 1963 children's favourite about a cat and a dog who trek 250 miles home.

☆　☆　☆

Leslie Dixon made her debut as a screenwriter in the late 80s with the Bette Midler/Shelly Long comedy *Outrageous Fortune* (Arthur Hillier, 1987), a female variant on the mismatched buddy genre that traded on Midler's kitsch persona. Dixon subsequently found a niche for herself as a writer of female-centred comedies, whether as the hired pen for *Overboard* (Garry Marshall, 1987), which starred Goldie Hawn as a snobby socialite who suffers from amnesia only to be 'trained' to be a good housewife by her former handyman; or as the uncredited dialogue polisher for Bette Midler in *Big Business* (Jim Abrahams, 1988), which teamed Midler with Lily Tomlin as a pair of mismatched identical twins. Dixon is very much the Hollywood player. She describes her background as 'Berkeley bohemian', she dropped out of college, travelled a while and finally came to Hollywood when she was in her late twenties. By then she had decided that she wanted to be a screenwriter and believed the only way to take the profession seriously was to relocate to the industry's capital. Only in Los Angeles, Dixon believes, can a screenwriter thrive and that means making all the right industry connections.

> It's the first thing that I tell anyone interested in screenwriting to do. It's how I am able immediately to differentiate between the people who are serious about wanting to get into this business and the people who are dilettantes. It's just that if I hadn't moved to LA, I would be typing in someone else's office right now.

Dixon's maxim worked for her. After a short time settling in, she sold her first script to Columbia. Shrewdly, if a little presumptuously, she reasoned that the story *AKA* would be bought by somebody since it has the lead play four different characters: 'I figured that would appeal to some actor's ego.' It's a familiar story – *AKA* waits to be made, but it bought Dixon the attention she wanted. She was soon called in to meet producers Robert Court and Ted Field, who were looking for a writer to work on a female buddy comedy that was eventually to be *Outrageous Fortune*. They had been toiling away on the project for several years without success. As Dixon explained in 1987:

> I went away and thought about it, and realised that one of the problems with all the drafts they had commissioned was that time and again they had hired men to write them. And that shouldn't necessarily be a problem, but these particular men did not have a feminine sympathetic side to their nature and couldn't get into a woman's frame of mind.[5]

114

It is in this context that a *New York Times* profile could state that Dixon 'believes – popular wisdom notwithstanding – that a female screenwriter today is at a happy advantage.' In Dixon's case her gender landed her a job at the point in her career when she desperately needed to make her mark. Quizzed on this comment three years later, Dixon is not so ready to enthuse about the prospects for women writers:

It depends who you are and what kind of work you do. For me, I'll get calls that the male screenwriter will not get because I like to write for women and I understand them. If I happen to be having a good day, I can bring a dimension to the role that may attract a female star, and in an environment that is catering less and less to actresses that seems to be a marketable skill. But it is by no means a crusade on my part, no conscious feminist rabble-rousing, but being a female I do understand other females to a large degree. So when I sit down to write I don't necessarily write female protagonists, although I did in *Outrageous Fortune*. Actually I am more interested in male/female stories, rather than female/female stories, but I find myself incapable of not fleshing out the female roles because it is so much more fun to write when you have a three-dimensional character. An understanding of women makes me want to write them, not to the exclusion of everything else.

Indeed, the niche that Dixon has found for herself has not proved to be limiting, but then so far she has played safe with her material. *Outrageous Fortune* was hardly a prototype *Thelma and Louise*: it's a comedy relying exclusively on the clashing screen personas of the comediennes Long and Midler, the daffy and the vulgar. After the film was released, Dixon was offered 'millions of movies and TV shows with women in them'. She has also been approached to work on scripts for Arnold Schwarzenegger. 'It did not work out because of my schedule, but I loved it that they thought of me. The type of pictures that he makes now aren't that different from *Outrageous Fortune* – the storyline and genre are basic formulas – and it would be fun to put him up against a strong woman character. I would have a ball!'[6] But while there is quantity on offer, quality is low:

Some of the writing assignments that I have been sent to do or that the studios have twisted my arm to do have been some of the dopiest premises that I have ever seen. I don't think that I would have ever set out to write a script about amnesia (*Overboard*) or have told a story about a mismatched bunch of identical twins (*Big Business*). They are some of the hokiest and most overused premises but somehow I got stuck with them. Working on them has taught me to be less snobby about such concepts. A lot of the things that I have worked on are writing assignments that go back to the beginning of my career when I was lucky to have a job.

Dixon has subsequently teamed up with her husband Tom Ropelewski. Together they have taken on rewrite assignments as well as collaborating on an original work, a comedy, *Madhouse* (1990), which Ropelewski also directed. Rather than aiming to direct herself, Dixon has opted to produce her next script:

> If I have an original script which I care about, then I am prepared to take very little money for it to produce it in exchange for certain controls – like choice of director and lead actors. I can't force the studio to put people in there that I do want but the studio can't put people in there that I don't want. They also can't rewrite me. It's a tremendously difficult thing to negotiate but I paid for it. I don't hold it against anyone who wants to make two million dollars in a calendar year. That's wonderful and I wish I was making that kind of money. But I am not, because on an original script I have got to a point where I know I have only so many times that I can be completely demoralised and then maybe I would lose heart altogether.

Dixon is adamant that it's a condition that affects all screenwriters regardless of gender:

> Every screenwriter feels that they have had a bad ride. We are a guild of whiners and complainers. Talk to a few men and they will all tell you what has happened to their brilliant screenplay. Writers are very sensitive people and they get very upset about things that happen to their script, and it's not just women, believe me. I don't know any studio executive that looks at the gender of the name on the title page and then says, I don't like this script. They just read it and if it's good – or if it does the job, or if it attracts an actor or director that can make the movie, which is really the bottom line – that writer is going to work.

What Dixon fails to mention is the more insidious aspect of who gets to write what in Hollywood. She herself got a break when she was hired to write a formula comedy for two female stars because the producers decided that a woman might be better at the job. While the doors were open in that instance, on how many other occasions do they remain closed? Dixon admits, 'There's a certain level of directors that I will never work with unless I sit down with them and invent a script in a room. The Rob Reiners and the Ron Howards – they have their own companies and don't read outside them, such is the company structure.' Indeed it is worth noting that to date only two women have had scripts produced by either Reiner's or Howard's companies, Castle Rock Entertainment and Imagine Films respectively: Nora Ephron's *When Harry Met Sally* and Laurice Elehwany's *My Girl*.

☆　☆　☆

> I am interested in doing a horror movie that would speak about the anger a woman feels when she is being dealt with on just a sexual level by men. It would probably be very brutal, then I would be criticised for not doing sensitive women's pictures. It's a difficult act to manage.
>
> Penelope Spheeris

If women writers are still mainly typecast as exponents of 'softer' material, what happens if a writer decides to transgress those boundaries and wants to write thrillers or action pieces for the mainstream market? More importantly, what happens if she wants to rethink the roles for women within the terms of those genres? Women such as Penelope Spheeris have been writing, and directing, different and difficult stories for the low-budget/exploitation market for the last twenty years, but without crossing over to the mainstream as her male counterparts have done: 'I believe one reason I have been held at arm's length in the business is that my films have always expressed a certain amount of brutality and anger, and that scares men. They don't want to see women dealing with such emotions.'

Certainly the studios seem to have an uneasy time with the women who make such attempts. Clair Noto has the dubious honour of being one of Hollywood's more highly regarded writers without having had any of her screenplays produced. Her screenplay *The Tourist*, written for Universal in 1979, was cited as one of the top ten unproduced scripts of the decade in *American Film*'s poll of Hollywood executives (April 1987). The tourist of the title is Grace Ripley, a sister from another planet, who arrives in a decaying Manhattan of the near future. Her mission is to scour the city, which now lathers in an orgiastic hedonism, for the one person who will help her back home again. With its vision of live sex clubs and 'duals' – interplanetary androgynes whose gender mutates according to the sexual apparatus of their last partner – Noto creates a perverse and dark vision, like that of David Cronenberg.

Ridley Scott, Paul Schrader and Francis Coppola are among the directors who have been attached to the script, which has done a merry-go-round trip between Universal and Warner Bros and back to Universal; while Joel Silver, the renegade independent producer responsible for *Die Hard* and *Lethal Weapon* among others, tried to buy it from Universal. Indeed the script has had a roasting in development hell, notching up over a million dollars in pre-production costs in the intervening thirteen years. As Noto comments: 'What kills *The Tourist* every time is that there's one conservative person at each studio who's really *disturbed* by it: it's not *cuddly* science fiction.' The fact that it is a female protagonist on the loose in this sleazy world also might have something to do with it.

Noto, who was brought up on the East Coast, trained in fine arts, eventually becoming a film editor for the television network ABC. She arrived in Los Angeles in the mid-70s when a script she had written about a Italian kid growing up in New York was bought by a production company. Though this first script was also never produced, it did bring her to the attention of an agent at the William Morris Agency, who took her on. 'At first I wasn't sent out on any meetings; that was the big joke because eventually I landed my first meeting with Ray Stark.' Stark was then one of the most influential producers in Hollywood (behind such hit films of the 1970s as *The Way We Were*). 'The conversation went, "How about a female James Bond, do you think that you can write it?" "You bet I could!"' Stark hired her on the strength of the script as well as a comic-strip she had written. 'There was never a question in his mind as to whether I could do it or not because I was a woman – I went in there because I could write adventures.' From then on she was in constant demand, her scripts running through the gamut of genres that normally had men on the case. 'I think that my agent was stunned. I think they were in shock that this girl was getting these assignments one after another from these big people.'

Noto is still a courted writer, but she has a bizarre relationship with her adopted home town. 'The way that I was brought up and taught to be true to myself serves me in very good stead as an artist, but it serves me in very bad stead in this particular arena. You have to be prepared to take a beating here – a beating within an inch of your life.' And from her experience Noto believes that women have to fight back harder. 'When I started out I know that I was on a lower salary than the male writers of comparable age and track record who were with my agent. Even when *The Tourist* was at its hottest, they were getting more than I was.' Noto has also had to put up with patronising producers.

> I had a meeting with an influential British producer who was interested in my work. There was a director associated with him who really wanted to work with me, but in the course of the meeting this producer implied that women couldn't know that much about film history and started mentioning British films that he thought would be very obscure to me. I wanted to say: 'Look, I've seen every documentary that the GPO made, I've seen all Lindsay Anderson's early shorts.' It made me feel very testy.

After so long without a visible success, it might seem strange that Noto persists. But screenwriting is her art – she is passionate about it and it provides her with an income.

> I'm not a prose writer, I am a dramatist. Even when I write letters, my letters tend to read like film scripts. Good dialogue is like line drawing. If you are drawing a knee and you have to articulate that knee with only a line, you've got no form, no chiaroscuro, no colour, you have to be on the mark. That's the substance of good dialogue.

Noto's scripts are usually about female protagonists, but not squeaky clean heroines, rather women with flawed and ambiguous personas. She insists on examining the side of female experience that is more often neatly stowed away.

> My characters are the psychos, the aliens, the scumbags – I like the outsiders. For instance, I am interested in the world of such mythical women as Medea, the woman who kills her own children. Medea is real – she comes from a very particular psychological complaint. I have been pitching a story to one actress' company about a woman who doesn't kill her child but uses him to get what she wants. She abandons her husband and goes on the road with the kid. He's the perfect kid and has to find a way to exist with his lunatic mother.

Other projects include a story that Noto describes as a female version of *Taxi Driver*:

It's based on an incident that happened a couple of years ago in which a young woman – the archetypal nice Jewish girl – just walked into a school and shot these children. It transpires that this girl has been ill since she was about sixteen. She stabbed her husband, yet people kept pushing her along until she decides she is not going to be pushed along any more and she kills these kids.

Noto is interested in the subtext of such crimes:

What do such acts reveal? I believe that these things have to be addressed, but not just as social ills. People call my agent, but they always want some simplified social twist on these crimes so that they can do them as movie murder of the week for TV. While these crimes say something about society, it is ultimately an individual's reaction to their own life and it should be told as such. It's like it's got to be told in some way so that no one gets upset by hearing it.

Indeed Noto believes that while she is hired to write the scripts, these stories have ultimately proved too frightening for the Hollywood establishment. She agrees that it is a conservatism that affects both men and women in her profession. Interestingly, though, she feels that she often has the strongest opposition to her scripts from other women in the industry. While she has a considered approach to her material and believes herself to be mindful of its exploitative potential, it seems to be the core idea of the project that most commonly disturbs her critics. Noto claims that the actresses who are clamouring for bolder roles, and who have the production companies that are able to jump-start projects, come to her for scripts but ultimately shy away from what she has to offer. Their most common reaction is that her scripts are just 'too dark'. She refers to one particular incident:

In 1988 I got into the most trouble with my script *The Girl in the Box* that was to be produced by the company that had distributed such films as Agnès Varda's *Vagabonde* in the States. It was based on a famous case in which a young woman was abducted by a couple in northern California. I worked extensively with the young woman and with the perpetrators [who were by then in prison]. It was a story about sexual obsession – this man gets his wife to help him kidnap the girl in order for her to become his sex slave, does all sorts of horrible things to her and eventually goes completely mad. The young woman manages to escape after seven years.

When word spread that Noto was working on the project, the production company was bombarded with calls from women's groups and actresses who protested about the idea without even having read the script. Noto argues that her script did not degrade women but was 'about human fragility'.[7]

Such vehement reactions to Noto's work highlight the problems for screenwriters who want to create stories about women that detract from overtly positive or heroic female images. Or, like *The Girl in the Box*, they might seem on the surface to be in the same league as those films which have exploited women over and over again. The long history of women's representation in Hollywood cinema, in which they have been trapped in the good/bad polarisation, seems to preclude detours into more subtle and potentially more complex territory. Arguably, the production process – from the demands of the financiers, the director's slant on the story, to the casting – may well strip more interesting characters and their stories of their carefully delineated nuances, thus reducing a Medea-type story to a suspect tale about a mad monster mother. As Noto confirms: 'Dan O'Bannon (who wrote *Alien* and *Total Recall*, among other films) is doing a rewrite of *The Tourist* for Universal – they are going to make it but it will not be my script. It will be a man's side of that female heroine. I can't fight that any more, I have white streaks in my hair.'

☆   ☆   ☆

Hilary Henkin, who has been working as a screenwriter since the early 80s, is one of the few women to have had a crack at the action genre and got her scripts produced. In the rowdy *Roadhouse*, which had Patrick Swayze kick-boxing his way across the screen, she proved that she could handle the requisite biffs and pows along with the best of them. She also wrote the original screenplay for *Lost Angels*, about a band of disaffected teenagers in San Fernando Valley (though she lost the credit in arbitration). She is interested in the marginal and twilight world of the outlaw, but her experience in Hollywood echoes that of Noto's in terms of how her off-kilter heroines are received. Henkin wrote the original script for the female cop thriller *Fatal Beauty*, but it was extensively rewritten, ended up as a dismal hash and was unsurprisingly dismissed by critics. Henkin refuses to see it.

> What happened to Rita Rizzoli [the heroine of *Fatal Beauty*] is a perfect object lesson as to what happens to a female character who does not play a wife or mother or girlfriend. Rita is driven, obsessive, violent and sexual. *Fatal Beauty* took its cue from a number of the super-chick B pictures from the 1950s and 1960s. They paved the way for Rita. It was a sort of high-falutin' B picture in the sense that Rita was driven on a mission in the same way that Dirty Harry was driven on a mission. Dirty Harry's mission was to find criminals. I thought about what a female version of that type of character would be like. Here's a woman who uses her sexuality, finds the person that she is looking for, tantalises them, then gets the information that she needs and kills them. It's not an intellectual idea, it is delightfully trashy and the notion of doing that really appealed to me.
>
> But what happened to Rita seems to be the object lesson of what happens to all those characters. It comes down to back story. It seems

120

that similar sorts of male characters within the genre are allowed to indulge their obsession, with almost no reason, and when they indulge their obsession they are applauded by the film-making establishment and the audience. But the notion of the female character who does things for the sake of doing them seems to be frighteningly out of control for the system and its perception of how the audience would react to that idea.

As I wrote Rita, she was alone, she had never been married, she never went out on dates. She spent her Friday nights at home with the radio on carving dumdum bullets. She starts out with this list in fine feminine handwriting of all the unsolved murders that have been perpetrated in her city. It was her objective to find the killers of all these people and she wouldn't rest until she did. They [the victims] were her family. And how did she get that family? It's just the way that it works out, nobody but she wanted them. But the studio didn't think that an audience wanted to see such a violent woman. Hence they built in a back story. The movie went through many incarnations on the way to production. It was turned into a comedy, and from being a comedic tragi-comedy, it became a broad comedy. Rita was given the quintessential abused female back story – which gives her a motive, but it is a far less profound motive than she might have had, had she just left the room as originally intended.

Henkin makes a speciality of gritty, stylised pieces. 'It seemed to me that the drama was more excessive – and that excessiveness is what I find intriguing.' The experience with *Fatal Beauty*, however, leads her to believe that it is easier to follow convention and write such genre material with male protagonists. 'It is very difficult to write obsessive female characters and have them accepted by the Hollywood establishment.' Actresses come to her, wanting to toughen their image.

We have these meetings where they say they want to do something different. I say, 'Would you be willing to kill somebody in the story?' They say 'no'. So the meeting's over. Until those actresses want to go to those dangerous places they will continue to make safe and sweet women's pictures. But there should be room for everything. It would be nice to have some not so sweet women's pictures.

Obsessive men are no problem. Her work has attracted such stars as Robert De Niro, for whom she has written a violent story about child pornography based on Philip Carlo's novel *Stolen Flowers* (it's yet to be made), and Sylvester Stallone, for whom she has also written a script, *Executioner*, in which his character sorts out a new breed of anarchist mobsters. Her other produced script is *Roadhouse*, in which Patrick Swayze plays Dalton, a drifter with a doctorate in philosophy who ends up as a bouncer at a roadside night spot. There he slugs it out with a local rogue and his henchman who have been terrorising the nearby town. Henkin describes it as both a 'bar-room brawl picture' and 'the classic tale of a mythic hero with a past'. Dalton is her archetypal protagonist – 'a man of few words who follows a strict moral code'. To use Henkin's own phrase, the film is delightfully trashy.

For Henkin, gender has not been an obstacle in terms of being hired for the pieces that interest her.

> I have never had any trouble being accepted, nor have I ever been paid less than a man. I would walk away if I was offered less. I have always had a very clear notion of what I wanted to write or what I was capable of writing. I write specifically one kind of piece and that was what I became noticed for in Hollywood. I don't know many women who write these sorts of pieces and I don't know why they don't. There are certain types of people drawn to certain types of material. I did what was right for me. I am sure that if I corrupted every part of my personality I could probably find a thousand stories about the family. But right now, after being in the writing profession for twelve years, I promise you that I have no idea what a breakfast room scene would be like. I don't know what they talk about – do they talk about college or the washing machine? Do they ask to pass the cereal?

As Henkin has commented: 'If I wrote *Ordinary People*, Dad would come to the table with a plate of eggs and Mom would pull out the machete. Then they'd solve their relationship in the kitchen. We'd see what was really what.'[8]

She admits that people seem to be quite surprised that the Hilary Henkin who writes this material is a woman.

> When I first arrived in town a long time ago, I would walk into the offices and I would be looked at as though I was someone's assistant. They would be expecting Hilary Henkin to walk in – there was always this moment when they would look over my shoulder, look down and then up but then by the time they had done this the second time around, they would ask 'Hilary?' with a quizzical tone in their voice.

Ardently resisting the notion that women should not write negative female characters, Henkin finds the critics' presumptions about her gender equally revealing:

> When the magazine *Rolling Stone* found out that a woman had written *Roadhouse* – which to them seemed to make fun of women throughout the picture – it was problematic for them. My answer to that has always been that I will write any character the way that I see fit. If they don't care for my vision of who should be made fun of because they are a tart – or whatever the male equivalent of that may be – that is simply not my issue. I find it comical that women writers are given responsibility for having more sense than male writers. Sure, you know what you are doing, but why don't they say that to a male writer. It's like laying the responsibility in our laps. It's certainly a lofty responsibility, but not quite a fair one.

But it is a responsibility that Henkin seems to take seriously:

> It's interesting to separate the writer's dilemma from the female writer's dilemma because the writer's dilemma in itself is so difficult. It makes you wonder, can it be more difficult? I walked away from *Fatal Beauty* because I wouldn't write the female character differently from the way that I felt she should be written.

Having learnt her lesson, Henkin is set to be her own producer for her next script, *Romeo is Bleeding*, which does feature another tough, 'larger-than-life heroine', Mona De Marco, in order to keep her vision of that character intact.

> I want to safeguard that script. I wish that I could have *Romeo...* made as it is and not have to be the person responsible for producing as well as writing it. But I am anxious to control the process of production and see that what I have written ends up on the screen. I will do a rewrite on this and a rewrite on that, but *Romeo...* is different. That is why I have turned down stars and turned down directors. I have made a deal with myself, and that is why I am producing it. It will be the first and last picture that I produce.

Romeo is Bleeding is a classic hard-boiled thriller, with Mona De Marco the classic villainess at the story's dark heart.

> Mona is a woman who is literally unstoppable and utterly sexual. I designed her around a vision of Rita Hayworth. The story takes place in a romantic battleground where the crime and the acts of violence are real acts – they are not metaphorical. With Mona, it doesn't matter what you do, she keeps on coming back and she is never frightened. She's much more courageous and more clear-thinking as times get tougher – unlike many female characters who seem to dissolve when real thought is required and become panic-stricken and helpless. Mona is the opposite. She likes the pressure and the more pressure she is under the more violent she becomes, and the better criminal she becomes.

In fact, for Henkin the more violence the better. She believes that violence and revenge are classic dramatic motifs. But she is keen to clarify what violence – a subject that is often simplified – can mean. 'I heard a director once say, "You know, when you pick up a gun you realise that there is a lot of power there." I thought to myself what kind of ridiculous notion is that to base something dramatic upon.' Indeed, Henkin is interested in the psychological roots of the desire to pick up the gun in the first place. 'There is the violence that every hit man knows in his heart of hearts. But there is also the violence known by the person who picks up a gun and kills members of their own family. Why do people kill their loved ones? Where does the passion to do that come from? What does it mean for men and what does it mean for women? I want to know how violence can erupt in certain types of love.' Eradicate violence from the screen, Henkin argues, and one eradicates central questions about the human condition.

And certainly she does not view violence as something that she should shy away from because of her gender: 'Women deal with violence all the time. The notion that women can't or shouldn't write about violence is a total fallacy.' Her women characters can be as violent and sadistic as the men. Likewise her male and female characters can equally be the object of violence – Henkin does not believe in making a special case for women. She does, however, believe in following certain rules for such scenes: 'In *Fatal Beauty*, Rita finds herself in a lot of potentially violent situations. It is not really a matter of whether the violence is directed towards a woman, but a matter of how the female character reacts to that violence.' Henkin cites a film such as *Extremities* (directed by Robert M. Young from a play by William Mastrosimone) in which a woman is raped, then terrorised by her assailant before she exacts her revenge.

> I hate seeing such films, because in the first place they are about help-less female victims. My heroines might be treated badly but they will react to the situation as equals and not as helpless victims. I know that is not always the situation in the real world and I don't know what you do about that. But I want to make my female characters powerful. Certainly there is no female character that I have written who isn't able to overpower a man with some sort of cleverness.

After much perseverance on Henkin's part, her female dynamo, Mona, has finally made the transfer from page to screen. But the green light has not come from a Hollywood studio. *Romeo is Bleeding* has been financed via the British-based company Working Title, with the British director Peter Medak at the helm. It is a victory for Henkin, though she exercises a certain caution.

> Here is where it becomes interesting. It seems as though it will be eas-ier to accept a character like Mona – a larger-than-life mythological vil-lain who keeps a gun in her stocking, or whatever she does at the time – because she is amusing and sexy. She is far easier to accept than some-one with the same intent who lives in a house, doesn't cause any trou-ble, goes about her life and has dreams of evil. That's far more scary.

☆　　☆　　☆

What I feel must happen is that there should be a debunking of the myths that have existed until now. What has predominated until now is the male myth and the male commercial perspective which says, 'Oh, we need some myths for women', which results in *Pretty Woman* or *Superwoman* – the male superhero in a woman's body. I don't feel that we know what our myths are – we haven't found them yet and we are in the real throes of the process of trying to find them.

Independent writer/director Maggie Greenwald believes that the genre definitions need to be redefined for a truly radical rethink about representations of women on screen. Her adaptation of Jim Thompson's hard-edged novel *The Kill-Off* was the first of three films released in 1990 in a new wave of screen interest in the writer; it was also the one with the lowest budget. There was some surprise that a woman had chosen to adapt a story about a festering small town caught up in a web of malicious gossip spun on the telephone by a cantankerous, bedridden Luane DeVore. But Greenwald argues that it stands on its head conventional notions of what a woman's film should be about. 'Everything that is striking about *The Kill-Off* has to do with the fact that the film is made by a woman. My film is truly a woman's film because it is strong and visceral.' It has an emotional power that cannot possibly be construed as sentimental.

Greenwald challenges the possibilities of what films that are typified by their 'emotional' content can do. *The Kill-Off* erupts with dark sentiments about a morally bankrupt human nature which affects the women as much as the men. For Greenwald it is the atrophied state that needs to be examined:

> *The Kill-Off* is not so much creating a new mythology as destroying the old and showing how dead all male and female myths are. Every character in the film, both male and female, is an archetype. The only two characters who have the remotest chance of survival are the two that find a minimal kind of love together. It's important for me as a film-maker to create these archetypes and then destroy them before I can go on to show more positive images and create new myths.

Greenwald is cautious, however, about how to approach the creation of new heroines within the terms of genres that she admires:

> I love Westerns: it is the action, the freedom, the cinematic setting; it is the myth of the loner against the world which is a character that I identify with. Westerns and the equivalent samurai films such as Akira Kurosawa's *Yojimbo* and *Tsubaki Sanjuro*[9] are some of my favourite movies. I have been trying to figure out what would be appropriate for a woman to play in that same sort of role. I think of the opening shot of *Yojimbo* – you have this incredible vista, the hero steps in, you see this strong male back and then he scratches his head. The tone of the movie is instantly set up in one shot. We have this huge landscape and we are looking down a valley – and there's this strong figure, clothed as a warrior, but as soon as he scratches his head we know that it is funny. What would be the female equivalent of that? Just to take that character and make it a woman would not work because it is a lie. I would have to find an emotional level at which it could work.

The Western provides the biggest challenge for female screenwriters who want to rethink the genre in terms of the kinds of lead roles it can offer women. In the 70s, Eleanor Perry might have conceived a feminist

Western as a simple case of ensuring that the lead wasn't a hooker. But it is more complicated than that. It is a genre preoccupied with – and troubled by – masculinity. As Geoffrey Nowell-Smith has pointed out: 'Essentially the world of the Western is one of activity/masculinity, in which the women cannot figure except as receptacles (or occasionally as surrogate males).'[10] Arguably, putting the women in chaps is not enough, though critics such as Pam Cook have referred to the feminist potential of such films as *Calamity Jane* (the 1953 musical in which Doris Day smudges up her peachy complexion to play the tomboy Calamity), and particularly Nicholas Ray's *Johnny Guitar* (1954). In Ray's film Joan Crawford plays Vienna, a former dance-hall girl who now runs a saloon. 'Never seen a woman who was more like a man,' drawls one of her curmudgeonly employees. But she switches comfortably between her masculine and feminine guises, the trim black trews and a white ball-gown, while maintaining equal stakes in the story. For Cook, however, the film's feminism lies in its critique of the Western's male values:

> Destructive masculine drives have gone out of control, creating a world dominated by death, betrayal and revenge. … Vienna has had enough of death and revenge; she and Johnny leave the ranchers, bankers and outlaws to their own devices. At the end of *Johnny Guitar*, still in pants, still more than equal to any man, having successfully resisted all attempts to bring her down, Vienna bids farewell to the Western.[11]

The actual history of the West, however, is rich in literature about women forging their identities out on the open range. The film-maker Nancy Kelly, who has chronicled aspects of contemporary rural life in her documentaries *Cowgirls* and *A Cowhand's Song*, recognised that one such biography, *A Thousand Pieces of Gold* by Ruthanne Lum McCunn, would translate well to screen. Completed in 1990, the film, made in collaboration with the screenwriter Anne Makepeace on the smallest of budgets, follows the story of a young Manchurian woman who is sold by her father and ends up living in an Idaho mining town on the Gold Rush frontier, after being auctioned in San Francisco. No doubt purists would define it as a film set in the West rather than a true Western. Indeed, the critic Ginette Vincendeau describes it as a melodrama with all the traditional conflicts of that genre, pointing out that though the film uses the iconography of the Western, as soon as it moves from the open spaces of the Chinese landscape to America the drama is confined to indoor settings. 'The story is about a woman who is a victim, but eventually becomes strong enough to overcome all the obstacles.'[12] The film engages with the heroine's struggle to overcome prejudice – not only against her sex but against her race – and make her stake in a harsh and hostile land.

In recent years the woman to take the most radical approach to the Western is the independent director-writer Kathryn Bigelow in her film *Near Dark* (1987, co-written by Eric Red), a contemporary tale set in dust-bowl America. Her interest, however, was more in genre-blending than gender-bending, for the movie poached on the Western's terrain and iconography to revitalise the mythology of the vampire genre. And as Pam Cook has remarked, Bigelow brilliantly uses each genre to 'comment on the values of the other'.[13] A transient night-riding posse of ragged vampires roam the roadhouses and motels of the prairie towns and terrorise the clean-living folks, with their spurs glinting in the dark rather than the more traditional pointy teeth. The film erupts with similar anxieties about the American dream that underpins the Western genre, as the protagonists get caught in a shoot-out of repressed desires. Preoccupied with the law of the good and bad father, *Near Dark* nevertheless remains true to the Western tradition in that it focuses on a hero's, rather than a heroine's, quest.

Bigelow readdressed the issue of gender in a masculine genre in her next film, *Blue Steel* (1990, also co-written by Eric Red). The film made new ground when it broke rank with the routine *policier* by focusing its story on a young woman cop. The heroine is the rookie Megan Turner (played by Jamie Lee Curtis), who within hours of getting her silver buttons is dressed down and suspended by her superiors for killing an armed robber. But the incriminating gun is nowhere to be found because one of the witnesses, a commodities trader named Eugene, has taken a fancy to it. And also to Megan. Soon corpses start turning up around the city, peppered with bullets inscribed with her name.

Blue Steel examines what happens when women are armed and how men react to them. Megan is surrounded by violent men: her father who beats up her mother, her hectoring superiors, the schizoid Eugene, who develops a lethal infatuation with her. But Megan's decision to join the force alienates those around her. A potential date is deterred when she jokes that she became a cop because 'I like to slam people's heads against walls.' Bigelow slams the film in people's faces, its power relying more on her fetishistic direction than on the script, with its mangled plotting. Bigelow proves to be a skilled director of action sequences. But ultimately *Blue Steel* is about the deeply wounded, for violence brings nothing to Megan but grief, as she begins to lose the people around her. In the film's last image, we see her dressed in a borrowed police uniform a couple of sizes too large for her, and on the verge of a collapse after the final exhausting shoot-out: the image of a woman defeated and out of her depth, a little girl in the wrong dressing-up clothes.

Bigelow's dissection of a genre demonstrated new possibilities for the visceral women's cinema that Greenwald talks of. It is the emotional punches that are most effective in the film. With the added muscle of Oliver Stone (co-producer with Edward Pressman), *Blue Steel* was the first film of its kind to be pushed into the mainstream, though significantly it fared far better on video than in the cinema. But if the 'women's picture' still had mostly 'soft' associations, the following year's *Thelma and Louise* – written by first-timer Callie Khouri – was going to blow that all away.

☆　☆　☆

I was fed up with the passive role of women. They were never driving the story because they were never driving the car.[14]

127

In November 1990 the *New York Times* ran an article on the filming of a new Ridley Scott feature. Headlined 'Ridley Scott Tries to Make it Personal', the story emphasised how the project was a change of tack for the director with a reputation for an often overbearingly glossy style. 'I've never really dealt with a film where the absolute is relationships, rather than adventure, in the broad stroke,' he commented. 'This is a film about two women; the visual has to be in parentheses.' And while the female warrior, Ripley, in Scott's *Alien* might seem to have prefigured his latest heroines, those acquainted with his films must have been astonished at the idea of the man who directed *Blade Runner* and *Black Rain* turning his attention to a 'women's' picture in which 'the absolute is relationships'.

Not since Susan Seidelman's low-budget *Desperately Seeking Susan* (1985, written by Leora Barish) had a film about women so caught the audience's imagination. *Thelma and Louise*'s breezy adventure, with a poignantly tragic edge, was one of the very few films in recent years that could boast two heroines, let alone two working-class heroines. Thelma is a mousy and down-trodden housewife with a slob husband who holds the reins. Louise is a diner waitress who has a complicated and unresolved relationship with her younger musician boyfriend. The two women are the best of friends despite differences in age and temperament; the older Louise is worldly-wise while Thelma at first seems quite naive.

The film starts as they both prepare for a weekend away from their deadbeat and problematic lives in Arkansas. But their holiday trip soon turns into a lifetime on the run when a furious Louise takes a gun that Thelma has packed for protection and pumps some bullets into Harlan, a truck stop lecher, after he rapes her best friend. The two women find themselves on the 'most wanted' list and are sent speeding through the scorched desert landscape of the American southern states in their Thunderbird convertible, heading for Mexico. But they avoid Texas, the location of an undisclosed traumatic incident that bedevils Louise and which the audience must assume was also a rape.

Hitting the trail of many a male buddy duo before them, they learn to savour the freedom – and the hazards – of the open road and toughen their souls while the sun tans their skin. But as they reach the monumental Grand Canyon, their journey takes a fatal turn as the army of FBI agents on their tail finally corners them. Rather than hand themselves in to be judged by a law that may not necessarily be on their side – as Thelma observes, 'The law is a tricky shit', especially when a truck stop full of witnesses observed her smooching with Harlan – the two women prefer to take a final flight over the edge.

European art movie buffs might have spotted similarities between *Thelma and Louise* and Alain Tanner's *Messidor* (1977), which follows two young women hitchhikers as they rob stores on their travels around Switzerland. Schlock movie experts could compare the film to *The Great Texas Dynamite Chase* (1976, also known as *Dynamite Women*), featuring two female bandits as they zip through the state on a bank-robbing spree. But with Ridley Scott behind *Thelma and Louise*, the theme of the female rebel was accommodated in a mainstream Hollywood movie. Under his

pumped-up direction, and with Thelma and Louise's snappy characterisation by Geena Davis and Susan Sarandon, an exhilarating whoosh of
adrenalin was injected into a story about women.

And it hit a nerve. Few road movies end up on the cover of *Time* magazine, but *Thelma and Louise* shook audiences and critics alike, clocking up
the kind of controversy that turns a film into a historic event.[15] American
critics and columnists were divided, but the point of discussion was not so
much the movie's creative merit. The word 'feminist' yo-yoed through
their copy as they tried to determine the film's ideological stance. Amy
Taubin of the *Village Voice* and Janet Maslin of the *New York Times* celebrated the film as feminist, while Sheila Benson of the *Los Angeles Times*
described it as a denial of everything that feminism stood for. Some male
critics were particularly caustic: Richard Johnson of the *New York Daily
News* called it 'degrading to men, with pathetic stereotypes of testos-
terone-crazed behaviour', while John Leo of the *U.S. News and World*
went as far as to call the story 'a fascist idea'.

Thelma and Louise's scriptwriter Callie Khouri (who failed to receive a
mention in the *New York Times* location report) soon learnt about the bur-
den of expectations attached to a film that treats women differently. Indeed,
the fact that two women were running around with a .38 in a Hollywood
movie seemed to make everyone jumpy, even if the film is more about the
friendship between Thelma and Louise than their dexterity with firearms.
She found the critics' passionate reactions to the film very revealing.

> I think that people should not just look at my film but also at the way
> that it has been criticized to gauge the prevailing attitudes towards
> women in film at the moment. *Thelma and Louise* is not about femi-
> nists, it's about outlaws. We see plenty of movies of the genre with men.
> I don't see why it shakes everybody up to see it with women.

To explain the furore, Khouri looks to the broader context of the general
social mood in America at the time of the film's release in 1991 when
issues around women were receiving much scrutiny. 'There was such a
backlash around the Equal Rights Amendment and the bill on abortion.
The atmosphere became so hysterical, like men imagined that women
were going to be storming their bathrooms!' Indeed, it was in the same
year that the well-publicised Anita Hill/Clarence Thomas case also elicited
a huge response on the issue of sexual harassment at work. It is indicative
of the atmosphere then that a film about two women taking the law into
their own hands should win such a controversial tag. 'I have never really
experienced such honest-to-God sexism in action until I started reading
the reviews of *Thelma and Louise* and seeing the critics look at a film differently because it is about two women.'

Khouri takes particular exception to the criticism that the film is
degrading to men:

> You can't do a movie without villains. You have to have something for
> the heroines or anti-heroines to be up against, and I wasn't going to

contrive some monstrous female, but even if this were the most men-bashing movie ever made – let all us women get guns and kill men – it wouldn't even begin to make up for the 99 per cent of all movies where the women are there to be caricatured as bimbos or to be skinned and decapitated. If men feel uncomfortable in the audience it is because they are identifying with the wrong character. Interestingly enough, though, during test screenings prior to the film's release, it scored the highest points amongst 25-year-old males.

Khouri is wary of describing *Thelma and Louise* as a feminist picture, although she was driven by feminist principles to write the screenplay, which was her first. She didn't originally set out to be a screenwriter. Like the legion of other hopefuls, she wanted to be an actress. Growing up in Paducah, Kentucky, she attended Purdue University where she planned to major in theatre studies. But she soon abandoned the course, dissatisfied with the inadequate range of roles on offer to women in the student productions ('I can't tell you how many times I played a prostitute'). After a stint in Nashville as an apprentice for a local theatre, she decided to head for Los Angeles, where she soon drifted into the music video business, finally working her way up to being a producer. 'It was a very distressing experience. It's so obvious, but in pop promos women are little other than objects.'

But for Khouri, the situation was not very different in the movies:

> It is such a rare thing to go to a movie and think, God, that was a really interesting female character. I feel that the roles generally available to women in Hollywood films are incredibly stereotypical: the girlfriend, the wife, the moll, the prostitute, the rape victim, the woman dying of cancer. I wanted to do something outside these terms.

Khouri was motivated to write a screenplay that challenged these stereotypes and broadened the range of roles. But the genesis of *Thelma and Louise* was found when she stretched the notion of being outside and beyond those stereotypes to its logical conclusion and decided that her heroines had to be outlaws. She was intrigued by the idea: 'It's the notion that for a woman to become whole, she has to go completely outside of what is traditionally acceptable for her. Then I started thinking about what would happen if someone who had never done anything bad suddenly found themselves in such a situation.' The premise for the script was simple. Sometime in 1987 Khouri jotted in her notebook: 'Screenplay idea: two women go on a crime spree. They're leaving town, both leaving behind their jobs and families. They kill a guy, rob a store, get hooked up with a young guy.'[16] She completed the script in six months, occasionally consulting a scriptwriting manual.

Khouri conceived the story very much as an allegorical journey as Thelma and Louise make a break from their dreary, repetitive lives. 'The two realise that they have committed a crime and that is why they are on the run. Louise says to Thelma, "You get what you deserve."' *Thelma and*

Louise does seem to defer self-consciously to the genre expectations of the fugitive film. At an early point, just as the two women embark on their journey, Thelma slips the pistol that she's always kept in her bedside drawer at home into the glove compartment of the car. Louise exclaims, 'Why the hell did you bring that?' to which Thelma retorts: 'Oh, come on, Louise … psycho-killers, bears, snakes.' It's as if they have been watching too many movies or TV shows and now it's their turn to be in one. Framing themselves in a polaroid snapshot at the beginning of the film, Thelma and Louise enter into a film and fantasy world. Thelma's raid on a grocery store is seen through the lens of the security surveillance system. The avuncular and pragmatic cop on their case (played by Harvey Keitel) turns out to be a film buff who watches midnight movies while Thelma and Louise continue on their journey. He talks to them on the phone long-distance, keeping them in touch with the reality of their situation. Interestingly, Khouri intended the detective to be the 'moral sense of the audience. He is us.'

Indeed, it is within the moral and allegorical framework of the story that Khouri justifies the fatalistic finale. Cornered by a regiment of gun-toting cops who wield their machines with far more menace than the two heroines ever would, Thelma and Louise embrace each other and then drive over the edge into the blue. But as the critic Amy Taubin points out:

> Given that a handful of open-ended outlaw films already exist, why should Thelma and Louise not have been allowed their days in Mexico drinking margueritas? Or conversely – given that the temper of the times makes it not unlikely that women who defend themselves against a rapist or otherwise defy the patriarchy are risking death – shouldn't we be forced to look at Thelma and Louise's bloody bodies at the bottom of the Grand Canyon, and thus to realise our complicity in their death?[17]

Khouri (and Scott) argues that such an ending would be too depressing. She wanted the conclusion to be triumphant.

> All the way through I was really writing towards the ending – I remember knowing that the image was going to be really spectacular. Thelma and Louise have outgrown the world, they are two women who have no place in it. Besides, realistically they were not going to be able to go back to living normal lives because they would have ended up in jail. I just kept on seeing this image of Thelma at the kitchen sink at the beginning of the film and knowing that she was never, never, never going to be there again.

Ideally, Khouri wanted to direct the story herself, but knew that was unlikely. Even within low-budget parameters, few financiers would have risked giving the green light to someone who had no directing experience. As a first-time writer she felt lucky to get even a few meetings with prospective producers. But the first response was daunting: 'The first couple of meetings I had, they said they loved the characters but did they have to kill the guy?' The script was saved by Scott. 'I was stunned, not when he decided to direct it – that decision came later, but when he decided to produce it.'

Khouri admits that initially she felt ambivalent about the idea, since if she could not direct it she would have liked another woman to do so. But then she reasoned that a heavyweight like Scott would at least get the film made. He also assured her that little of the script would be changed, and key to the contract agreement was that the ending would remain intact. But the casting of Sarandon did slightly moderate the character of Louise since as written she was nearer in age to Thelma. During the film's shoot both Davis and Sarandon apparently chipped in with a few comments on dialogue and it is interesting to compare the draft of the script that was doing the rounds before Scott's involvement and the film as made. The dialogue is pared down, which is not unusual in the process of taking a script to screen, but significantly the scenes removed are those which take time to illuminate and examine the women's friendship.

Not surprisingly, with Scott at the helm, the project instantly changed gear from being a low-budget road-movie, which is traditionally conceived as a character-based genre – two people, a car and a landscape – to a Hollywood extravaganza. (Though Khouri points out that for Scott, the prince of pyrotechnics, the $17.5 million budget was minimal: 'If it had been guys rather than women, they would have blown up a few more trucks and that would have bumped up the budget.') It is a case of how a director's stamp can blur a script's own vision. Ironically, when the film calls for all-stops-out direction at the finale, its power begins to wither. Though Khouri states that she is pleased with it, that spectacular ending which she had hoped for never really takes off.

Scott chose to lighten the mood as the heroines' journey draws to a close, adding his own comic sketch scene in which a Rasta cyclist encounters a police car that Thelma and Louise have left behind in the middle of nowhere. The scene is the only one in the film which has no bearing on Thelma and Louise's story, and seems to detract from it at a point when the tragic nature of their journey should be most manifest. Likewise the friends' rapturous farewell as they hurtle over the precipice in their car fails to deliver any real emotional punch. The image runs in slow motion, the car is briefly suspended in mid-air, and then the film immediately breaks into a crassly zippy credit sequence with a montage of 'snaps' from the rest of the film. How much more devastating it might have been had the director allowed the audience to pause and contemplate the heroines' final dramatic act.

Thelma and Louise's ending has fuelled numerous debates. But the most pertinent answer must be on the T-shirts emblazoned with the legend 'Thelma and Louise live forever'. It has ceased to be just another movie and has become an event. Its success has also opened up the way for potential change in Hollywood and made it possible for the studios more readily to accept that films carried by female leads shouldn't, as Penelope Spheeris puts it, just be about 'ironing and crying'.

If you are going to have a movie that is a thriller and if you are going to have all the principals as women – and I can't think of a film that has that – you are going to have one woman wearing the black hat and one woman wearing the white hat and another woman being the best friend. It's what the dramatic structure demands and why shouldn't women get to play all those parts?

Amanda Silver

The dust had barely settled around *Thelma and Louise* when another film boasting two female protagonists zoomed to the top of the US box-office charts. But the women in this film were hardly buddies on the move. Hailed as a *Fatal Attraction* for the 90s, *The Hand that Rocks the Cradle* is about the enmity that develops between two women as one attempts to wreck the other's happy home. Actually, it is more of a killing and crying sort of film. Claire Bartel has everything: part-time career, spacious home, husband, daughter and another child on the way. Peyton Mott has nothing: her husband has committed suicide, her house has been repossessed, resulting in a miscarriage that leaves her incapable of having children. But little does Claire know that Peyton blames her for it all. For Claire filed a malpractice suit against her unscrupulous gynaecologist, Peyton's husband, after he assaulted her during a consultation. Nor is Claire aware of Peyton's real identity when she comes smiling by six months later offering her services as a nanny to the Bartels. Peyton is the seemingly sunny angel in the house who turns out to be the harbinger of destruction. She tries to lure Claire's children away from her, even secretly breast-feeds the new baby. She incites Claire to believe that her husband is having an affair with her best friend Marlene and then makes moves upon him herself. All this helps to turn the fulfilled and happy Claire into a suspicious and jittery bundle of nerves, pushing her closer and closer to the edge.

The plot of *The Hand that Rocks the Cradle* is formulaic in its structure, and it is not surprising that the young screenwriter Amanda Silver started writing it as her graduation thesis while she was completing the screenwriters' programme at the University of Southern California. Her script follows the successful 'high concept' design of such thrillers as *Fatal Attraction*, *Pacific Heights* and *The Stepfather* in which a seemingly happy domestic set-up is threatened by an interloper, whether it is a spurned lover, a psychotic tenant or a psychotic would-be father. But the twist of *The Hand that Rocks the Cradle* is that for the first time the concept is used to pit a woman against a woman. (Even though in the final showdown of *Fatal Attraction* the Glenn Close character is killed by the wife, the real quarrel is between Close and Michael Douglas.) Like Callie Khouri, Silver wanted to write about women for her first feature. Like Khouri, she opted for the 'switcheroo' tactic, taking a genre and rejigging it with a touch of gender swapping, though the genesis of her script is somewhat obscure:

I was interested in the dramatic structure of *Othello* and I had always thought that it would make a good thriller. To me Iago represents the dark side of Othello – all his doubts. Iago was preying on things that were already there. I wanted to translate that to two female characters. I thought, how could I get one woman close enough to another to prey upon her fears?

Silver's answer was to put them together in a domestic setting, the traditionally female realm. The house becomes the women's battleground, with the children and husband the prized trophies. Silver concedes that she could have put the two women in the work-place but she felt that the home and family provided more 'juicy opportunities to exploit'. These opportunities involve Peyton picking at Claire's sense of herself as a mother and wife. As Claire's friend Marlene jokingly declares: 'A woman's a failure these days if she doesn't bring in $50,000 a year and still make time for blow-jobs and home-made lasagne.' Is Claire a good enough wife and mother, but also has she become too much the mother at the expense of other aspects of herself?

Silver also intended the film, like *The Stepfather*, to be a mild satire on the values of those smugly ensconced behind the white picket fences and lovingly tended gardens. Exploiting the juicy opportunities is not difficult: the Bartels are such a patently nice, philanthropic family. She's a part-time horticulturist, he's a plant geneticist. They take in Solomon, a handyman with a learning difficulty. They're too saintly to be true. The audience should be desperately waiting for the heartily diabolic Peyton to snipe the Bartels down.

The Hand that Rocks the Cradle cranks up the formula. But like *Thelma and Louise*, it provided a disconcerting spectacle for some. American feminist Susan Faludi, author of *Backlash: The Undeclared War Against American Women*,[18] felt that it was a perfect example of the phenomena she had documented in her book. There she examines how in the 1980s the American media, among other institutions, began to conspire to make women believe that they are fettered rather than liberated by feminism. She describes how working mothers have been persuaded to feel guilty about leaving their children in day-care or with nannies. This is exactly the fear played upon in *The Hand that Rocks the Cradle*. Faludi also took to task the central premise of the film. 'What strikes me as interesting and upsetting is that the criminal here is the dead gynaecologist, but the wife's rage is directed at another woman, who is just another victim. ... It seems like we only have one film a year where women are actually allowed to be buddies.'[19]

Silver, who calls herself a feminist, points out in reply that Claire's friend Marlene provides a glowing example of the loyal female friend. But she does not believe that it is her responsibility as a writer to worry about what is 'politically correct or not'.

Men get to be everything in the movies, they get to be good, they get to be bad, they get to be friends and they get to be enemies. I feel that women should get to play all those parts. They should be allowed to be strong, they should be allowed to be vicious. But if they are never allowed to be weak or to be neurotic or to care about babies, then you are talking about robots, you are not talking about drama.

She did not intend the film to be a message to working mothers about the perils of leaving their children with others, though as a working mother herself she believes that if the film prompts a discussion about the difficulties of balancing work with children that is not such a bad thing. 'In my film I am exploiting a concern that is already out there. I see it as a catharsis for fears that already exist.'

Indeed *The Hand that Rocks the Cradle* exploits anxieties about innumerable matters from undesirable child care to child abuse through to corrupt gynaecologists. There is also, in the form of Peyton, the troubling spectre of the childless woman. Cinema's small band of female psychotics tend to fit either of two categories: women rejected by men (*Fatal Attraction*, *Play Misty for Me*) or women who have been driven into madness over a lost child (spot the backstory in *Misery*), monstrously perverted versions of the stereotypical nurturing and caring female. The latter are typically older women: latter-day 'crones'. In this respect, the young and attractive Peyton does not conform, though Silver admits that she originally conceived her as 'an almost campy, over the top figure' and toned her down in the various rewrites to being a more realistic character. She concedes, however, that the motivation for Peyton's psychotic behaviour does follow a convention. 'Babies and men. It is a male conception of what motivates a woman to go nuts. But then I thought of the biblical story in which two women fight over a baby. It has a very primal connection and works dramatically, so I milked it for all it was worth.'

The old stories are always the more acceptable. Indeed Silver admits that it was 'embarrassingly' easy to sell the script to a studio. While Silver herself was hardly a Hollywood novice (she was an executive assistant at Tri-Star pictures before turning to screenwriting, while her grandfather was the screenwriter Sidney Buchman), her husband Rick Jaffa had worked in Hollywood as an agent at William Morris and had also written a couple of scripts which had been sold to Hollywood Pictures. He was able to find people to read *The Hand that Rocks the Cradle* and the script was soon sold, also to Hollywood Pictures. There it went through the usual rewrite process, which Silver describes as a relatively pain-free experience.

A lot of it was compromise – but I felt good because I didn't feel that the original vision had been compromised at all, it was only little things. Though during the rewriting process there would only be myself and one other female production executive in a roomful of men. You are usually talking about men's conception of women, which [I believe to be] different. I felt very lucky with the group of men I was working with. One of them was my husband [who was executive producer on the film] and the Hollywood Pictures people were very 'hands off' for them. I felt that everyone was making a big effort not to impose sexist or male fantasies on Peyton.

Arguably Silver's smooth dealings on the production of the script have much to do with her contacts and her own knowledge of the industry. But the fact that *The Hand that Rocks the Cradle* is a thriller about women which sticks to such familiar home territory also helps. As Hilary Henkin discovered with Rita in *Fatal Beauty*, it is easier for the executives to impose their view on a female character when she strays into territory that is seen as strictly belonging to the boys.

Notes

1. Unless credited otherwise, all the screenwriters' quotes are from interviews conducted by the author in the winter of 1990. Callie Khouri was interviewed in June 1991, Amanda Silver in June 1992.
2. *The Times*, 15 November 1989.
3. *Premiere*, March 1992.
4. Interview with Penelope Spheeris, *American Film*, vol. 10 no. 6, April 1985.
5. *New York Times*, 25 January 1987.
6. Though Dixon did not give details of the Schwarzenegger projects she was approached to write, as her comment suggests they were likely to be of the *Kindergarten Cop* and *Twins* variety.
7. In comparison, Jennifer Lynch's notorious *Boxing Helena* makes an interesting case. In 1987, the 19-year-old Lynch was approached by Phillipe Caland, a Lebanese-French financier and owner of a Chicken Kitchen fast food chain, who was looking for a female writer to flesh out his one-line idea about a man who dismembers a woman and puts her in a box. Her initial reaction was to be suspicious of Caland's intentions. 'I thought, "How dare you want to hire a woman to do something like this just because it would be easier and cooler for people to handle?"' Later, she decided to work on the project, claiming that the idea intrigued her. While there is a certain disingenuousness about the whole affair, the main blame may be apportioned to Caland. Some producers no doubt feel that to have a woman behind such material would lend it a politically correct credibility, or, more probably, a sensational angle to sell the film on.
8. Henkin interviewed by Laurie Ochoa, *American Film*, November 1988.
9. Kurosawa's films follow the exploits of the mercenary samurai Sanjuro, an eccentric anti-hero whose bouts of violence are seen in the context of the ugly society he inhabits. Sergio Leone borrowed the idea for his film *A Fistful of Dollars*.
10. Geoffrey Nowell-Smith, 'Minnelli and Melodrama', in Christine Gledhill (ed.), *Home is Where the Heart is* (London: BFI Publishing, 1987), p. 72.
11. Pam Cook's essay on women in the 'Culture and History' section of Edward Buscombe (ed.), *The BFI Companion to the Western* (London: André Deutsch/British Film Institute, 1988), p. 243.
12. Ginette Vincendeau, 'Third Opinion', BBC Radio Three, broadcast 25 June 1993.
13. *Monthly Film Bulletin*, January 1988.
14. Callie Khouri in *Time*, 24 June 1991.
15. The following survey of US press responses was featured in Richard Schickel's article on the film in *Time*, 24 June 1991.
16. *New York Times*, 5 June 1991.
17. Amy Taubin, *Sight and Sound*, July 1991, p. 19.
18. The book was published in Britain under the title *Backlash: The Undeclared War Against Women* (London: Chatto & Windus, 1991).
19. *Guardian*, 11 March 1992.

Epilogue

Hollywood's Year of the Woman and After

Always on the look-out for some excuse to celebrate, the estimable fellows of the American movie industry marked 1993 as the Year of the Woman. The highlight of the Hollywood calendar, the Oscar ceremony, overflowed with brief but earnest eulogies to all those women who have worked both on and behind the screen. Women screenwriters were among those saluted – no names were mentioned but a two-minute collage of clips from their movies was screened. Women, the audience were reminded by the comperes, could write everything, not just romances.

But the Hollywood films produced and distributed in 1993 testify to a slightly different picture. Where are the women writing Arnold Schwarzenegger or Jean Claude Van Damme films? If a woman had written, say, *The Fugitive*, with Harrison Ford as a wrongly accused man on the run, we could believe that those women who are interested in such genres are getting a fair chance to play the field (the last block-busting adventure movie to have a woman writer on board was the 1984 *Indiana Jones and the Temple of Doom*, scripted by Gloria Katz and her partner William Huyck, while Diane Thomas gave the adventure yarn a refreshing overhaul in 1984 with *Romancing the Stone*), and perhaps even bring a new dimension to this kind of tale. But they are still almost invariably hired to write stories that are relationship and family-centred. Apart from Nora Ephron's *Sleepless in Seattle*, there is Holly Goldberg Sloan's *Made in America*, a farcical comedy about miscegenation anxieties in which Whoopi Goldberg plays a wacky widow who discovers that her test-tube daughter's natural father is a white-trash car salesman. Leslie Dixon has made a huge success as the co-screenwriter (with Randi Mayem Singer, from Anne Fine's novel) of *Mrs Doubtfire*, a provocative family fantasy starring Robin Williams as a father who has to masquerade as a British nanny in order to have access to his children.

Or take Kate Lanier's *What's Love Got to Do with It*, which updates the concerns of such films about female performers as *A Star is Born* or *Love Me or Leave Me* in concentrating on Tina Turner's relationship with her abusive husband Ike; a relationship from which she is finally, triumphantly, able to walk away. Sara Kernochan (whose previous credits include the arty sex romp *9¹/₂ Weeks*) co-scripted *Sommersby*, a love story set during the Civil War. The 'woman's film' is even getting the sequel treatment with *My Girl II* and *Fried Green Tomatoes II* in pre-production. The latter was scripted by Kathy McWorter, whose yet to be made romantic comedy *The Cheese Stands Alone* commanded a high fee. These are films made only when female audiences are being valued and courted.

Even *Indecent Proposal* (written by Amy Holden Jones), which styled itself as an 'erotic thriller' (the erotic now seems to have replaced the melodramatic when it comes to female-led thrillers), aims to appeal primarily to a female audience, though women in the audience may be less than happy about the story of a bartered bride who is whisked away for the night by a handsome millionaire so that she and her doting husband can pay their bills. With its thesis that women are property to be swapped around, however independent they think they may be, *Indecent Proposal* hardly does women any favours. It is a traditional romance with all the trappings.

The biggest surprise, then, is that this Amy Holden Jones is the same Amy Jones who also wrote and directed *Love Letters* (1985), a Roger Corman low-budget movie that merited considerable critical attention. An ironic play on the conventions of the 'women's movie', the film followed a brilliant young career woman's obsessive affair with a married man. Jones's heroine, rather than being consumed by the dangerous liaison, comes to a self-understanding that enables her to walk away bereft but wiser. An intimate film full of careful observations on the hazards of relationships, *Love Letters* rewrote the romance genre. Such a revaluing of a genre is lost in *Indecent Proposal*.

The fact that Jones has had to give up directing to make a career for herself in Hollywood says much; her other scripts include the agreeably zesty girls-coming-of-age story *Mystic Pizza* (1988), and the children's movie about a lovable dog, *Beethoven* (1991). After the success of *Indecent Proposal*, Jones landed the job of scripting the remake of *Niagara*, a story of passion and murder which launched Marilyn Monroe as a lead actress in the 50s. With Sharon Stone touted to play the Monroe role, it has box-office potential. But again one may surmise how Jones the writer-director may have dealt with such material.

Hollywood, however, is a contrary place. Arguably, Jones's chances of returning to direct are better now than ever, but they will improve further if she sticks to subjects traditionally associated with women. Not only is Nora Ephron now established as a director with her comedies *This is My Life* and *Sleepless in Seattle*, but Caroline Thompson has also directed her first feature, another version of the children's literary classic *Black Beauty*. Callie Khouri, too, has a deal to direct one of her scripts, a 'Southern family saga'. Meanwhile Leslie Harris and Julie Dash were hailed as the first black women writer/directors to complete features, with *Just Another Girl on the IRT* and *Daughters of the Dust*, respectively.

It is indicative of the problems that face black film-makers that it took Dash nearly ten years to raise the money for her film.¹ Set at the turn of the century, *Daughters of the Dust* tells the story of the Peazants, an

African-American Gullah family from the islands off the coast of Georgia, as they prepare to make the voyage to the mainland. It is an elegiac appraisal of the African-American past that pays particular attention to the women in the family, with Dash drawing on the legacy of the writers Toni Morrison, Alice Walker and Gloria Naylor. Meanwhile Harris follows in the tradition of the new wave of urban movies by black male directors (*Straight Out of Brooklyn*, *Boyz in the Hood*, *Juice*) and gives the genre a female perspective. Her film is about a Brooklyn schoolgirl who is keen to pursue a career in medicine but whose plans go awry when she becomes pregnant. The moral may be that while the boys' troubles start when they mess around with guns and drugs, the young women's troubles start when they mess around with sex.

In tracing the legacy of *Thelma and Louise*, I found one attempt to 'clone' the two women on the road formula with *Leaving Normal* (1992), though this did not involve a woman writer. Directed by the *thirtysomething* co-creator Edward Zwick and scripted by Edward Solomon, the story follows a cocktail waitress who teams up with a battered housewife and takes the road north to Alaska. But with no crime and little violence, this cosy version of the 'girls with guns caper' failed to score at the box-office.

For action girls, one has to turn to *The Assassin*, which started production a year after the release of *Thelma and Louise*. It found a perky heroine in the wild girl who is civilised, Pygmalion-style, and turned into a sleek killer for the state. Indeed, her training is as much about feminising her as anything else. But as she discovers her femininity and emotions, she becomes a liability to herself and is almost unable to pull off the job. If the studios were hesitant about green-lighting movies about boisterous women, this one was hardly a gamble since it was a total recall of writer/director Luc Besson's *Nikita*. Television action writer Alexandra Seros was originally hired to adapt the French script with Besson directing, but they were later replaced by Robert Getchell (a 'women's picture' writer who also scripted *Sweet Dreams* and *Stella*) and the director John Badham, though Seros did retain a credit on the final film.

So what of other sharp-shooting sisters and those who wish to create them? The fact that *The Assassin* did not hit the top of the box-office chart might bode badly for future action girls. But after thinking long and hard about the Western format, Maggie Greenwald devised *The Ballad of Little Jo*. Greenwald did put her heroine in chaps: cross-dressing, she passes for a man out on the frontier – eighty years on from Gene Gauntier's Belle, the girl spy. Greenwald is convinced that her film would have been impossible to fund without the success of *Thelma and Louise*. It is significant, though, that she found the money from independent production companies, with part of the modest budget coming from outside the US (it was produced for $4 million by the American independent Fine Line in conjunction with the UK-based Manifesto Sales company).

The Ballad of Little Jo, like *Blue Steel* before it, might point the way forward for those writer/directors who want to revise male-dominated genres. It is based on the true story of Josephine Monaghan, a young woman who lived as a man in order to survive in the West in the mid-nineteenth century. Only the bare bones of her story are known. From a wealthy, upper-class New York family, she had a child out of wedlock who was adopted by her sister after Josephine was thrown out by her father. Her only option was to go West. She eventually ended up in Idaho, having taken on a male guise so that she could make a living. Her true identity was only discovered on her death.

Using these fragments of one woman's life, Greenwald set out to create a new myth for the West.

It struck me that it had all the ingredients of a classic Western story – one of a rugged individualist who headed out West to carve a place for herself there. The cross-dressing thing wasn't so important to me. I was concerned with what might have happened to her to take on that disguise and why she might have decided to sustain it.[2]

Maggie Greenwald on the set of The Ballad of Little Jo. *Photo by Bill Foley.*

140

In the film it becomes painfully obvious why Josephine would be likely to become Jo, when she is assaulted by a passing posse. But it is not a simple transition as she hacks her long hair and takes on the accessories of manhood, wearing them at first like uncomfortable armour. It is a sad ritual of survival, as Jo relinquishes her past, including the memory of her child, with her female self at first as good as dead to the world.

Under Greenwald's contemplative direction, and with Suzy Amis's beautifully controlled performance as Jo, *The Ballad of Little Jo* basks in a new-found role for a woman as well as questioning the rules by which gender roles in hitherto male-dominated genres are governed. It scrutinises the lore and law of the Western, including the right to bear arms. For Jo is no gunslinger and the moment she is finally prompted to reach for the trigger is pivotal.

The Ballad of Little Jo points one way forward, while the degree to which it was controlled by women (it was produced by Brenda Goodman, along with Fred Berner, while Manifesto's Aline Perry gave the go-ahead to the financing of the film) suggests a blueprint for the future.

It is telling that the British writer Lynda La Plante, who has so brilliantly rethought roles for women in the ground-breaking British TV series *Widows* (in which a group of gangsters' wives plan their own heist) and *Prime Suspect*, still waits to see the latter drama turned into a feature in the US. It was optioned by one of the studios, who decided that the story of Detective Chief Inspector Jane Tennison's investigation into a series of murders of prostitutes needed to be rewritten by a man. One might also take heed of the case of *Bad Girls*, another female Western that was greenlighted in 1993. Scripted by newcomer Yolande Turner with additions by Becky Johnston, it is about a band of prostitutes who are goaded into avenging the rape of one of their number. The director was to be Tamra Davis, who had previously made a modest but accomplished directorial debut with *Guncrazy*, a downbeat tale of two teenagers on the run in redneck California. But several weeks into the production of *Bad Girls*, Davis was replaced by Jonathan Kaplan (whose films *The Accused* and *Heart Like a Wheel*, about a woman racing driver, have given him a reputation as one of Hollywood's 'feminist' men), who brought his own writer, Ken Friedman, to polish the script. The studio, Fox, wanted the spectacle of a trigger-happy female posse, while Davis (who claims *Johnny Guitar* as one of her favourite films) wanted to stay faithful to the Turner and Johnstone script, which was more concerned with the relationships between the women. It is ironic that this should have happened during Hollywood's Year of the Woman.

For the modern-day Betty Schaefer, writing a script might not be enough; more often she wants to direct too. She's fought for a space in the writers' building and proved for far too long that she can excel in one craft. As cinema approaches its hundredth birthday, the modern-day Schaefer knows that, for those who wish it, a woman's lot is on the lot as much as anywhere else. It's the postscript to Hollywood's Year of the Woman that the script girl would like the industry to take to heart.

Notes

1. The issues facing the black woman screenwriter may be different from those facing the white woman screenwriter, something the Writers Guild of America recognises. Their membership directory provides lists of 'protected classes', and those who request it can have their names included under such headings as 'American Indian', 'Black', 'Latino' as well as 'Women'. While there are a number of black women screenwriters who wish to be identified as such (including Toni Cade Bambara and Vida Spears), the majority work in television. In the past a number of prominent black women novelists and playwrights have been summoned by Hollywood. In 1941 Zora Neale Hurston served as a story consultant at Paramount, though she went to Los Angeles primarily to write her autobiography. While she was there she tried to persuade them to adapt her novels into screenplays, though without success. Later, Lorraine Hansberry adapted her play *A Raisin in the Sun* (1961) for Columbia, while Maya Angelou worked on screenplays in the 70s. Certainly, for those who want to work in film and who want to deal in black subject matter the opportunities have been pretty scarce, and that is perhaps why black women such as Dash and Harris have to be motivated enough to write and direct and raise the money for their films as well. Whether Hollywood will avail them of handsome budgets for their next films awaits to be seen. But since, as Dash has pointed out, 'Ultimately Hollywood defines what the black film is' (as Hollywood also defines what the 'feminist' film is), their financial independence from the majors may not be a shortfall but actually crucial.
2. From an interview with the author conducted in November 1993. Some of this material appeared in an article by the author, 'Western Women', in *Guardian Weekend*, 4 December 1993.

Select Bibliography

Acker, A., *Reel Women – Pioneers of the Cinema*, New York: B.T. Batsford, 1991.

Behlmer, R., ed. *Memo from David O. Selznick*, New York: Viking, 1972.

Beranger, C., *Writing for the Screen*, Dubuque, IA: William C. Brown, 1950.

Brownlow, K., *The Parade's Gone By*, London: Secker & Warburg, 1968.

———— *Behind the Mask of Innocence*, London: Jonathan Cape, 1990.

Buscombe, E., ed., *The BFI Companion to the Western*, London: André Deutsch/BFI Publishing, 1988.

Carey, G., *Anita Loos*, New York: Alfred A. Knopf, 1988.

Carr, C., *The Art of Photoplay Writing*, New York: The Hannis Jordan Co., 1921.

Caspary, V., *The Secret of Grown-ups*, New York: McGraw-Hill, 1979.

Ceplair, L. and Englund, S., *The Inquisition in Hollywood*, Berkeley and Los Angeles: University of California Press, 1979.

Chase, D., *Film Making: The Collaborative Art*, Boston: Little Brown & Co, 1975.

Clark, R., ed., *Dictionary of Literary Biography, Volumes 25 & 26, American Screenwriters*, Detroit, Mich.: Gale, 1984.

Coffee, L., *Storyline: Recollections of a Hollywood Screenwriter*, London: Cassell, 1973.

Corliss, R., *Talking Pictures: Screenwriters in American Cinema*, Woodstock, N.Y.: The Overlook Press, 1974.

Czitrom, D. J., *Media and the American Mind*, Chapel Hill: University of North Carolina Press, 1982.

Dick, B. F., *Hellman in Hollywood*, London: Fairleigh Dickinson Press, 1982.

Emerson, J., and Loos, A., *Breaking into Movies*, New York: The James A. McCann Co., 1921.

Ephron, H., *We Thought We Could Do Anything: The Life of Screenwriters Phoebe and Henry Ephron*, New York: Norton, 1977.

Ephron, N., *When Harry Met Sally*, New York: Alfred A. Knopf, 1990.

Faludi, S., *Backlash: The Undeclared War Against Women*, London: Chatto & Windus, 1991.

Fenton, J.R., *Women Writers: From Page to Screen*, New York: Garland Publishing, 1990.

Filene, C., ed., *Careers for Women*, Boston: Houghton Mifflin, 1934.

Foreman, A., *Women in Motion*, Bowling Green, Ohio: Bowling Green University Popular Press, 1983.

Friedrich, O., *City of Nets*, London: Headline, 1987.

Glyn, A., *Elinor Glyn*, London: Hutchinson, 1955.

Goldman, W., *Adventures in the Screen Trade*, New York: Warner Books, 1983.

Haskell, M., *From Reverence to Rape: The Treatment of Women in the Movies*, New York: Holt, Rinehart and Winston, 1974.

Hellman, L., *An Unfinished Woman*, London: Macmillan, 1969.

―――― *Scoundrel Time*, London: Macmillan, 1976.

Higham, C., *Cecil B. DeMille*, London: W.H. Allen, 1974.

Johnston, C., *The Work of Dorothy Arzner – Towards a Feminist Cinema*, London: British Film Institute, 1975.

Kay, K., and Peary, G., eds. *Women and the Cinema: A Critical Anthology*, New York: E. P. Dutton, 1977.

Klotman, P. *Frame by Frame: A Black Filmography*, Bloomington: Indiana University Press, 1979.

―――― 'The Black Writer in Hollywood, Circa 1930: The Case of Wallace Thurman', in M. Diawara, *Black American Cinema*, London: Routledge, 1993.

Langman, L., *A Guide to American Screenwriters – The Sound Era, 1929–82*, New York: Garland Publishing, 1984.

Leff, L. J., and Simmons J. L., *The Dame in the Kimono: Hollywood Censorship and the Production Code. From the 1920s to 1960s*, London: Weidenfeld and Nicolson, 1990.

Loos, A., *Kiss Hollywood Goodbye*, London: Quality Book Club, 1976.

Marion, F., *How to Write and Sell Film Scripts*, New York: Garland, 1978, reprint.

―――― *Off with Their Heads*, New York: Macmillan, 1972.

Martin, A., and Clark, V., eds. *What Women Wrote: Scenarios, 1912–1929*, University Publications of America – Cinema History Microfilm Series, 1987.

Marx, S., *Mayer and Thalberg: The Make-Believe Saints*, New York: Random House, 1975.

McBride, J., *Hawks on Hawks*, Berkeley and Los Angeles: University of California Press, 1982.

McCarthy, T. and Flynn, C., *Kings of the B's*, New York: E. P. Dutton, 1975.

McGilligan, P., *Backstory: Interviews with Screenwriters of Hollywood's Golden Age*, Berkeley and Los Angeles: University of California Press, 1986.

―――― *Backstory 2: Interviews with Screenwriters of the 1940s and 1950s*, Berkeley and Los Angeles: University of California Press, 1991.

―――― *George Cukor: A Double Life*, London: Faber & Faber, 1992.

Meade, M., *Dorothy Parker: What Fresh Hell Is This?*, London: Heinemann, 1988.

Navasky, V., *Naming Names*, New York: Viking Press, 1980.

Peiss, K., *Cheap Amusements*, Philadelphia, PA, Temple University Press, 1986.

Perry, E., *Blue Pages*, Philadelphia and New York: J. B. Lippincott, 1979.

Rose, J., *Marie Stopes and the Sexual Revolution*, London: Faber and Faber, 1992.

Rosen, M., *Popcorn Venus*, New York: Coward, McCann and Geoghegan, 1973.

Schatz, T., *The Genius of the System*, New York: Pantheon, 1988.

Schwartz, N. L., *The Hollywood Writers' Wars*, New York: Alfred A. Knopf, 1982.

Scott, E. F., *Hollywood: When the Silents Where Golden*, New York: McGraw-Hill, 1972.

Server, L., *Screenwriter: Words Become Pictures*, New Jersey: Mainstream Press, 1987.

Slide, A., *Early Women Directors*, New Jersey: A. S. Barnes, 1977.

Smith, S., *Women Who Make Movies*, New York: Hopkinson and Blake, 1975.

Spoto, D., *The Dark Side of Genius: The Life of Alfred Hitchcock*, New York: Ballantine, 1984.

Stemple, T., *Framework*, New York, Continuum, 1988.

Thomas, B., *King Cohn*, New York: McGraw-Hill, 1990.

―――― *Thalberg*, New York: Doubleday, 1969.

Tibbets, J. C., *Introduction to the Photoplay*, Shawnee Mission, Kansas: National Film Society, 1977.

Todd, J., *Women and Film*, New York: Holmes and Meier, 1988.

Truffaut, F., *Hitchcock*, London: Secker & Warburg, 1968.

Viertel, S., *The Kindness of Strangers*, New York: Holt, Rinehart and Winston, 1969.

Select Filmography

Sound Period 1928–94

The following credits are for scripts both singly and co-written. Writing partnerships are credited where they have been relevant to the whole or the majority of the career.

For a silent film filmography refer to Ann Martin and Virginia M. Clark (eds.), *What Women Wrote: Scenarios, 1912–1929*, Cinema History Microfilm Series, University Publications of America, 1987. This also includes some scripts.

Zoë Akins

1930	*Sarah and Son*; *Anybody's Woman*; *Right to Love*
1931	*Once a Lady*; *Women Love Once*; *Working Girls*
1933	*Christopher Strong*
1934	*Outcast Lady*
1936	*Accused*; *Camille*; *Lady of Secrets*
1938	*The Toy Wife*
1939	*Zaza*
1947	*Desire Me*

Katherine Albert (with Dale Eunson)

1951	*On the Loose*
1953	*The Star*

Jay Presson Allen

1964	*Marnie*
1972	*Cabaret*; *Travels with My Aunt*
1975	*Funny Lady*
1980	*Just Tell Me What You Want*
1981	*Prince of the City*
1982	*Deathtrap*
1983	*Never Cry Wolf*
1991	*The Year of the Gun*

Doris Anderson

1929	*Wolf of Wall Street*; *Charming Sinners*; *Marriage Playground*
1930	*Anybody's Woman*; *Grumpy, Fast and Loose*; *True to the Navy*
1931	*The Gay Diplomat*; *Men Call It Love*; *Woman Pursued*
1932	*Wild Girl*
1934	*Glamour*; *I Give My Love*; *Love Birds*
1935	*Straight From the Heart*; *Without Regret*
1936	*And So They Were Married*
1937	*Girl From Scotland Yard*; *King of Gamblers* (aka *Czar of the Slot Machines*); *Sophie Lang Goes West*
1938	*Give Me a Sailor*
1939	*Beauty for the Asking*
1940	*Women in War*
1942	*Mrs Wiggs of the Cabbage Patch*
1946	*That Brennan Girl*
1950	*Never a Dull Moment*

Maya Angelou

1972	*Georgia, Georgia*

Edna Anhalt

1947 *Bulldog Drummond Strikes Back* (with Edward Anhalt)
1948 *Embraceable You*
1949 *The Younger Brothers*
1950 *Sierra; Return of the Frontiersman; Panic in the Streets* (with Edward Anhalt and Richard Murphy)
1952 *The Member of the Wedding* (with Edward Anhalt); *The Sniper* (with Edward Anhalt)
1955 *Not as a Stranger* (with Edward Anhalt)
1957 *The Pride and the Passion* (with Edward Anhalt)

Alice Arlen

1984 *Silkwood*
1985 *Alamo Bay*
1988 *Cookie*

Gladys Atwater

1937 *Criminal Lawyer; The Man Who Found Himself*
1938 *Crashing Hollywood; Crime Ring; This Marriage Business*
1939 *Parents on Trial*
1942 *American Empire*
1953 *The Great Sioux Uprising*

Gwen Bagni

1949 *Captain China*
1952 *Untamed Frontier*
1953 *Law and Order*
1968 *With Six You Get Eggroll*

Betty Bainbridge

1933 *Secrets of Hollywood*

Jane and Pip Baker

1970 *Captain Nemo and the Underwater City*

Anne Bancroft

1980 *Fatso*

Leora Barish

1986 *Desperately Seeking Susan*

Elizabeth Beecher

1941 *Underground Rustlers*
1942 *The Lone Rider in Cheyenne; The Silver Bullet, Little Joe the Wrangler*
1943 *Tenting Tonight on the Old Camp Ground; Haunted Ranch, Land of the Hunted Men; Wild Horse Stampede; Cowboy Commandos; Bullets and Saddles; Death Valley Rangers; Cowboy in the Clouds*
1944 *Swing in the Saddle; Cyclone Prairie Rangers; Saddle Leather Law*
1945 *Sing Me a Song of Texas; Rough Ridin' Justice; Rough Riders of Cheyenne*

Barbara Benedek

1982 *The Big Chill*
1989 *Immediate Family*
1990 *Men Don't Leave*

Dorothy Bennett

1943 *When Johnny Comes Marching Home; Follow the Band; It Comes Up Love; Mr Big*
1944 *Show Business; Sensations of 1945*
1945 *Patrick the Great*

Sally Benson

1943 *Shadow of a Doubt*
1944 *Meet Me in St Louis*
1946 *Anna and the King of Siam*
1949 *Come to the Stable*
1950 *Conspirator; No Man of Her Own*
1953 *The Farmer Takes a Wife*
1963 *Summer Magic*
1964 *Viva Las Vegas*
1965 *Joy in the Morning*

Clara Beranger

1929 *The Idle Rich*
1930 *This Mad World*
1933 *His Double Life*
1934 *Social Register*

Kathryn Bigelow

1981 *The Loveless*
1987 *Near Dark*
1990 *Blue Steel*

Bridget Boland

1962 *Damon and Pythias*
1969 *Anne of the Thousand Days*

Muriel Roy Bolton

1942 *Henry Aldrich, Editor; This Time for Keeps*
1943 *Henry Aldrich Haunts a House; Henry Aldrich Swings It*
1944 *Passport to Adventure; Henry Aldrich – Boy Scout; Henry Aldrich Plays Cupid; She's a Sweetheart; Meet Miss Bobby Socks*
1945 *Grissly's Millions; My Name is Julia Ross*
1948 *Mickey; The Spiritualist*

Lizzie Borden

1983 *Born in Flames*
1986 *Working Girls*

Marie Boyle

1930 *The Big Trail*

Leigh Brackett

1945 *The Vampire's Ghost*
1946 *The Big Sleep; Crime Doctor's Manhunt*
1959 *Rio Bravo*
1961 *Gold of the Seven Saints*
1962 *Hatari!*
1967 *El Dorado*
1970 *Rio Lobo*
1973 *The Long Goodbye*
1980 *The Empire Strikes Back*

Rita Mae Brown

1982 *The Slumber Party Massacre*

Adele Buffington

1928 *River Woman; Times Square*

1929 *Phantom City*
1930 *Swellhead; Just Like Heaven; Extravagance*
1931 *Freighters of Destiny; Aloha*
1932 *A Man's Land; Ghost Valley; Haunted Gold; Forgotten Women; High Speed*
1933 *The Eleventh Commandment; The Iron Master; West of Singapore*
1934 *Beggar's Holiday; The Moonstone; Picture Brides; When Strangers Meet; Cheaters*
1935 *Powdersmoke Range; Keeper of the Bees*
1936 *Hi, Gaucho*
1937 *Circus Girl; The Duke Comes Back; Michael O'Halloran; The Sheik Steps Out; Any Man's Wife*
1941 *Arizona Bound; The Gunman From Bodie; Forbidden Trails*
1942 *Below the Border; Ghost Town Law; Down Texas Way; Riders of the West; West of the Law; Dawn of the Great Divide*
1943 *The Ghost Rider; The Stranger From Pecos; Six Gun Gospel; Outlaws of the Stampede Pass; The Texas Kid*
1944 *Raiders of the Border*
1945 *The Navajo Trail; Flame of the West; Bad Men of the Border; The Lost Trail; Frontier Feud*
1946 *Drifting Along; Wild Beauty; Shadows on the Range*
1948 *Overland Trails; Crossed Trails; The Valiant Hombre*
1949 *Crashing Thru; Shadows of the West; West of Eldorado; Haunted Trails; Western Renegades; Raiders of the Dusk; Range Land*
1950 *West of Wyoming; Gunslingers; Jiggs and Maggie Out West; Six Gun Mesa; Arizona Territory*
1951 *Overland Telegraph*
1953 *Cow Country*
1958 *Bullwhip*

Elizabeth (Betty) Burbridge

1931 *Law of the Rio Grande; Mounted Fury; Between Fighting Men; Neck and Neck; Chinatown After Dark; Anybody's Blonde; Is There Justice?*

1932 *Hellfire Austin; The Racing Strain; Sin's Pay Day*
1933 *Dance Hall Hostess; Phantom Thunderbolt*
1934 *Rawhide Mail; Boss Cowboy; Redhead*
1935 *Tracy Rides; The Singing Vagabonde; Get That Man; Honeymoon Unlimited; Reckless Roads; Rescue Squad; Calling All Cars*
1936 *The Crime Patrol*
1937 *Come on Cowboys; Springtime in the Rockies; Paradise Express*
1938 *The Purple Vigilantes; Outlaws of Sonora; Under Western Stars; Wild Horse Rodeo; Riders of the Black Hills; Gold Mine in the Sky; Heroes of the Hills; Man From Music Mountain; Pals of the Saddle; Prairie Moon; Santa Fe Stampede; Red River Range*
1939 *The Night Riders; Three Texas Steers; Wyoming Outlaw; Colorado Sunset; New Frontier; The Kansas Terrors; Rovin' Tumbleweeds*
1940 *Rancho Grande; Gaucho Serenade; Under Texas Skies*
1941 *Thunder over the Prairie; Raiders of the Badlands*
1942 *Stardust on the Stage*
1943 *Santa Fe Scouts; Frontier Fury; Robin Hood of the Range*
1944 *Oklahoma Raiders; West of the Rio Grande; Song of the Range*
1945 *The Cisco Kid Returns; In Old Fashioned Mexico; Oregon Trail; The Cherokee Trail; The Cherokee Flash*
1946 *Alias Billy the Kid; Home on the Range; Man From Rainbow Valley; Out California Way*
1947 *Where the North Begins; Trail of the Mounties*
1948 *The Return of Wildfire*
1949 *The Daring Caballero*

Vera Caspary

1935 *I'll Love You Always*
1941 *Lady From Louisiana*
1946 *Bedelia*
1947 *Out of the Blue*

1950 *Three Husbands*

Sonia Chernus

1976 *The Outlaw Josey Wales* (with Philip Kaufman)

Cynthia Cidre

1989 *In Country*
1992 *Mambo Kings*

Lenore J. Coffee

1929 *Desert Nights*
1930 *Bishop Murder Case; Mothers Cry*
1931 *The Squaw Man; Possessed*
1932 *Downstairs; Night Court; Arsene Lupin*
1933 *Torch Singer*
1934 *All Men Are Enemies; Evelyn Prentice; Four Frightened People; Such Women Are Dangerous*
1935 *Vanessa, Her Love Story*
1936 *Suzy*
1938 *Four Daughters; White Banners*
1940 *My Son, My Son; The Way of All Flesh*
1941 *The Great Lie*
1942 *The Gay Sisters*
1943 *Old Acquaintance*
1944 *'Til We Meet Again; Marriage is a Private Affair*
1946 *Tomorrow is Forever*
1947 *Escape Me Never*
1949 *Beyond the Forest*
1951 *Lightning Strikes Twice*
1952 *Sudden Fear*
1954 *Young at Heart*
1955 *The End of the Affair; Footsteps in the Fog*
1959 *Cash McCall*

Adele Comandini

1929 *The Girl From Woolworth's*
1930 *Playing Around; Love Racket*
1934 *A Girl of the Limberlost; Jane Eyre*
1936 *The Country Beyond*
1937 *Three Smart Girls*
1938 *The Road to Reno*
1940 *Beyond Tomorrow; Her First Romance*

1942 *Always in My Heart*
1943 *Good Luck Mr Yates*
1945 *Christmas in Conneticut; Danger Signal; Strange Illusion*

Betty Comden (all titles co-written with Adolph Green)

1947 *Good News*
1949 *The Barkleys of Broadway; On the Town*
1952 *Singin' in the Rain*
1953 *The Band Wagon*
1958 *Auntie Mame*
1960 *The Bells are Ringing*
1964 *What a Way to Go!*

Dorothy Cooper

1948 *A Date with Judy; On an Island with You*
1950 *Duchess of Idaho*
1951 *Rich, Young and Pretty*
1953 *Small Town Girl*
1957 *Let's Be Happy*
1958 *Flood Tide*

Olive Cooper

1935 *Confidential; Hot Tip*
1936 *Dancing Feet; Happy Go Lucky; Hearts in Bondage; Laughing Irish Eyes; Navy Born; The Return of Jimmy Valentine*
1937 *Jim Hanvey – Detective; Join the Marines; Lady Behave; Rhythm in the Clouds*
1938 *Annabel Takes a Tour; Cocoanut Grove; Orphans of the Street*
1939 *The Mysterious Miss X; She Married a Cop*
1940 *Young Bill Hickock; The Border Legion*
1941 *Robin Hood of the Pecos; In Old Cheyenne; The Singing Hills; Sheriff of Tombstone; Down Mexico Way; The Great Train Robbery; Ice-Capades*
1942 *Cowboy Serenade; Call of the Canyon; Affairs of Jimmy Valentine*
1943 *King of the Cowboys; Idaho; Nobody's Darling; Shantytown*
1944 *Song of Nevada; My Best Girl; Three Little Sisters*

1945 *Sioux City Sue; The Bamboo Blonde*
1949 *The Big Sombrero; Outcasts of the Trail; Bandit King of Texas*
1950 *Hills of Oklahoma*

Joyce H. Corrington (with John Corrington)

1971 *The Omega Man; Von Richthofen and Brown*
1972 *Boxcar Bertha*
1973 *Battle for the Planet of the Apes*
1974 *The Arena*

Valerie Curtin (with Barry Levinson)

1979 *… And Justice for All*
1980 *Inside Moves*
1982 *Best Friends*
1984 *Unfaithfully Yours*
1992 *Toys*

Julie Dash

1992 *Daughters of the Dust*

Marjorie David

1987 *Shy People*

Suzanna DePasse

1972 *Lady Sings the Blues*

Helen Deutsch

1944 *The Seventh Cross; National Velvet*
1947 *Golden Earrings*
1949 *Shockproof*
1950 *Kim; King Solomon's Mines*
1951 *It's a Big Country*
1952 *Plymouth Adventure*
1953 *Lili*
1954 *Flame and the Flesh*
1955 *The Glass Slipper; I'll Cry Tomorrow*
1956 *Forever Darling*
1964 *The Unsinkable Molly Brown*
1967 *Valley of the Dolls*

Karen De Wolf

1934 *By Candlelight; Countess of Monte Cristo; Love Captive*

1935 *Public Opinion; Society Fever*
1936 *Bulldog Edition; Doughnuts and Society*
1937 *Borrowing Trouble; The Jones Family in Hot Water; Love in a Bungalow*
1938 *Always in Trouble; Passport Husband; Safety in Numbers; Walking Down Broadway*
1939 *Saga of Death Valley; Everybody's Baby*
1940 *Pioneers of the West; Blondie Plays Cupid*
1941 *Go West, Young Lady; Blondie in Society; Blondie Goes Latin; Her First Beau; Tillie the Toiler*
1941 *Shut My Big Mouth; Meet the Stewarts; Blondie for Victory; Blondie's Blessed Event*
1943 *Footlight Glamour; It's a Great Life; The Darling Young Man*
1944 *Nine Girls*
1945 *Getting Gertie's Garter*
1946 *The Cockeyed Miracle*
1947 *Bury Me Dead; Stepchild*
1948 *Adventures of Casanova*
1949 *Johnny Allegro; Slightly French; Make Believe Ballroom; Holiday in Havana*
1950 *When You're Smiling*
1953 *Count the Hours; Appointment in Honduras*
1954 *Silver Lode*

Joan Didion
(with John Gregory Dunne)

1971 *Panic in Needle Park*
1972 *Play It as It Lays*
1976 *A Star is Born*
1981 *True Confessions*

Beulah Marie Dix (credits post-1928)

1929 *Girls Gone Wild; Trent's Last Case; Black Magic*
1930 *Girl of the Port; Midnight Mystery; Conspiracy*
1931 *Three Who Loved*

Leslie Dixon

1987 *Outrageous Fortune; Overboard*

1989 *Loverboy*
1993 *Look Who's Talking Now; Mrs Doubtfire*

Mary Agnes Donoghue

1988 *Beaches*
1991 *Deceived*
1992 *Paradise*

Nancy Dowd

1977 *Slapshot*
1978 *Coming Home*
1984 *Swing Shift*

Carole Eastman (aka Adrien Joyce)

1967 *The Shooting*
1969 *The Model Shop*
1970 *Five Easy Pieces*
1970 *Puzzle of a Downfall Child*
1975 *The Fortune*
1991 *Man Trouble*

Laurice Elehwany

1991 *My Girl*

Delia Ephron

1992 *This is My Life*

Nora Ephron

1984 *Silkwood*
1986 *Heartburn*
1988 *Cookie*
1989 *When Harry Met Sally*
1992 *This is My Life*
1993 *Sleepless in Seattle*

Phoebe Ephron
(with Henry Ephron)

1949 *Look for the Silver Lining*
1950 *Jackpot*
1951 *On the Riviera*
1952 *Belles on Their Toes; What Price Glory?*
1954 *There's No Business Like Show Business*
1955 *Daddy Long Legs; Girl Rush*
1956 *Carousel; The Best Things in Life are Free*
1957 *Desk Set*

1963 *Captain Newman, M.D.*

Carrie Fisher

1990 *Postcards From the Edge*

Janice Fisher

1987 *The Lost Boys*

Margaret Fitts

1949 *The Sun Comes Up*
1950 *Stars in My Crown*
1952 *Talk About a Stranger*
1955 *Moonfleet*

Fannie Flagg

1991 *Fried Green Tomatoes at the Whistle Stop Café*

Lucille Fletcher

1948 *Sorry, Wrong Number*

Naomi Foner

1988 *Running on Empty*
1993 *A Dangerous Woman*
1994 *Beyond Rangoon*

Caroline Francke

1933 *Bombshell*

Harriet Frank Jnr (from 1958 all titles co-written with Irving Ravetch)

1948 *Silver River; Whiplash*
1958 *The Long Hot Summer*
1959 *The Sound and the Fury*
1960 *The Dark at the Top of the Stairs; Home From the Hill*
1963 *Hud*
1967 *Hombre*
1972 *The Cowboys*
1974 *Conrack; The Spikes Gang*
1979 *Norma Rae*
1985 *Murphy's Romance*
1990 *Stanley and Iris*

Ketti Frings

1941 *Hold Back the Dawn*

1944 *Guest in the House*
1949 *The File on Thelma Jordan; The Accused*
1950 *Dark City; The Company She Keeps*
1952 *Come Back Little Sheba; Because of You*
1954 *About Mrs Leslie*
1955 *Foxfire; The Shrike*

Anne Froelick

1941 *Shining Victory*
1944 *The Master Race*
1945 *Miss Susie Slagle's*
1947 *Easy Come, Easy Go*
1950 *Harriet Craig*

Maude Fulton

1929 *Nix on Dames*
1930 *Captain Applejack; Steel Highway*
1931 *Command Performance; The Maltese Falcon*
1932 *Under Eighteen*
1933 *Broadway Bad; Broken Dreams*
1936 *The Song and Dance Man*

Ruth Goetz (with Augustus Goetz)

1949 *The Heiress*
1952 *Carrie*
1958 *Stage Struck*

Holly Goldberg Sloan

1993 *Made in America*

Martha Goldhirsh

1990 *Sibling Rivalry*

Frances Goodrich (with Albert Hackett)

1933 *Penthouse; The Secret of Madame Blanche*
1934 *Fugitive Lovers; Hide-Out; The Thin Man*
1935 *Ah, Wilderness; Naughty Marietta*
1936 *Rose Marie; After the Thin Man*
1937 *The Firefly*
1939 *Another Thin Man; Society Lawyer*
1944 *Lady in the Dark; The Hitler Gang*
1946 *It's a Wonderful Life; The Virginian*

1948	Easter Parade; The Pirate; Summer Holiday
1949	In the Good Old Summer Time
1950	Father of the Bride
1951	Father's Little Dividend; Too Young to Kiss
1953	Give a Girl a Break
1954	The Long, Long Trailer; Seven Brides for Seven Brothers
1956	Gaby
1958	A Certain Smile
1959	The Diary of Anne Frank
1962	Five Finger Exercise

Ruth Gordon (all except *The Actress* co-written with Garson Kanin)

1948	A Double Life
1949	Adam's Rib
1952	The Marrying Kind; Pat and Mike
1953	The Actress

Barra Grant

1978	Slow Dancing in the Big City

Eve Greene

1932	Prosperity
1933	Beauty for Sale; Day of Reckoning; Tugboat Annie
1934	Operator 13; This Side of Heaven; You Can't Buy Everything
1935	The Great Impersonation; Storm over the Andes
1936	Yours for the Asking
1937	Her Husband Lies; When Love is Young
1938	Stolen Heaven
1939	Little Accident
1941	The Night of January 16th
1942	Joan of Ozark; Sweater Girl
1944	Strange Affair
1947	Born to Kill

Maggie Greenwald

1989	The Kill-Off
1993	The Ballad of Little Jo

Eleanore Griffin

1943	War of the Wildcats
1948	Tenth Avenue Angel

1955	Good Morning, Miss Dove; A Man Called Peter

Frances Guihan

1929	Midstream
1935	The Throwback; Bulldog Courage
1936	The Cowboy and the Kid; Ride 'Em Cowboy; Boss Rider of Gun Creek; The Cowboy Star; Empty Saddles
1937	Westbound Mail; Sandflow; Left Handed Law; Black Aces; Law for Tombstone; Sudden Bill Born; Boss of Lonely Valley
1938	Frontier Scout

Blanche Hanalis

1966	The Trouble with Angels
1968	Where Angels Go ... Trouble Follows
1973	From the Mixed-up Files of Mrs. Basil E. Frankweiler

Lorraine Hansberry

1961	A Raisin in the Sun

Patricia Harper

1942	Prairie Pals
1943	Western Cyclone; Black Market Rustlers; Blazin Frontier
1944	The Drifter; Trigger Trail; Trail to Gunsight
1945	The Topeka Terror; Code of the Lawless
1947	Range Beyond the Blue; Border Feud; Ghost Town Renegades; Frontier Fighters

Leslie Harris

1993	Just Another Girl on the I.R.T.

Joan Harrison

1939	Jamaica Inn
1939	Rebecca
1940	Foreign Correspondent
1941	Suspicion
1942	Saboteur
1944	Dark Water

Lillie Hayward

1930 *On the Border*
1932 *Big City Blues; Miss Pinkerton; They Call it Sin*
1933 *Lady Killer*
1934 *Bedside; Big-Hearted Herbert; Housewife; Registered Nurse*
1935 *Front Page Woman; Personal Maid's Secret; The White Cockatoo*
1936 *The Walking Dead*
1937 *Penrod and Sam; That I May Live; Blonde Trouble; Her Husband's Secretary; Night Club Scandal; That Man's Here Again*
1938 *Her Jungle Love; Sons of the Legion*
1939 *Disbarred; King of Chinatown; Television Spy; Unmarried*
1940 *The Biscuit Eater*
1941 *Aloma of the South Seas*
1942 *Heart of the Rio Grande; On the Sunny Side; The Undying Monster*
1943 *My Friend Flicka; Margin for Error*
1944 *My Pal Wolf*
1945 *Tahiti Nights*
1946 *Black Beauty; Child of Divorce; Smoky*
1947 *Banjo*
1948 *Northwest Stampede; Blood on the Moon*
1949 *Follow Me Quietly; Strange Bargain*
1951 *Cattle Drive*
1952 *Bronco Buster; The Raiders*
1955 *Sante Fe Passage*
1957 *Tarzan and the Lost Safari*
1958 *The Proud Rebel; Tonka*
1959 *The Shaggy Dog*
1960 *The Boy and the Pirates; Toby Tyler*
1962 *Lad: A Dog*

Amy Heckerling

1977 *Getting It Over With*
1990 *Look Who's Talking*
1991 *Look Who's Talking Too*

Jo Heims

1960 *The Threat*
1962 *The Devil's Hand*
1963 *Gunhawk*
1967 *Double Trouble; Tell Me in the Sunlight*
1968 *The First Time*
1969 *Play Misty for Me*
1972 *You'll Like My Mother*
1973 *Breezy*

Lillian Hellman

1935 *The Dark Angel*
1936 *These Three*
1937 *Dead End*
1941 *The Little Foxes*
1943 *The North Star*
1947 *The Searching Wind*
1961 *The Children's Hour*
1966 *The Chase*

Hilary Henkin

1987 *Fatal Beauty*
1988 *Roadhouse*
1994 *Romeo is Bleeding*

Beth Henley

1986 *Crimes of the Heart; True Stories*
1989 *Miss Firecracker*

Debra Hill (with John Carpenter)

1978 *Halloween*
1980 *The Fog*
1981 *Halloween II*

Elizabeth Hill

1934 *Our Daily Bread*
1938 *The Citadel*
1941 *H.M. Pulham, Esq*

Ethel Hill

1932 *Scarlett Brand*
1933 *Ship of Wanted Men; Fog*
1934 *Blind Date; Fury of the Jungle; The Most Precious Thing in Life; Whirlpool*
1935 *The Best Man Wins; Eight Bells; Party Wire; The Public Menace*
1937 *It Happened in Hollywood; Let's Get Married*
1938 *Just Around the Corner*
1939 *The Little Princess*
1940 *Maryland*
1941 *Dance Hall; For Beauty's Sake; Small Town Deb*

1943   *War of the Wildcats*
1944   *Man From Frisco*
1945   *Twice Blessed*
1946   *Two Smart People*

Gladys Hill

1967   *Reflections in a Golden Eye*
1970   *The Kremlin Letter*
1975   *The Man Who Would Be King*

Karen Leigh Hopkins

1990   *Welcome Home Roxy Carmichael*

Tracy Hotchner

1981   *Mommie Dearest*

Dorothy Howell

1929   *The Donovan Affair*
1930   *Men Without Law; Guilty?; Soldiers and Women; Rain or Shine; The Squealer; Ladies Must Play; For the Love o' Lil; The Last of the Lone Wolf*
1931   *Arizona; Dirigible; Platinum Blonde; 50 Fathoms Deep; Miracle Woman*
1932   *Behind the Mask; Big Timer; Final Edition; Love Affair; The Menace*
1934   *Whirlpool*
1954   *Quest for the Lost City*

Gale Anne Hurd
(with James Cameron)

1984   *The Terminator*

Frances Hyland

1929   *Two Men and a Maid; The Voice Within*
1930   *Peacock Alley; Lost Zeppelin; Kathleen Marouveen; Extravagance; Third Alarm*
1931   *Morals for Women; Single Sin*
1932   *Guilty or Not Guilty; The Thirteenth Guest; Unholy Love*
1933   *The Intruder; Officer 13; A Shriek in the Night; The Sin of Nora Moran*
1934   *Money Means Nothing; A Woman's Man*
1935   *Hilldorado; My Marriage; Smart Girl; Thunder in the Night*

1936   *Star for a Night; Under Your Spell; The Crime of Doctor Forbes*
1937   *City Girl; 45 Fathers*
1938   *Change of Heart; Island in the Sky; Keep Smiling; While New York Sleeps*
1939   *Charlie Chan in Reno; Winner Takes All; Everybody's Baby*
1940   *The Cisco Kid and the Lady; Free, Blonde and 21; Girl From Avenue A*
1942   *In Old California; You're Telling Me*
1943   *Someone to Remember*
1945   *The Cheaters*
1946   *Murder in the Music Hall; In Old Sacramento*

Patricia Irving

1986   *Jumpin' Jack Flash*

Susan Isaacs

1985   *Compromising Positions*
1987   *Hello Again*

Diane Johnson

1980   *The Shining*

Monica Johnson
(with Albert Brooks)

1984   *Modern Romance*
1988   *Lost in America*

Agnes Christine Johnston

1929   *Divine Lady; Man and the Moment; The Shannons of Broadway*
1932   *Three Wise Girls*
1933   *Lucky Devils; Headline Shooter*
1935   *When a Man's a Man*
1938   *Out West with the Hardys*
1939   *The Hardy's Ride High*
1940   *All Women Have Secrets; Seventeen*
1941   *Double Date; Life Begins for Andy Hardy*
1942   *Andy Hardy's Double Life; The Courtship of Andy Hardy*
1944   *Andy Hardy's Blonde Trouble; Janie*
1946   *Black Beauty; Janie Gets Married; The Time, the Place and the Girl*
1947   *Black Gold*

Becky Johnston

1986 *Under the Cherry Moon*
1992 *The Prince of Tides*
1994 *Bad Girls*

Amy Holden Jones

1985 *Love Letters*
1987 *Maid to Order*
1988 *Mystic Pizza*
1993 *Indecent Proposal; This Thing Called Love*
1994 *The Getaway*

Fay Kanin (all except those asterisked with Michael Kanin)

1942 *Sunday Punch*
1952 *My Pal Gus*
1954 *Rhapsody*
1956 *Teacher's Pet*
1961 *The Right Approach*
1962 *The Swordsman of Sienna*
1982 *Friendly Fire**

Gloria Katz (with Williard Huyck)

1968 *The Devil's Eight*
1973 *American Graffiti*
1975 *Lucky Lady; Messiah of Evil*
1979 *French Postcards*
1984 *Indiana Jones and The Temple of Doom*
1984 *Best Defence*
1986 *Howard the Duck*

Rose Kaufman (with Philip Kaufman)

1979 *The Wanderers*
1989 *Henry and June*

Gina Kaus

1942 *The Wife Takes a Flyer*
1949 *The Red Danube*
1953 *The Robe; All I Desire*
1958 *Tempestous Love*

Frances Kavanaugh

1941 *Dynamite Canyon; The Driftin' Kid; Riding the Sunset Trail; Lone Star Lawmen*
1942 *Western Mail; Where the Trails End; Trail Riders*
1943 *The Law Rides Again; Blazing Guns; Death Valley Rangers*
1944 *Westward Bound; Arizona Whirlwind; Outlaw Trail; Sonora Stagecoach; Harmony Trail*
1945 *Wildfire; Saddle Serenade; Song of Old Wyoming*
1946 *Romance of the West; God's Country; The Caravan Trail; Colorado Serenade; Driftin' River; Tumbleweed Trail; Stars over Texas; Wild West*
1948 *The Enchanted Valley; Prairie Outlaws*
1950 *Forbidden Jungle; The Fighting Stallion*

Virginia Kellogg

1933 *Mary Stevens M.D.*
1937 *Stolen Holiday*
1947 *T-Men* (story)
1949 *Caged; White Heat* (story)

Barbara (Bobby) Keon

1938 *The Adventures of Tom Sawyer*
1943 *Jane Eyre*

Sarah Kernochan

1986 *9½ Weeks*
1993 *Sommersby*

Callie Khouri

1991 *Thelma and Louise*

Dorothy Kingsley

1944 *Broadway Rhythm; Bathing Beauty*
1946 *Easy to Wed*
1948 *A Date with Judy; On an Island with You*
1949 *Neptune's Daughter*
1950 *The Skipper Surprised His Wife; Two Weeks with Love*
1951 *Angels in the Outfield; It's a Big Country; Texas Carnival*
1952 *When in Rome*
1953 *Small Town Girl; Dangerous When Wet; Kiss Me Kate*

1954 Seven Brides for Seven Brothers
1955 Jupiter's Darling
1957 Pal Joey; Don't Go Near the Water
1959 Green Mansions
1960 Can-Can; Pepe
1967 Valley of the Dolls

Patricia Knop

1986 9½ Weeks
1987 Siesta
1989 Wild Orchid
1994 Delta of Venus

Kate Lanier

1993 What's Love Got to Do With It?

Agnes Brand Leahy

1930 Only the Brave; The Social Lion
1931 Fighting Caravans; Caught; The Beloved Bachelor
1932 Evenings for Sale; Forgotten Commandments; The Night of June 13th; No One Man; Sky Bride
1933 The Lone Cowboy; Hell and High Water; Pick-Up

Connie Lee Bennett (with Karen De Wolf unless asterisked)

1942 Blondie for Victory; Blondie's Blessed Event
1943 Footlight Glamour; It's a Great Life; The Daring Young Man
1944 Nine Girls
1945 Leave it to Blondie*; Life with Blondie*
1946 Blondie's Lucky Day*
1947 Blondie's Big Moment*; Blondie's Holiday*

Gladys Lehman

1929 Broadway Hoofer; The Fall of Eve; Red Hot Speed
1930 A Lady Surrenders; The Little Accident; Personality; The Cat Creeps; Embarrassing Moments
1931 Seed; Many a Slip; Strictly Dishonourable
1932 Back Street; Nice Women; They Just Had to Get Married

1933 Hold Me Tight; White Woman
1934 Death Takes a Holiday; Double Door; Enter Madame; Little Miss Marker
1936 Captain January; The Poor Little Rich Girl; Reunion
1937 Midnight Madonna; Slave Ship
1938 The Lady Objects; She Married an Artist; There's Always a Woman
1939 Blondie Brings Up Baby; Good Girls Go to Paris
1940 Hired Wife
1941 Her First Beau; Nice Girl?
1942 Rio Rita
1943 Presenting Lily Mars
1944 Two Girls and a Sailor
1945 Her Highness and the Bellboy; Thrill of a Romance
1947 This Time for Keeps
1948 Luxury Liner
1951 Golden Girl

Isobel Lennart

1942 The Affairs of Martha; Once Upon a Thursday
1943 Lost Angel; A Stranger in Town
1945 Anchors Aweigh
1946 Holiday in Mexico
1948 The Kissing Bandit
1949 East Side, West Side; Holiday Affair
1950 A Life of Her Own
1951 It's a Big Country
1952 My Wife's Best Friend; Skirts Ahoy!
1953 The Girl Next Door; Latin Lovers
1955 Love Me or Leave Me
1956 Meet Me in Las Vegas
1957 This Could Be the Night
1958 Merry Andrew; The Inn of Sixth Happiness
1960 Please Don't Eat the Daisies; The Sundowners
1962 Period of Adjustment; Two for the Seesaw
1967 Fitzwilly
1968 Funny Girl

Sonya Levien

1929 The Younger Generation; Trial Marriage; They Had to See Paris; Frozen Justice; South Sea Rose
1930 Song o' My Heart; So This is London; Liliom; Lightnin'

1931   The Brat; Daddy Long Legs; Delicious; Surrender
1932   After Tomorrow; Rebecca of Sunnybrook Farm; Tess of the Storm Country
1933   Berkeley Square; Cavalcade; Mr Skitch; State Fair; Warrior's Husbands
1934   As Husbands Go; Change of Heart; The White Parade
1935   Beauty's Daughter; Here's to Romance; Navy Wife
1936   Reunion; The Country Doctor
1938   The Cowboy and the Lady; Four Men and a Prayer; In Old Chicago; Kidnapped
1939   Drums Along the Mohawk; The Hunchback of Notre Dame
1941   Ziegfeld Girl
1945   The Valley of Decision; State Fair
1946   The Green Years
1947   Cass Timberlane
1948   Three Daring Daughters
1951   The Great Caruso; Quo Vadis
1952   The Merry Widow
1954   The Student Prince
1955   Hit the Deck; Interrupted Melody; Oklahoma!
1956   Bhowani Junction
1957   Jeanne Eagels

Anita Loos (credits post-1928)

1931   The Struggle
1932   Red Headed Woman
1933   The Barbarian; Hold Your Man
1934   Biography of a Bachelor Girl; The Girl From Missouri
1935   Riff Raff
1936   San Francisco
1937   Mama Steps Out; Saratoga
1939   The Women
1940   Susan and God
1941   Blossoms in the Dust; They Met in Bombay; When Ladies Meet
1942   I Married an Angel
1949   Father Was a Fullback

Mary Loos (with Richard Sale)

1946   Rendezvous with Annie
1947   Calendar Girl; Driftwood; Hit Parade of 1947

1948   The Dude Goes West; The Inside Story
1949   Mother is a Freshman; Mr Belvedere Goes to College
1950   When Willie Comes Marching Home; Ticket to Tomahawk; I'll Get By
1951   Meet Me After the Show
1953   The French Line; Woman's World
1955   Gentlemen Marry Brunettes

Ida Lupino

1949   Not Wanted
1950   Outrage
1953   The Bigamist
1954   Private Hell 36

Jeanie Macpherson (credits post-1928)

1929   The Godless Girl; Dynamite
1930   Madam Satan
1933   The Devil's Brother
1938   The Buccaneer

Frances Marion (credits post-1928)

1928   Bringing Up Father
1930   Their Own Desire
1930   Anna Christie; The Big House; Rogue Song; Let Us Be Gay; Good News; Min and Bill
1931   The Secret Six; The Champ
1932   Blondie of the Follies; Cynara
1933   Secrets; Dinner at Eight; Peg o' My Heart; The Prizefighter and the Lady
1935   Riff Raff
1936   Camille
1937   The Good Earth; Knight Without Armour; Love from a Stranger
1940   Green Hell

Sara Y. Mason (with Victor Heerman)

1928   Alias Jimmy Valentine
1929   The Broadway Melody
1930   The Girl Said No; Love in the Rough; They Learned About Women
1931   Man in Possession
1932   The Age of Consent; Shopworn
1933   Chance at Heaven; Little Women

1934 *The Age of Innocence; The Little Minister*
1935 *Break of Hearts; Magnificent Obsession*
1937 *Stella Dallas*
1939 *Golden Boy*
1949 *Little Women*
1954 *Magnificent Obsession*

Melissa Mathison

1979 *The Black Stallion*
1982 *The Escape Artist; E.T. the Extra-Terrestrial*
1990 *Son of Morningstar*

Elaine May

1971 *A New Leaf; Such Good Friends*
1976 *Mikey and Nicky*
1978 *Heaven Can Wait*
1987 *Ishtar*

Mary McCall, Jr.

1932 *Street of Women*
1934 *Babbitt; Desirable*
1935 *Dr Socrates; A Midsummer Night's Dream; The Secret Bride; The Woman in Red*
1937 *I Promise to Pay; It's All Yours; Women of Glamour*
1938 *Breaking the Ice; Dramatic School*
1939 *Maisie*
1940 *Congo Maisie; Gold Rush Maisie*
1941 *Kathleen; Maisie Was a Lady; Ringside Maisie*
1944 *The Sullivans; Maisie Goes to Reno*
1945 *Keep Your Powder Dry*
1949 *Dancing in the Dark; Mr Belvedere Goes to College*
1952 *Ride the Man Down; Thunderbirds*
1959 *Juke Box Rhythm*

Bess Meredyth (credits post-1928)

1929 *Wonder of Women*
1930 *Chasing Rainbows; In Gay Madrid; The Sea Bat; Our Blushing Brides; Romance*
1931 *Laughing Sinners; The Phantom of Paris; The Prodigal; Cuban Love Song*

1932 *Strange Interlude; West of Broadway*
1933 *Looking Forward*
1934 *The Affairs of Cellini; The Mighty Barnum*
1935 *Folies Bergere; Metropolitan*
1936 *Half Angel; Under Two Flags*
1937 *The Great Hospital Mystery*
1940 *The Mark of Zorro*
1941 *That Night in Rio*
1947 *The Unsuspected*

Nancy Meyers (with Charles Shyer)

1980 *Private Benjamin*
1984 *Protocol; Irreconcilable Differences*
1987 *Babyboom*
1991 *Father of the Bride*

Jane Murfin

1929 *Street Girl; Dance Hall*
1930 *Seven Keys to Baldpate; The Pay Off; Leathernecking; Lawful Larceny; The Runaway Bride*
1931 *Friends and Lovers; Too Many Crooks*
1932 *What Price Hollywood?; Young Bride; Rockaby; Way Back Home*
1933 *After Tonight; Ann Vickers; Double Harness; Our Betters; The Silver Cord*
1934 *Crime Doctor; The Fountain; The Life of Verfie Winters; The Little Minister; Romance in Manhattan; Spitfire; This Man is Mine*
1935 *Alice Adams; Roberta*
1936 *Come and Get It*
1937 *I'll Take Romance*
1938 *The Shining Hour*
1939 *Stand Up and Fight; The Women*
1940 *Pride and Prejudice*
1941 *Andy Hardy's Private Secretary*
1943 *Flight for Freedom*
1944 *Dragon Seed*

Czenzi Ormonde

1951 *Strangers on a Train*
1958 *Step Down to Terror*
1959 *1,001 Arabian Nights*

Gail Parent

1978 *Sheila Levine is Dead and Living in NY*
1979 *The Main Event*

Dorothy Parker

1934 *Here is My Heart*
1935 *One Hour Late*
1936 *Lady Be Careful; The Moon's Our Home; Suzy; Three Married Men*
1937 *A Star is Born; Woman Chases Man*
1938 *Sweethearts; Trade Winds*
1941 *Week-End for Three*
1942 *Saboteur*
1949 *The Fan*

Laura Perelman
(with S. J. Perelman)

1936 *Florida Special*
1939 *Ambush*
1940 *The Golden Fleecing*

Eleanor Perry

1963 *David and Lisa; Ladybug Ladybug*
1968 *The Swimmer*
1969 *Last Summer; Trilogy*
1970 *Diary of a Mad Housewife; The Lady in the Car with Glasses and a Gun*
1973 *The Man Who Loved Cat Dancing*

Anna Hamilton Phelan

1985 *Mask*
1988 *Gorillas in the Mist*

Dori Pierson

1988 *Big Business*

Polly Platt

1968 *Targets*
1978 *Pretty Baby*

Gertrude Purcell

1930 *Follow the Leader*
1931 *Girl Habit; The Royal Family of Broadway*
1932 *Night Mayor; No More Orchids; Vanity Street*
1933 *Another Language; Child of Manhattan; Cocktail Hour*
1934 *Palooka; She Was a Lady*
1935 *The Girl Friend; If You Could Only Cook*
1936 *Make Way for a Lady; Witness Chair*
1937 *Hitting a New High; Music for Madam; Super Sleuth*
1938 *Mother Carey's Chickens; Service de Luxe*
1939 *Destry Rides Again; The Lady and the Mob*
1940 *A Little Bit of Heaven; One Night in the Tropics*
1941 *Ellery Queen and the Murder Ring; The Invisible Woman*
1942 *In Old California; Ice Capades Revue*
1944 *Follow the Boys; Reckless Age*
1945 *Paris Underground*
1947 *Winter Wonderland*

Ayn Rand

1945 *You Came Along; Love Letters*
1949 *The Fountainhead*

Judith Rascoe

1974 *Road Movie*
1979 *Who'll Stop the Rain? aka Dog Soldiers*
1981 *Endless Love*
1989 *Eat a Bowl of Tea*
1990 *Havana*

Tina Rathbone

1988 *Zelly and Me*

Dorothy Reid (credits post-1928)

1934 *Road to Ruin; Woman Condemned*
1935 *Honeymoon Limited; Women Must Dress*
1938 *Prison Break*
1940 *Drums of the Desert; The Haunted House; The Old Swimmin' Hole; On the Spot; Tomboy*
1941 *Redhead*
1947 *The Hal Roach Comedy Carnival; Curly*
1948 *Who Killed "Doc" Robbin?*
1949 *Impact*

1951 *Rhubarb*
1955 *Footsteps in the Fog*

Elizabeth (Betty) Reinhardt

1940 *Gold Rush Maisie*
1941 *Maisie Was a Lady*
1942 *Maisie Gets Her Man*
1943 *His Butler's Sister*
1944 *Laura*
1946 *Cluny Brown; Sentimental Journey*
1947 *Carnival in Costa Rica*
1948 *Give My Regards to Broadway*
1950 *Hit Parade of 1951*

Patricia Resnick

1978 *A Wedding*
1979 *Quintet*
1980 *Nine to Five*
1985 *Maxie*
1989 *Second Sight*
1992 *Straight Talk*

Alma Reville (US films only)

1935 *Strauss' Great Waltz*
1936 *The Passing of the Third Floor Back*
1941 *Suspicion*
1943 *Shadow of a Doubt*
1945 *It's in the Bag*
1948 *The Paradine Case*
1950 *Stage Fright*

Craig Rice

1942 *The Falcon's Brother*
1943 *The Falcon in Danger*

Silvia Richards

1947 *Possessed*
1948 *Secret Beyond the Door*
1951 *Tomahawk*
1952 *Ruby Gentry, Rancho Notorious*

Janet Roach

1985 *Prizzi's Honour*
1988 *Mr North*

June Roberts

1990 *Mermaids*

Marguerite Roberts

1933 *Jimmy and Sally; Sailor's Luck*
1934 *Peck's Bad Boy*
1935 *College Scandal*
1936 *Florida Special; Forgotten Faces; Hollywood Boulevard; Rose Bowl*
1937 *Turn of the Moon; Wild Moon*
1938 *Meet the Girls*
1940 *Escape*
1941 *Honky Tonk; Ziegfeld Girl*
1942 *Somewhere I'll Find You*
1944 *Dragon Seed*
1947 *Desire Me; If the Winter Comes; The Sea of Grass*
1949 *Ambush; The Bribe*
1951 *Soldiers Three*
1962 *Diamond Head*
1963 *Rampage*
1965 *Lorett's Many Faces*
1968 *Five Card Stud*
1969 *True Grit*
1970 *Norwood*
1971 *Red Sky at Morning; Shoot Out*

Mary Rodgers

1977 *Freaky Friday*
1981 *The Devil and Max Devlin*

Louise Rose

1973 *Sisters*

Ruth Rose

1933 *King Kong; Son of Kong; Blind Adventure*
1935 *The Last Days of Pompeii; She*
1949 *Mighty Joe Young*

Jeanne Rosenberg

1979 *The Black Stallion*
1985 *Journey of Natty Gann*
1990 *White Fang*

Judith Ross

1979 *Rich Kids*

Stephanie Rothman

1967 *It's a Bikini World*
1971 *The Velvet Vampire*

1972 Group Marriage
1974 The Working Girls; Terminal Island

Jean Rouverol Butler

1950 So Young, So Bad
1952 The First Time
1963 A Face in the Rain
1968 The Legend of Lylah Clare

Kathleen Knutsen Rowell

1983 The Outsiders
1984 The Joy of Sex

Florence Ryerson

1929 Pointed Heels
1930 Call of the West
1931 Drums of Jeopardy; The Reckless
      Hour
1933 The Crime of the Century
1934 Have a Heart; This Side of Heaven; A
      Wicked Woman
1935 The Casino Murder Case
1936 Mad Holiday; Moonlight Murder;
      Tough Guy
1938 Everybody Sing
1939 The Ice Follies of 1939; The Kid
      From Texas; The Wizard of Oz
1940 Henry Goes Arizona

Susan Sandler

1987 Crossing Delancy

Sara Schiff

1989 Lord of the Flies

Doris Schroeder

1934 Crimson Romance
1934 Hop-a-Long Cassidy; The Eagle's
      Brood; Bar 20 Rides Again
1936 Call of the Prairie; Three on the
      Trail; Heart of the West
1940 Legion of the Lawless; Bullet Code;
      Prairie Law; Oklahoma Renegades;
      Texas Terrors
1941 The Phantom Cowboy; Two Gun-
      Sheriff; Kansas Cyclone; Gangs of
      Sonora; A Missouri Outlaw
1942 Arizona Terrors; Jesse James Jnr.;
      Westward Ho; Pirates of the Prairie

1945 Bandits of the Badlands
1946 Fool's Gold; Days of Buffalo Bill;
      Death Valley
1947 Dangerous Venture
1948 Sinister Journey; False Paradise;
      Strange Gamble
1949 The Gay Amigo

Marjorie Schwartz

1991 The Butcher's Wife

Kathryn Scola

1931 The Lady Who Dared; Wicked
1933 Baby Face; Female; Lady of the
      Night; Lilly Turner; Luxury Liner;
      Midnight Mary
1934 Fashions of 1934; A Lost Lady; The
      Merry Frinks; A Modern Hero
1935 The Glass Key; One Hour Late
1936 It Had to Happen
1937 Second Honeymoon; Wife, Doctor
      and Nurse
1938 Alexander's Ragtime Band;
      Always Goodbye; The Baroness
      and the Butler
1939 Hotel for Women
1940 The House Across the Bay
1941 Lady From Cheyenne
1943 The Constant Nymph; Happy Land
1945 Colonel Effingham's Raid
1949 Night Unto Night

Susan Seidelman

1982 Smithereens

Alexandra Seros

1993 The Assassin

Amanda Silver

1991 The Hand That Rocks the Cradle

Randi Mayem Singer

1993 Mrs Doubtfire

Tess Slesinger

1937 The Bride Wore Red; The Good
      Earth
1938 Girl's School

161

1940 *Dance, Girl, Dance*
1941 *Remember the Day*
1942 *Are Husbands Necessary?*
1945 *A Tree Grows in Brooklyn*

Dodie Smith

1944 *The Uninvited*
1951 *Darling, How Could You*

Carol Sobieski

1977 *Casey's Shadow*
1980 *Honeysuckle Rose*
1981 *Annie*
1982 *The Toy*
1989 *Winter People*
1991 *Fried Green Tomatoes at the Whistle Stop Café*

Edith Sommer

1950 *Born to Be Bad; Perfect Strangers*
1959 *The Best of Everything; Blue Denim*
1962 *Jessica*
1964 *The Pleasure Seekers*
1966 *This Property is Condemned*

Bella Spewack
(with Samuel Spewack)

1933 *The Cat and the Fiddle; Clear All Wires; The Nuisance; Should Ladies Behave?*
1934 *The Gay Bride*
1935 *Rendezvous*
1937 *Vogues of 1938*
1938 *Boy Meets Girl; The Chaser; Three Loves Has Nancy*
1940 *My Favourite Wife*
1945 *Weekend at the Waldorf*

Anne Spielberg

1988 *Big*

Amy Spies

1985 *Girls Just Want to Have Fun*

Joan Tewkesbury

1974 *Thieves Like Us*
1975 *Nashville*
1979 *The Tenth Month*

1982 *A Night in Heaven*
1987 *The Accused* (uncredited)
1989 *Cold Sassy Tree*
1990 *Susie and Simpson*

Sylvia Thalberg

1930 *Montana Moon*
1931 *New Moon; This Modern Age*
1932 *When a Fella Needs a Friend*
1933 *Christopher Bean*
1934 *Now and Forever*
1936 *A Son Comes Home*

Diane Thomas

1984 *Romancing the Stone*

Caroline Thompson

1990 *Edward Scissorhands*
1991 *The Addams Family*
1992 *The Secret Garden*
1994 *Black Beauty*

Joan Torres

1972 *Blacula*
1973 *Scream, Blacula, Scream*

Wanda Tuchock

1929 *Hallelujah*
1930 *Billy the Kid; Not So Dumb*
1931 *Sporting Blood; Susan Lenox, Her Fall and Rise*
1932 *Letty Lynton; Little Orphan Annie; New Morals for Old*
1933 *Bed of Roses; No Other Woman*
1934 *Finishing School*
1935 *O'Shaughnessy's Boy*
1938 *Hawaii Calls*
1939 *The Llano Kid*
1940 *Youth Will Be Served*
1941 *For Beauty's Sake*
1944 *This is the Life; Ladies of Washington; Sunday Dinner for a Soldier*
1945 *Nob Hill; Within These Walls*
1947 *The Foxes of Harrow; The Homestretch*

Barbara Turner

1973 *The Affair*
1984 *Cujo*

Bonnie Turner

1992 *Wayne's World*
1993 *Coneheads; Wayne's World 2*

Catherine Turney

1945 *Mildred Pierce*
1946 *The Man I Love; My Reputation; Of Human Bondage; One More Tomorrow; A Stolen Life*
1947 *Cry Wolf*
1948 *Winter Meeting*
1950 *No Man of Her Own*
1952 *Japanese War Bride*
1957 *Back From the Dead*

Betty Tusher

1968 *Psych-Out*

Gladys Unger

1932 *Wayward*
1934 *Cheating Cheaters; Coming Out Party; Countess of Monte Cristo; Embarrassing Moments; Glamour; Great Expectations; Romance in the Rain*
1935 *Alias Mary Dow; The Mystery of Edwin Drood; Rendezvous at Midnight; Strange Wives; Sylvia Scarlett*
1937 *Daughter of Shanghai; Night of Mystery*

Eve Unsell

1931 *Secret Call; Unfaithful; Up Pops the Devil*

Gabrielle Upton

1959 *Gidget*
1962 *Escape from East Berlin*

Kay Van Riper

1937 *A Family Affair*
1938 *Judge Hardy's Children; Out West with the Hardys; You're Only Young Once*
1939 *Andy Hardy Gets Spring Fever; Babes in Arms; The Hardys Ride High*

1941 *Lady Be Good*

Virginia Van Upp

1934 *Pursuit of Happiness*
1935 *So Red the Rose*
1936 *Easy to Take; My American Wife; Poppy; Timothy's Quest; Too Many Parents*
1937 *Swing High, Swing Low*
1938 *You and Me*
1939 *Cafe Society; Honeymoon in Bali*
1941 *Bahama Passage; One Night in Lisbon; Virginia*
1943 *The Crystal Ball; Young and Willing*
1944 *Cover Girl; The Impatient Years; Together Again*
1945 *She Wouldn't Say Yes*
1946 *Gilda*
1951 *Here Comes the Groom*
1952 *An Affair in Trinidad*

Salka Viertel

1933 *Queen Christina*
1934 *The Painted Veil*
1935 *Anna Karenina*
1937 *Conquest*
1941 *Two-Faced Woman*
1947 *Deep Valley*

Irmgard von Cube

1947 *Song of Love*
1948 *Johnny Belinda*
1952 *The Girl in White*

Jane Wagner

1978 *Moment by Moment*
1981 *The Incredible Shrinking Woman*

Luci Ward

1936 *The Law in Her Hands; Murder by an Aristocrat*
1937 *Land Beyond the Law; Cherokee Strip; Melody for Two; Mountain Justice*
1938 *Call of the Mesquiteers; Panamint's Bad Man; Man from the Music Mountain; Overland Stage Raiders; Sante Fe Stampede; Red River Range*

1939 *New Frontier; The Arizona Kid;
Beyond the Sacramento*
1942 *The Lone Star Vigilantes; Lawless
Plainsmen; Bad Men of the Hills;
Vengeance of the West*
1943 *The Fighting Buckaroo; Law of the
Northwest*
1944 *Sundown Valley; Riding West;
Raiders of Ghost City; Cowboy from
Lonesome River; Sagebrush Heroes*
1945 *The Frozen Ghost*
1946 *Badman's Territory*
1947 *Trail to San Antone*
1948 *Black Bart; Return of the Badmen*
1949 *Six Gun Music; Rustlers*
1956 *Blackjack Ketchum, Desperado*
1957 *The Night the World Exploded*
1967 *The Ride to Hangman's Tree*

Claudine West

1930 *The Soul Kiss*
1931 *The Guardsman; Just a Gigolo;
Private Lives*
1932 *Payment Deferred; Smilin' Through;
The Son-Daughter*
1933 *Reunion in Vienna*
1934 *The Barretts of Wimpole Street*
1937 *The Good Earth*
1938 *Marie Antoinette*
1939 *Goodbye, Mr Chips; On Borrowed
Time*
1940 *The Mortal Storm*
1942 *Mrs Miniver; Random Harvest;
We Were Dancing*
1943 *Forever and a Day*
1944 *The White Cliffs of Dover*

Mae West

1933 *I'm No Angel*
1934 *Belle of the Nineties*
1935 *Goin' to Town*
1936 *Go West, Young Man; Klondike
Annie*
1937 *Every Day's a Holiday*
1940 *My Little Chickadee*

Hagar Wilde

1937 *Bringing Up Baby*
1944 *Guest in the House*
1945 *The Unseen*

1949 *I Was a Male War Bride; Red, Hot
and Blue*
1950 *Shadow of the Eagle*
1954 *This is My Love*

Martha Wilkerson

1951 *Hard, Fast and Beautiful*

Mary Willingham

1951 *Hard, Fast and Beautiful*
1961 *Battle at Bloody Beach*
1964 *Bullet for a Badman*
1965 *Arizona Raiders*
1966 *Gunpoint*
1967 *Forty Guns to Apache Pass*

Elizabeth Wilson

1951 *Cave of Outlaws*
1958 *Raw Wind in Eden*
1964 *Invitation to a Gunfighter*

Linda Woolverton

1992 *Beauty and the Beast*

Dorothy Yost

1933 *Hello Everybody*
1934 *The Gay Divorcee*
1935 *Alice Adams; A Dog of Flanders;
Freckles; Laddie*
1936 *Bunker Bean; M'Liss; Murder on a
Bridle Path; That Girl From Paris*
1937 *Racing Lady; There Goes the
Groom; Too Many Wives*
1939 *Bad Little Angel; Four Girls in
White; The Story of Vernon and
Irene Castle*
1940 *Forty Little Mothers; Sporting Blood*
1945 *Thunderhead – Son of Flicka*
1946 *Smoky*
1948 *The Strawberry Roan*
1949 *Loaded Pistols; The Cowboy and the
Indians; The Big Cat*
1953 *Siginaw Trail*

Dalene Young

1980 *Little Darlings*
1983 *Cross Creek*

Index

170

Also available from BFI Publishing

PICTURING THE PAST
The Rise and Fall of the
British Costume Film

Sue Harper

From the riotous banqueting scenes of *The Private Life of Henry VIII* to the sexual banditry of *The Wicked Lady*, British costume film attracted controversy. This book charts the development of a flamboyant genre from the 1930s to the 1950s. A pioneering study which combines the interpretation of unknown archival material with attention to visual style, it establishes the ways in which historical film responded to social change and provided potent metaphors for its audiences.

Sue Harper demonstrates how producers such as Alexander Korda, Herbert Wilcox, Michael Balcon and the Ostrers constructed images of the past which drew, variously and selectively, on key themes in popular culture. She shows that official bodies feared the effects of historical film and attempted to influence it. She conducts a broad survey of contemporary audience response, establishing that it was for women and the working class that the costume film had an important and symbolic function.

Hardback
ISBN 0 85170 448 4
£35.00

Paperback
ISBN 0 85170 449 2
£14.95

Melodrama
STAGE PICTURE SCREEN

Jacky Bratton, Jim Cook, Christine Gledhill

Since the early seventies, melodrama has been the focus of some of the most provocative and illuminating debates in media studies as well as in women's studies, informing Theatre Studies, Art History, Music and Film.

This book draws on the papers presented at the international conference *Melodrama: Stage Picture Screen* held in London in 1992. The contributions by leading melodrama scholars derive from a range of disciplines and offer varying perspectives on melodrama's Debates, Transformations, Revisions and Politics. Taken individually, each of the essays yields a variety of insights; as a collection, they provide a comprehensive overview of the 'state of the art' of melodrama studies in the many disciplines which have something to say about the subject. The book also shows how stimulating, even indispensable, interdisciplinary approaches and conferences can be for the understanding of complex cultural phenomena such as Melodrama.

The editors were members of the Organising Committee for the Conference.

Hardback
ISBN 0 85170 437 9
£35.00

Paperback
ISBN 0 85170 438 7
£14.95